The Failure of Civil Society?

The Failure of Civil Society?

The Third Sector and the
State in Contemporary Japan

AKIHIRO OGAWA

Published by
State University of New York Press, Albany

For information, contact State University of New York Press, Albany, NY
www.sunypress.edu

Production by Eileen Meehan
Marketing by Anne M. Valentine

Library of Congress Cataloging-in-Publication Data

Ogawa, Akihiro, 1968-
    The failure of civil society? : the third sector and the state in contemporary
Japan / Akihiro Ogawa.
        p. cm.
    Includes bibliographical references and index.
    ISBN 978-0-7914-9395-3 (hardcover : alk. paper)
    ISBN 978-0-7914-9396-0 (pbk. : alk. paper)
    1. Nonprofit organizations—Japan.   2. Nonprofit organizations—
Government policy—Japan.   3. Civil society—Japan.   4. Non-governmental
organizations—Japan.   I. Title.

HD2769.2.J3O35 2009
338.7'4—dc22   2008025084

10 9 8 7 6 5 4 3 2 1

For Deborah

Contents

Illustrations

Figures

Pictures

Table

Acknowledgments

First I have to thank the secretariat staff members and volunteers of my field site nonprofit organization (NPO) for their patience with and interest in my daily presence. During my research, I was very much inspired by actions and conversations with all of the participants of the NPO, in particular, my research collaborators—Takemoto Hirokazu, Shirai Toru, Sato Shigeo, Shimada Yasuko, Takabayashi Mari, the late Kojima Mariko, Itami Natsuko, Ito Misao, Sahara Shigemoto, Tsutsumi Takayuki, Yoshikawa Kinya, Nakazawa Tsuneo, Ishibe Hideo, Inoue Kuniko, Ito Hiroko, and Kitajima Shizuko.

I would like to acknowledge my advisors—Theodore Bestor, Davydd Greenwood, and Victor Koschmann—for my graduate work at Cornell University, where the idea for this book was originally developed. Ted made me realize the power of ethnography when I faced a deadlock with my research methodology. Action Research strategy, advocated by Davydd, confirmed to me the meaning of doing research in my own society. The Action-Research way of thinking caused a sort of paradigm shift in my brain. Vic gave me the insight to locate this ethnographic project in postwar Japanese historical and political contexts. His perspective enriched this project.

During my graduate course work, fieldwork, and writing stage, I received many insightful comments, advice, and encouragement regarding this project from the following: Jeff Kingston, Gerald Curtis, Victoria Lyon Bestor, Bernd Lambert, Vilma Santiago-Irizarry, Peter Katzenstein, Miyazaki Hirokazu, Deguchi Masayuki, Glenda Roberts, John C. Campbell, Brett de Bary, Osawa Machiko, Rafael Humpert, Nakamura Mayumi, David Leheny, Chin-Sung Chung, Gordon Mathews, Guven Peter Witteveen, Andrew M. Gardner, David M. Hoffman, Sekiya Yuichi, Robert Pekkanen, Nakamura Yusuke, Frank Schwartz, Sally Falk Moore, Susan Pharr, Jennifer Chan, Mori Shigeki, Shankar Sankaran, Seung-Mi Han, Mitsui Hideko, Adam Yuet Chau, Merry White, Mineko Sasaki-Smith, Joshua Hotaka Roth, Patricia Steinhoff, Hagen Koo, Peter Cave, Roger Goodman, Susan Wright, Helen Siu, Takahashi Mutsuko, Mats Karlsson,

Okubo Kuniko, Patricia Weitsman, David L. Hoffmann, and two anonymous reviewers at State University of New York Press—all who inspired my thoughts on Japanese NPOs and encouraged me to think about my project in international comparative perspectives. The writing of this book was primarily supported by the Advanced Research Fellowship in the Program on U.S.-Japan Relations at Harvard University. I thank the Institute of Social Science at the University of Tokyo, where I was sponsored by Professor Ishida Hiroshi, for providing me with an ideal environment for writing the earlier version of this book. I also thank Nancy Ellegate and Allison Lee at State University of New York Press for their assistance. I appreciate as well all of the computer help I received from Tracey Nauright.

My persistent interest in civil society was generated and accelerated by real-world experiences in journalism before going back to graduate school. I am grateful to all of the people I met as a reporter at *Kyodo News*. Among them, I learned a lot, especially from Miyashita Shoji and Midori, Aoyama Yoshiko, Harada Momoyo, Watanabe Yoshiyuki, Furuya Sugio, and Suzuki Eiji, who make continuous grassroots efforts to advocate what they believe and try to change the world through their professions and beyond.

And, finally, to Deborah Weitsman Ogawa: I greatly appreciated your support. Always, you were the first reader for me. Your comments stimulated my way of thinking and broadened my perspectives. Since we met in Tokyo as colleagues at *Kyodo*, where we jointly covered the Tokyo Stock Exchange (what a romantic place!), we have moved repeatedly—to New York, where this project was started as my graduate agenda, Ithaca, again Tokyo, Boston, again New York, and finally Stockholm—over the past decade. During these days we also experienced the most precious moment of our life—the birth of Hannah Karin.

The earlier version of chapter 4 of this book appeared as "Invited by the State: Institutionalizing Volunteer Subjectivity in Contemporary Japan," in *Asian Anthropology* 3 (2004: 71–96), and chapter 7 as "Initiating Change: Doing Action Research in Japan," in *Dispatches from the Field: Neophyte Ethnographers in a Changing World* (Long Grove, IL: Waveland Press, 2006, edited by Andrew Gardner and David M. Hoffman). The author thanks Greg Irwin for permission to use his translation of *Hana* (*Flowers*) or *Near the River in the Spring* from the book *Japan's Best Loved Songs of the Season* (*Eigo de utau nihon no uta*) (Tokyo: Japan Times, 1998). The photographs in chapters 3 (except for pictures 3.4 and 3.8), 6 (picture 6.4), and 7 (picture 7.1) were provided by Sumida gakushu garden for this publication. Unless otherwise noted, the remaining photographs are mine.

Because of the confidential nature of the materials upon which this book draws, no identifying individual names for data sources are provided. Except where otherwise indicated, all quotations are taken from my field notes, and all translations are mine. Furthermore, Japanese individuals' names are written with the surname first. Conversions from Japanese yen to U.S. dollars are made at a constant rate of 110 yen to the dollar.

Chapter 1

Introduction

Key Questions

The *Nihon Keizai Shimbun*, a Japanese business daily, reported on January 26, 2003, an interesting episode regarding the ongoing phenomenon of nonprofit organization (NPO) incorporation following the 1998 NPO Law (formally the Law to Promote Specified Nonprofit Activities, enacted in 1998) in Japan. The paper said that one of the most profitable industries in the currently sluggish Japanese economy is the *hanko* business. *Hanko* is a seal that is symbolic of formal approval among both individuals and corporations in Japanese society. Its function is equivalent to that of the signature in Western countries. The number of franchise shops manufacturing *hanko* has nearly doubled in the past three years. Traditionally, making *hanko* required high-level engraving skills. Today, however, the introduction of the computer in the *hanko* industry has streamlined production. In Japanese society, *hanko* is often required in the administrative procedures of the government. According to the newspaper article, individuals usually have only five *hanko* over a lifetime. The current demand should therefore be limited. If this is the case, then why is the business thriving? The business daily attributed the surge to the dramatically increasing number of NPOs created under the 1998 NPO Law. Since the law's enactment, more than 30,000 NPOs have been incorporated (as of March 31, 2007), as Figure 1.1 shows, and the number is still increasing at a relatively constant and consistent pace across the country.[1] In the process of gaining recognition as an NPO, an organization is required to submit documents to the government with a *hanko*. *Hanko* makes the documents more formal and is used to enhance the trustworthy image of NPOs in Japanese society. It symbolizes formal participation in society. The logic is that receiving NPO status increases opportunities for active social participation.

Seeing this emerging phenomenon, I started this project with a simple question: What is going on under the institutionalization of the

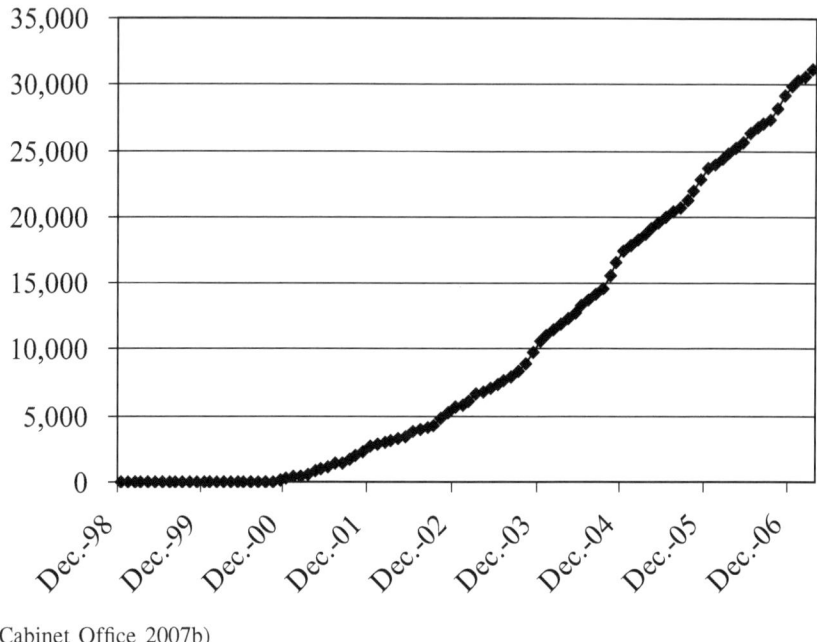

(Cabinet Office 2007b)

Figure 1.1 Number of NPOs as of March 31, 2007

NPO sector? Since the late 1990s, the NPO has excited great attention and debate among both ordinary Japanese and political elites, as well as considerable discussion in the popular press and in academic writings, as a key actor in civil society—a public sphere that broadly refers to nonstate institutions and associations that are critical to sustaining modern democratic participation. Until then, the Japanese term *NPO* (written "NPO" and pronounced *enu-pī-ō*)—specified nonprofit corporations, or *tokutei hieri katsudō hōjin* in Japanese legal terms—was not in popular use; in fact, it was virtually unknown. The term *NPO* first appeared in 1995, the year of the Great Hanshin-Awaji Earthquake on January 17, 1995, in a popular encyclopedia of contemporary Japanese vocabulary (*Gendai yōgo no kiso chishiki* various years). The NPO, a voluntary third-sector organization,[2] caught national attention and gained momentum in Japanese society, particularly after the great earthquake, when approximately 1.3 million volunteers acted to aid victims of the disaster (Economic Planning Agency 2000). The government bureaucracy's ineffective efforts to deal with the tragic situation paled in comparison to the impressive work of volunteers at the scene of the earthquake. The contributions of volunteers dramatized, on a national scale, the need for a social structure that would bolster a voluntary third sector. In the aftermath of the 1995 earthquake, efforts to ease rigid government control over the incorporation of NPOs began to receive strong support from political and business leaders and members of the media. It is believed that the result of this social movement was the passage of the NPO Law in March 1998 (see Pekkanen 2000 on the legislation process).

Before the 1998 NPO Law, the government intervened more aggressively in the incorporation of nonprofit, third-sector organizations. The Japanese Civil Code, which was written in 1898, more than 100 years ago under the Meiji government, regulated the major third-sector organizations, including *kōeki hōjin*, usually translated as public interest corporations or public interest legal persons under Article 34. There are two forms of public interest corporations—incorporated foundations (*zaidan hōjin*) and incorporated associations (*shadan hōjin*). In addition, various public interest organizations are authorized by special laws arising under, or attached to, Article 34. These special bodies include social welfare services corporations (*shakai fukushi hōjin*), medical services corporations or hospitals (*iryō hōjin*), private school corporations (*gakkō hōjin*), religious corporations (*shūkyō hōjin*), and offender rehabilitation corporations (*kōsei hogo hōjin*). Specified nonprofit corporations (commonly called NPOs) incorporated by the NPO Law—a main focus of this book—are categorized in the special group (Japan Association of Charitable Organizations 2001). An organization seeking to be incorporated is forced to undergo an administrative process. Permission (*kyoka*), approval (*ninka*), or recognition (*ninshō*) is granted at the discretion of the national or prefectural government agencies that had jurisdiction over the organization's field of activities, a common regulation technique.[3] According to Article 34 of the Civil Code, the government authorities require that the group submit a detailed plan of activities and select a governing board of publicly esteemed individuals. Once registered, an organization is obliged to submit a budget and a plan of activities before the beginning of each fiscal year, which starts on April 1 and ends on March 31 of the following year. At the end of the year, the organization presents a progress report and financial reports to the appropriate ministries. Incorporated groups need to adhere rigidly to reporting requirements or risk having their status revoked.[4]

Under the 1998 NPO Law, meanwhile, the incorporation process for third-sector organizations became quite (and amazingly) simple. The prefectural government now prepares templates for the necessary documents in a prospective NPO's application packet, including the cover page, articles of association (*teikan*), and budget forms. People who want to create an NPO have only to fill out the templates and choose activity areas from seventeen disciplines defined by the NPO Law, including social welfare, social education, community development, environment, disaster relief, community safety, and human rights.[5] I received a guidebook on NPOs that was distributed in the Tokyo Metropolitan Government office (see Tokyo Metropolitan Government 2000b). The guidebook indeed includes everything I would need to incorporate an NPO. People who are interested in incorporating NPOs need only take advantage of these templates. I also found that these kinds of documents could easily be downloaded from the Internet on each prefecture's Web site. Regarding incorporation, the governor of the prefecture in which the NPO is located—or the Cabinet Office in the case of an NPO with offices in at least two prefectures—is required to authenticate the establishment of the organization. The government's decision on any NPO application is based on a set of objective criteria. Thus an application undergoes a relatively straightforward recognition process rather than a permission or approval process that would involve the discretion of government agencies, which was formerly common practice. As of March 31, 2007, 99 percent of applications for NPO status under the NPO Law passed smoothly through the registration process (Cabinet Office 2007d).[6] When an application failed, it did so simply because it lacked certain documents. One leading NPO practitioner in Japan points out that "[t]he direct significance of the NPO Law is that by making it easier for many organizations engaged in civic activities to obtain corporate status, the law enables these organizations to enter into different contracts and arrangements" (Yamaoka 2000, 3). Real estate can now be held under the name of an NPO. A bank account can be opened under the name of an NPO. Contracts with other entities can be formed under the name of an NPO. For example, an NPO can rent an office, subscribe to a telephone company, and even make an entrustment contract with the government and businesses. Before the enactment of the NPO Law, these kinds of contracts were made under individuals' names.

So what are NPOs doing exactly? NPOs of various types have been incorporated across the country. During my fieldwork from 2001 through 2003 in Japan, almost every day newspapers reported on the establishment of new NPOs. I offer some images of Japanese NPOs from my newspaper clippings. As Figure 1.2 shows, the most popular activity area in which NPOs are created is the promotion of social welfare, health, or medical treatment. As of March 31, 2007, 58 percent of NPOs (or 18,140 NPOs) were registered in this category (Cabinet Office 2007c). Most of these

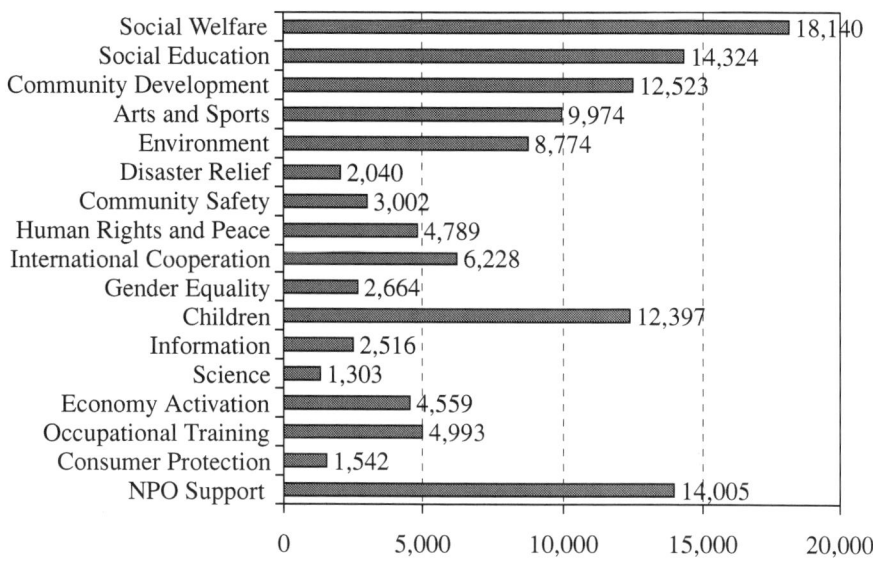

(Cabinet Office 2007c)

Note: Of 26,114 NPOs, or 83.9 percent of the total, registered in more than two areas of activity (Cabinet Office 2007a). In this subgroup, 5,504 NPOs registered in two areas, 5,724 NPOs registered in three areas, and 4,769 NPOs registered in four areas, and 206 NPOs even registered in all of the seventeen designated areas.

Figure 1.2 Areas of NPO Activities as of March 31, 2007. An NPO can cross-register in several activity domains.

organizations are called *kaigo* NPOs and specialize in providing care to the elderly. Such NPOs play a significant role in elder care, a task that was performed by female family members as well as the local government dispatching care workers to individual homes following the enactment of the Welfare Law for the Elderly in 1962. The second most popular type of NPO activity is the promotion of social education. My field site is included in this category. It is an NPO that promotes lifelong learning (*shōgai gakushū*) activities in a local downtown Tokyo community. Across the country, lifelong learning—once the province of the government—is increasingly administered by NPOs. Third, a representative organization in the category of culture, arts, and sports (which is ranked sixth) is an NPO in Tokyo's Toshima ward (*Asahi Shimbun*, February 5a, 2004). This NPO is in charge of developing arts programs for local residents. It is based at an abandoned junior high school that was closed due to the population decrease in the inner city of Tokyo. Other NPOs in this group provide assistance to museums. Members of these NPOs play signifi-cant roles in actual museum operations and contribute their knowledge, skills, and experiences as docents (*Nihon Keizai Shimbun*, February 28, 2004). Lastly, community safety is also a popular area. A typical NPO in this category is one that developed a unique type of alarm system following a recent crime wave (*Asahi Shimbun*, February 5b, 2004). An NPO in Shinagawa ward in Tokyo created an effective alarm buzzer for children that emits electric waves and sound. According to the newspaper article, when the buzzer is activated, an alarm sounds and the device sends electric waves to a "mother device" that can be more than fifty meters away. These wireless mother devices with display panels will be set up in public facilities and shopping areas, where they will transmit information to a central host computer.

Observing the phenomenon, the key research objective of this book is to explore what ordinary grassroots Japanese people are feeling and experiencing under the NPO, the seed of the institutionalization of Japanese "civil society," or *shimin shakai*, under the 1998 NPO Law, as well as to determine how the new concept of the NPO was introduced and interpreted among them. I document in detail the transition that Japanese society has undergone since the epoch-making NPO Law was implemented, allowing thousands of civic groups to be acknowledged as proactive participants in Japanese social and political life. In particular, as a case, I analyze the dynamic micro-politics of everyday interactions between the state and ordinary individuals in the creation and ongoing activities of an NPO. In so doing, I devote special attention to the way in which different levels of the Japanese government try to shape the NPO, or "civil society," into an existing social and political structure that actually supports the state's specific goals. I also illuminate how grass-roots people respond to the state's deliberate actions to institutionalize civil society in Japan. My research questions include the following: Can civil society successfully be constructed by a state? What are the ways in which states seek to shape their relations with their populations, and how effective are those policies likely to be? Ultimately, I believe that this book calls into question the relationship between the state and individuals in contemporary Japanese society while raising the broad issue of whether civil society can be intentionally created through the actions of the state. On this point, this book extends the value of the current study of policy in anthropology, argued in *Family and Social Policy in Japan: Anthropological Approaches* (Goodman 2002), by adding a very timely policy narrative. More practically, I believe that the narratives documented in this book should provide Japanese policy makers with a significant strategy for affecting third-sector or NPO policy. Further, there are important policy implications of the book for any state seeking to mold its society in specific ways.

Anthropology of Civil Society

The concept of civil society experienced an enormous theoretical rebirth following the collapse of communism in Eastern Europe in the 1980s. This book directly addresses a substantive lacuna that exists throughout the civil-society scholarship. Most of the work in the field contains normative theoretical formulations with ethnocentric Western intellectual origins (e.g., Arato 1981, 2000; Naruse 1984; Keane 1988, 1998; Habermas 1989, 1996; Shils 1991; Calhoun 1992; Cohen and Arato 1992; Curtis et al. 1992; Evans and Boyte 1992; Seligman 1992; Tester 1992; Walzer 1992; Kumar 1993; Pérez-Diaz 1993; Putnam 1993, 1995, 2000; Salamon 1994, 2001; Diamond 1994; Eberly 1994; Gellner 1994; Fukuyama 1995; Hall 1995; Verba et al. 1995; Levi 1996; Berman 1997; Diamond et al. 1997; Mathews 1997; Sakamoto 1997; Alexander 1998, 2003; Lehning 1998; Rueschemeyer et al. 1998; Wuthnow 1998; Salamon et al. 1999; Skocpol and Fiorina 1999; Ehrenberg 1999; Levy 1999; Florini 2000; Edwards et al. 2001; Warren 2001; Rosenblum and Post 2002; P. Smith 2002; Kaldor et al. 2003; Edwards 2004; Miyajima 2004; Salamon et al. 2004; Baker and Chandler 2005; Batliwala and Brown 2006; Redclift 2006). It seems that these studies, analytical and descriptive in quality, often have promoted static, patterned, highly abstract notions and models of the state and the individual. "Civil society" has even been used as a strategic term by those campaigning for goals such as democracy and justice.

The International Encyclopedia of the Social and Behavioral Sciences defines the idea of civil society in two distinct ways.[7] In the first definition, the civil society concept can be traced back to the notion of *societas civilis* in Cicero's writing (Cicero 1998), and its earlier foundation in Aristotle's concept of *koinonia politike* (Aristotle 1981). Civil society was synonymous with political structures and organizations. Here, civil society is conterminous with the state—that is, power relations ordered through law and institutions with the objective of ensuring social harmony (e.g., Locke [1690] 1980; Hobbes [1660] 1996). In the second formulation, civil society is understood as a self-regulating, self-governing body outside and often in opposition to the state, represented both as the nexus of societal associations expected to generate civility, social cohesion, and morality and as the site of reciprocal economic relations among individuals engaged in market-exchange activity. For Adam Ferguson ([1767] 1995), Adam

Smith ([1776] 1974), and Immanuel Kant ([1784] 1963), civil society is a normative category describing a social realm strictly distinguished from the state. Civil society, in these readings, describes a unity of individual lives—a sphere of solidarity and moral sentiment. Further, it is an arena of active citizenry and concern about public issues. In Hegelian-Marxist terms, meanwhile, the anatomy of civil society is to be sought in political economy (Hegel [1821] 1967; Marx [1843] 1978b, [1845] 1978a). For Hegel, civil society was the market. He focused on the right to the private ownership of property, the division of labor, and exchange as the central features of civil society, using the term *bürgerliche Gesellschaft*, which has been translated as bourgeois society (see Engels [1852]1975, 188). Marx narrowed the Hegelian sense of civil society. He equated civil society with bourgeois *capitalist* society, seeing it as another vehicle for furthering the interests of the dominant class under capitalism.

In the contemporary discourse on civil society, the scholarship surrounding the second definition outlined earlier is more relevant. Civil society signifies, as Craig Calhoun (2001) argues, the organization of social life on the basis of interpersonal relationships, group formation, and a system of exchange linking people beyond the range of intimate family relations and without reliance on direction by the government. Civil society is important to advocates of democracy, Calhoun continues, because it signifies the capacity of citizens to create amongst themselves the associations necessary to bring new issues to the public agenda, to defend both civil and human rights, and to provide for an effective collective voice in the political process. Indeed, civil society theorists focus on the capacity for self-organization of social relations outside the control of the state. For example, Francis Fukuyama (1995, 8) defines civil society as "the realm of spontaneously created social structures separate from the state that underlie democratic political institutions." Larry Diamond (1994, 4) regards civil society as "self-generating." Michael Walzer (1992, 89) presents civil society as "the space of uncoerced human association and also the set of relational networks—formed for the sake of family, faith, interest, and ideology—that fill this space." These networks include "unions, churches, political parties, social movements, cooperatives, neighbourhoods, schools of thought, societies for promoting or preventing this and that" (90). Jürgen Habermas (1996, 367) nicely summarizes the usage of civil society as follows:

> Civil society is composed of those more or less spontaneously emergent associations, organizations, and movements that, attuned to how societal problems resonate in the private life spheres, distill and transmit such reactions in amplified form

to the public sphere. The core of civil society comprises a network of associations that institutionalizes problem-solving discourses on questions of general interest inside the framework of organized public spheres.

This definition clearly rationalizes the democratic capacity of citizens to create amongst themselves the associations necessary to bring new issues to the public agenda, to defend civil rights, and to provide for an effective collective voice in contemporary social and political life.

In the context of the United States, the idea of civil society is linked not only to democracy but also to reliance on voluntary organizations. In this sense, Alexis de Tocqueville and Robert Putnam have been central to the debate on civil society. The discourse was based on an idealization of American communitarian ideas and practices. Tocqueville noted the propensity of Americans, who lived in relative equality compared to European class-based society, to form voluntary associations of all kinds for all purposes. In this tendency, Tocqueville perceived the strength of the American democracy. Tocqueville argued,

> The Americans . . . are fond of explaining almost all the actions of their lives by the principle of self-interest rightly understood; they show with complacency how an enlightened regard for themselves constantly prompts them to assist one another and inclines them willingly to sacrifice a portion of their time and property to the welfare of the state. (Tocqueville [1840] 1980, 122)

Tocqueville maintained that civic associations reinforced the spirit of collaboration that was vital to public affairs; political associations, in turn, taught habits that could be transferred to nonpolitical forms of cooperation. Through associational life, he claimed, American citizens are imbued with an ethic of self-interest.

Recently, however, social critics have noted the decline of civil society in the United States. This decline is often attributed to the expansion of the government and corporate sectors, which has coincided with the narrowing of the voluntary service and advocacy sector. Putnam's *Bowling Alone* (2000), for example, portrays a significant decline in associational habits among Americans. Citing surveys that have tracked levels of political participation and group membership over the past quarter-century, Putnam (1995) argues that Americans who came of age during the Great Depression and World War II have been far more deeply engaged in the lives of their communities than the generations that have followed them. According to Putnam, Americans must be concerned about depleting their stock of "social capital." Defining the core idea of social capital in the phrase "social networks have value," and arguing that increased "social contacts affect the productivity of individuals and groups" (Putnam 2000, 19), Putnam sees social capital as a distinct form of public good that is embodied in civic engagement and affects economic prosperity. In particular, he highlights voluntary associations as agents that create and sustain the bridging of social capital that enables people to get ahead. Putnam et al. (1993) further argue that a democratic government is more responsive and effective when it faces a vigorous civil society; a civic culture of "generalized trust" and social solidarity is an important prerequisite of a vital democracy. Such a culture is nourished by voluntary associations that are egalitarian rather than hierarchical and that treat citizens as participants rather than as clients. The civil society is most likely to foster solid social cooperation, to reinforce norms of reciprocity, and, thus, to make democracy work. The work of Putnam, who stresses the trust and reciprocity between people that facilitate collective action in terms of economic and political development at the regional and national levels, is particularly relevant to the contemporary civil-society scholarship.

Today, these discourses on civil society converge within a more practical but ideal discourse coined by the global associational revolution. Consider the following quote from Lester Salamon's milestone article on contemporary civil-society scholarship:

> A striking upsurge is underway around the globe in organized voluntary activity and the creation of private, nonprofit or nongovernmental organizations. From the developed countries of North America, Europe and Asia to the developing societies of Africa, Latin America and the former Soviet bloc, people are forming associations, foundations and similar institutions to deliver human services, promote grass-roots economic development, prevent environmental degradation, protect civil rights and pursue a thousand other objectives formerly unattended or left to the state. . . . Indeed, we are in the midst of a global "associational revolution" that may prove to be as significant to the latter twentieth century as the rise of the nation-state was to the latter nineteenth century. (Salamon 1994, 109)

Salamon argues that this associational revolution may be permanently altering the relationship between the state and individuals. He later continues his argument elsewhere:

> [T]he appropriate paradigm for the 21st century is one of partnership and a politics of collaboration—i.e., a "new governance" that emphasizes collaboration, not separate action, by the different sectors as the best hope for achieving meaningful progress. This is the true meaning of the "civil society" about which we hear so much today—not a sector, but a relationship among sectors, and between them and citizens, in which all are actively engaged in addressing public problems. (Salamon 2001, 37)

This rationale is further justified by Jessica Mathews in terms of a "power shift" in the post-cold war era. Mathews articulates a new dynamic of associational life, arguing, "They [states, markets, and civil society] are sharing powers—including political, social, and security roles at the core of sovereignty—with businesses, with international organizations, and with a multitude of citizens groups, known as nongovernmental organizations" (Mathews 1997, 50).

My own research is motivated primarily by a concern for the way civil society is discussed by these authors in particular and in the contemporary literature in general. In my view, the way of discussing civil society in the existing scholarship is a very privileged one. It largely ignores the experiences of ordinary grassroots people as seen within their local institutional frameworks, such as the Japanese NPO.

In the Japanese context that this book studies as a case, civil society, or *shimin shakai*, became a familiar term among social scientists who were mostly influenced by Marxism in the postwar period 1945–1970 (e.g., Ōtsuka 1946; Kawashima 1949; Shimizu 1951; Takashima 1953; Uchida 1953; Maruyama 1954; Mizuta 1954; Ōkouchi 1954; Matsushita 1966, 1971a, 1971b; Sakuta 1966; Hirata 1969; Fukuda 1971; Takabatake 1971; see Barshay 1992, 2003, 2004; Koschmann 1978, 1993, 1996; Takashima 1991; Matsushita 1994; Kokuminbunka Kaigi 1997; Garon 2002; Iokibe 1999; Carver et al. 2000; Takabatake 2001, 2004; Avenell 2006 for reviewing comprehensive historical developments on the civil society argument in this period). This categorizing preceded the recent international proliferation of civil-society literature in the West from the 1970s onward (see Carver et al. 2000 for further detailed argument). Since the 1990s in the revival of civil society in the West, as well as the surge of volunteerism following the Great Hanshin-Awaji Earthquake, civil society has once again been the focus of an enormous amount of attention in mainstream Japanese society, among political elites, in the popular press, and in academic writings (e.g., Amenomori 1993; Honma and Deguchi 1996; Yamamoto 1996, 1998, 1999; Curtis 1997; Saeki 1997; Broadbent 1998;

Ishitsuka 1998; Imai 1998, 2001; Lesbirel 1998; Mori 1998; Saito 1998; Yagi et al. 1998; Yamauchi et al. 1999; Vosse 1999; Pekkanen 2000, 2003, 2004a, 2004b, 2006; Imada 2001; Takao 2001; Hirata 2002; Hirowatari 2002; Sato 2002; Shigetomi 2002; Tsujinaka 2002; Osborne 2003; Schwartz and Pharr 2003; Alagappa 2004; Chan-Tiberghien 2004; Hasegawa 2004; Iriyama 2004; Kingston 2004; Yamaguchi 2004; Waley 2005; Yoshida 2005; Kawahara 2006; Ducke 2007; Haddad 2007).

These works primarily suggest that Japan does not have civil society in the Western sense, which I reviewed earlier. Uchida Yoshihiko, a historian of economic theory and one of the most enthusiastic Japanese scholars using the term *civil society*, said that civil society in Japan was immature (Uchida 1953), for example. The dominant view is that civil society is monolithic, with little delineation between the state and society. Japanese civil society or third-sector groups in fact will have this quasi-government characteristic. From this perspective, the political advocacy that exists is weak (primarily compared to the United States); the relationship between the state and society is very close, and little attention is paid to what is going on outside the state. Some argue that in a historical institutionalism framework—a dominant theoretical orientation in social sciences—Japan has been an "activist state" (Pharr 2003), successfully institutionalizing (through funding and favorable tax treatment) specific kinds of third-sector groups that significantly support such national ideology as developmentalism in the modernization process. Legal and institutional frameworks indeed contour the Japanese civic terrain (see Pekkanen 2003).

I agree with these arguments. But as an anthropologist I am most interested in exploring the historical and cultural dynamics—local practices, values, and beliefs—developed in the context of civil society. I believe that each society and culture molds its own version of civil society, reflecting its most important values, such as individual liberty, public solidarity, pluralism, and nonviolence, all of which sustain a dynamic civic culture. I assume that even in Western countries sociopolitical relationships are various and that the concept of civil society is, of course, not unified. On this point, Chris Hann (1996, 3; see also Hann and Dunn 1996), a social anthropologist, argues that civil society debates have been too narrowly circumscribed by modern Western modes of liberal individualism. In addition, he argues that the exploration of civil society requires careful attention to a range of informal interpersonal practices that are overlooked by other disciplines. In Hann's view, anthropologists have much to contribute to the investigation of the moral aspects of power, cohesion, and social order in contemporary societies. We anthropologists are facing "civil society's need for de-construction" (Benthall 2000).

Anthropologists have made relatively limited contributions to the discussion on civil society, as William Fisher (1997) points out in the *Annual Review of Anthropology*. In the area of Japanese anthropology, for example, there have been few detailed anthropological studies that have attempted to articulate what is happening within specific civil-society organizations such as NPOs and nongovernmental organizations (NGOs). Likewise, there are few anthropological analyses of the impact of Japanese NPO/NGO practices on the relations of power among individuals, communities, and the state. Little attention has been directly paid to the discourse within which concepts of civil society are presented as solutions to the problems of democracy. When we re-read ethnographies, however, we find that many anthropologists vividly describe such key features of civil society as reciprocity and exchange, the elaboration of communal advantage, modes of affiliation, and patterns of public participation. Such social behaviors were traditionally documented in earnest in ethnographies of territorial societies (e.g., Embree 1939; Dore 1958, 1978; R. Smith 1974, 1978; Hendry 1981; Smith and Wiswell 1982; Kelly 1985; Bestor 1989, 1990, 2004; Ben-Ari 1991; Robertson 1991; Traphagan 2004; Kawano 2005) and of social structure and group affiliations (e.g., Vogel 1963, 1975; Plath 1964; Befu 1963; Nakane 1967, 1970; Doi 1971; Dore 1973; Rohlen 1974, 1983; White 1987, 1991, 2002; Imamura 1987; Okimoto and Rohlen 1988; Hamabata 1990; Kondo 1990; Hamada 1991; Sato 1991; Goodman 1993, 2000; Allison 1994; Roberts 1994; Turner 1995; Ogasawara 1998; Robertson 1998; Traphagan 2000; Gill 2001; Nakamura 2002, 2006; Roth 2002; Miyazaki 2003; McVeigh 2004; Graham 2005). While anthropologists may not have consciously addressed the concept of civil society, I contend that they have been documenting crucial elements of this construct. Among a few exceptions are ethnographies produced during and after the late 1990s (Stevens 1997; LeBlanc 1999; Nakano 2000, 2005; Thang 2001; Moon 2002; Nakamaki 2002; Han 2004; Witteveen 2004). These projects directly focus on the civic sphere in Japan and consciously see volunteerism—a key phenomenon of civil society—as such a term, for example. Victoria Bestor (2002) gives a comprehensive review of the anthropological literature on the topic of civil society in Japan.

I myself was struck by the power of ethnography when I began to analyze the emerging NPO phenomenon in Japan. Sociocultural anthropologists are armed with ethnography. We are skilled field-workers, using open-ended, naturalistic inquiry methods and inductive reasoning to understand local perspectives. Doing ethnography is a serious interpretive endeavor that involves observing, documenting, and analyzing customs and behaviors. Ethnography provides "not only substantive information but perspectives on that information" (Peacock 2001, 121).

In fact, ethnographic research made it possible to trace three levels of analysis—ideological process, institutional patterning, and the everyday routines of individuals (Kelly 1993, 192). On this point, I was not confined to "studying up," in Laura Nader's (1972) sense. I took a more flexible research position in keeping with what Susan Reinhold (1994, 477–79) calls "studying through": tracing ways in which power, for example, creates webs and relations between actors, institutions, and discourses across time and space.

Ethnography describes real people in a systematic and an accurate manner. However, it does more than that. By revealing the general through the particular and the abstract through the concrete, an ethnographic work weaves facts into a form that highlights patterns, principles, meanings, and values. In so doing, ethnography can reveal "how things are really done" at a local level, as well as what effects they are having on ordinary, grassroots people in particular macro-processes. Meanwhile, going beyond means-ends analysis allows the examination of reflexive loops, making my own self-existence more apparent. Further, I particularly found that the ethnographic approach is uniquely suited to the study of societies in transformation, as it allows the researcher to pay attention to uncertainty.[8] Furthermore, what made ethnography most attractive to me was that it facilitated the inclusion of diverse voices. For me, ethnography is "an active form of democratic participation" (Greenhouse and Greenwood 1998, 3). Ethnographic inquiries seek to discover the perspectives that are embedded in the voices of others. George Marcus characterizes "voices" as follows:

> Voices are not seen as products of local structures, based on community and tradition, alone or as privileged sources of perspective. Rather they are seen as products of the complex sets of associations and experiences which compose them. (Marcus 1994, 49)

Collecting such voices as ethnographic evidence, anthropology can function as a public witness and can provide a record of our times. The ethnographic approach, fortified with multiple local viewpoints, helps us interpret deeper structural and cultural patterns and rationalities. In fact, this approach, by deconstructing the dominant political rationality, can reveal concepts that underpin the moral, ethical, and social order, which often are disguised by ideology and power (Wedel and Feldman 2005).

Civil society is not a model; it is an active, dynamic process that I myself experience. My research objective is not to argue about what civil society is but to discover what civil society does. This book thus provides a grounded analysis of grassroots practices and values expressed by local actors trying to frame common definitions of the Japanese NPOs incorporated under the 1998 NPO Law. Employing detailed ethnography, I argue that when one examines the Japanese NPO from the grassroots up, instead of from the top down (i.e., from the view of political elites and high-level institutions), a very different picture of social and political life in Japan emerges. Otherwise, the civil society argument itself will never be democratized.

What I sought in this book was an ethnography of civil society in contemporary Japan. I document people, places, and meanings as well as the concrete manifestations of civil society. At the same time, I seek to avoid simplistic essentialism or stereotyping of Japan's historical development, aiming to link Japanese civil society studies and experiences to the global discourse on civil society. I argue the state-led institutionalization of volunteer-based NPOs under the name of civil society, and I locate such Japanese NPOs, or "civil society," as a form of agency in neoliberalism, a dominant ideology in contemporary global politics and economies. Further, this book explicitly illuminates strong disagreements from below combined with grassroots resistance and frustration regarding the state's deliberate effort to construct such "civil society." The conflicts within the ongoing NPO phenomenon present powerful narratives—real voices and real experiences that have yet to be vibrantly documented as a form of ethnography. Recording these conflicts should enable a critical assessment of some recent normative approaches and destabilize some key understanding as well as advocating the merits of civil society under the existing scholarship.

Fieldwork

I conducted ethnographic fieldwork in total of twenty-four months for this project—from September 2001 through April 2003, with follow-up research in July and August 2005, in addition to September and December 2006. I worked as an unpaid staff researcher at an NPO that I call SLG (pseudonym), which was incorporated under the 1998 NPO Law. It was located in Kawazoe (pseudonym) in downtown Tokyo and promoted lifelong learning in the local community. In exchange for my administrative and planning work at SLG, I was given free rein to conduct research at the NPO.

There are some specific reasons I chose SLG as my research base. During the initial stage of my fieldwork, I was indeed looking for some "typical" NPOs under the NPO Law in Japanese society. However, I realized that it would be almost impossible to define what is typical at that point since Japanese NPOs had only a short history. Only two years had passed since the NPO Law was enacted when I started fieldwork. My field site SLG was originally established by the municipal government as a citizens' group in the mid 1990s. It provided lifelong learning opportunities to the local residents in place of the government. Following the enactment of the NPO Law in 1998, the group was reincorporated as an NPO under the strong leadership of the government. Actually, the case of SLG strongly reminded me of an "activist state" argument (Pharr 2003), as I introduced earlier, which describes Japan as successfully institutionalizing civil society groups that conveniently support current policy through funding and favorable tax treatment. An NPO like SLG itself might be nothing new. Yet I believed that SLG would provide me with a great case study on the state-led institutionalization of civil society. My key research interest is to know what grassroots Japanese people experience and feel within such a state-led institutionalization of civil society, in particular, during the molding process of civil society; my scholarly interest as an anthropologist is to document them as a form of original ethnography. SLG is extremely relevant to analyze when I go beyond such formal discourse on Japanese civil society, describe values and beliefs expressed and practiced by people, and present how the concept of civil society is interpreted and implemented at a Japanese grassroots level. My case study of SLG makes a unique contribution to the civil society scholarship in and outside of Japan.

In my fieldwork, I used conventional techniques of participant observation, conducted an extensive series of interviews, and complemented my observations and interview records with archival research as needed. For data collection, I believed that a micro-level approach would allow for a detailed analysis of everyday practices. The study of occasions and routines, I maintained, should reveal much of the machinery of the social structure. Meanwhile, I anticipated that macro-level forces and constraints would be observable at the microlevel, as these forces have meanings for individuals in their everyday lives. The call for a turn to everydayness is generated by research that brings with it a practice orientation (Bourdieu 1977; Giddens 1984). As Anthony Giddens (1984, 36) argues, "All social systems, no matter how grand or far-flung, both express and are expressed in the routines of daily social life." As an organizational researcher located at an NPO, I believed that there was great value in examining the everyday practices of organizational life that are usually taken for granted or dismissed as unimportant.

More specifically, I expected that the meetings I observed and the stories I heard in the organization would afford important information about the social structure and culture of the organization. At my field site, I regularly attended weekly staff meetings, course planning and volunteer recruitment meetings, and monthly directors' meetings. At these meetings, I collected evidence of basic organizational values such as rationality, pragmatism, and efficiency. Anthropologists conceptualize meetings as communication events that must be examined because they are embedded within a sociocultural setting—such as an organization, a community, or a society—as a constitutive social form (Schwartzman 1989, 1993; see also Flyvbjerg 1991; Kunda 1992 for ethnographic case studies). My approach at the field site was motivated by an appreciation of the idea that the world does appear to us through particular routines and gatherings composed of specific actors (or agents) attempting to press their claims and trying to make sense of what is happening to them. The meetings I attended contributed to the production and reproduction of everyday life of the NPO—that is, they were an *organizing* process of everyday life (Weick 1995).

I collected stories through the open-ended interview method. I mostly spoke with people at SLG in informal settings over coffee or drinks. To the anthropologist, stories are highly significant, as they represent how people interpret meaning. They shape and sustain individuals' *images* of the organization in which they work (Morgan 1986; see also Orr 1990; Van Maanen 1991). The anthropologist subjects these *images* to analysis in terms of their deployment of values, power, rules, discretion, organization, and paradox. In this way, stories play a key role in constituting meaning for organizational members. The stories one hears and tells, and the morals that are drawn from them, tend to constitute organizational realities to an extent that is often unrecognized. Even in a single organization, there may be several organizational realities. Various metaphors, skillfully knitted together, can accurately reflect the complex and multidimensional social realities that comprise organizations. Furthermore, my fieldwork at SLG was supplemented by conversations with NPO practitioners, Japanese NPO specialists in academia, and government officials in charge of NPO matters at different levels.

Further, I used extensive analysis of government documents from the National Diet Library in Tokyo, municipal libraries, and government facilities in order to supplement the data I collected at SLG. In addition, I attended workshops for NPO practitioners across the country and performed discourse analysis of NPO coverage in the mass media. Meanwhile, I introduce several pieces of literature from Japanese primary sources to this ethnography, since there are numerous rich interdisciplinary discussions on civil society or *shimin shakai* in the Japanese studies scholarship in the post-World War II era. By referring to the literature,

I believe that the full relevance of my argument on a new civil society organization—*NPO*—to the scholarship is solidified.

Action Research

Before going into the chapter overviews, I need to mention that this project takes Action Research (AR) as a key research stance. AR is a social research strategy that combines collaborative research and an impulse toward social change with a strong democratic emphasis (Greenwood and Levin 1998). It differs from conventional social science research, as it engages ordinary people in the research process and ultimately supports "a more just or satisfying situation for the stakeholders" (Greenwood and Levin 1998, 4). This strategy is also a social practice through which the researcher seeks to help marginalized people attain a degree of emancipation by making them autonomous and responsible members of society. It is also allied with the ideals of democracy; in this sense, it is proper to call AR a research strategy of the people, by the people, and for the people (Park 1997).

I understand AR to be a framework in which ordinary people can practice democracy by dealing with concrete problems that are of immediate concern to them. AR provides a forum for people to discuss what should be done to effect meaningful social change. In my project at SLG, I employed AR strategy to address the practical problems that arose in participants' daily struggles for social well-being. The "problems" discussed in this project are those that the participants recognized as important. SLG members were the individuals charged with solving these problems. They formulated, conducted, and learned from the research process. As a trained researcher, my role was to facilitate this process. Through participant observation, open-ended interviews, and document analysis, I helped uncover problems and possibilities for change; meanwhile, the SLG members and I were empowered to choose options freely. I facilitated the organization of a team to evaluate activities and to define the problems SLG members wanted to solve. SLG members began to accumulate knowledge and explore solutions using their own initiatives.

I chose this research strategy for a variety of reasons. The main reason directly relates to the meaning I found in doing this research. I came to the anthropology of civil society with an academic background in political science, public policy and administration, and history, as well as career experience as a reporter. Even though my academic discipline and the direction of my professional career have changed, my interest in research has remained intact. During the mid 1990s, before returning to graduate school, I worked as a reporter at a wire service in Japan, where I covered the Tokyo financial scene. At the press clubs of the Bank of Japan and the Tokyo Stock Exchange, I saw Japan taking steps to transform itself into a more deregulatory state in order to galvanize the economy and society. I had the opportunity to witness Japan's distinctive procedures for policy making, and I became familiar with the political process and its attendant constraints. During this time, journalists and scholars emphasized that Japan's bureaucratic state needed to become more transparent and accountable to its people so that it could respond more effectively to their needs (e.g., Ogawa 1997). However, a question remained: How could ordinary people speak up in public about the public good? I myself added other questions: How can I be involved in the action? What can I do to support the public good? Around the same time, Japanese society saw the emergence of NPOs, and I wondered whether this new third sector would offer an effective alternative to the existing bureaucratic structure. Would NPOs break through the inflexible political process in Japan?

By underlying my research with public interest anthropology, I become committed to the democratization of knowledge in research and practice (Sanday 1976, 1998, see also Yamashita 2004 for a Japanese context). My ultimate objectives as an anthropologist in doing this type of research are to help empower ordinary people and to forward the democratization of society by practicing action-oriented social research (Ogawa 2005, 2006a, 2006b). In fact, I eagerly engage ways to empower ordinary people at my field site by capturing grassroots voices in my collaborative ethnography. Therefore, I locate my ethnographic fieldwork as an attempt to design a blueprint for democratizing society. I believe that the availability of this research stance makes the discipline of anthropology one of the most viable fields for facilitating social change (Greenwood 1999).

Overview of Chapters

Chapter 2 is an ethnography of Kawazoe, the district in which I conducted fieldwork. Kawazoe is located in a *shitamachi* area (downtown neighborhood) in the eastern part of Tokyo. People began inhabiting the district hundreds of years ago. Providing ethnographic data on Kawazoe, such as information on local life, history, industries, and population, this chapter looks in particular at active, rich, local associational life in Kawazoe and introduces the kinds of social capital—social groups and networks—that are active in this urban Tokyo neighborhood. I locate my field site, an NPO called SLG, in this local associational landscape, focusing on how SLG was generated from and integrated into the local community. Meanwhile, chapter 3 describes the landscape of the ongoing NPO phenomenon as a form of organizational ethnography. As a case, I present the detailed, inside story of how SLG, an NPO promoting lifelong learning in a local community, was operated and developed in collaboration with existing entities, primarily the municipal government. In so doing, first, this chapter presents an actual grassroots experience organized under the name NPO. Further, I document the way in which the government has molded civil society by introducing the organizational form of the NPO to residents. This chapter also illustrates grassroots responses to the state's discourse on civil society making. These two chapters, combined with information on Japanese NPOs presented in this introductory chapter, provide basic knowledge of my field site for the chapters that follow.

Chapter 4 examines the state of volunteerism in Japanese society after the enactment of the 1998 NPO Law, exploring a key question: Who are volunteers? In my fieldwork, what I primarily observed and experienced was the mobilization of a type of subjectivity under the name of volunteerism. This subjectivity could be characterized as a Foucauldian coercive subjectivity—what I call "volunteer subjectivity." I have identified this phenomenon from a viewpoint heavily influenced by Michel Foucault's notion of governmentality, which refers not only to political processes or state agencies but also, in a more general sense, to the art of guiding people (Foucault 1991). I argue that this normative, self-disciplined subjectivity is important and ideal for society and is reproduced as a desirable social identity through education as a national project and a nationwide campaign promoting volunteerism. Citing the case of SLG at the micro-political level, I describe the way in which the state invites—or, more accurately, mobilizes—local residents to become volunteers and organizes them under an NPO. Furthermore, this chapter, as well as chapter 6, contributes to the current upsurge of Foucauldian anthropologies of modernity (e.g., Inda 2005) by adding an account from Japan.

Chapter 5 explores a case of associative democracy, focusing on policy collaboration in the area of lifelong learning between SLG and the municipal government in downtown Tokyo. The collaboration, currently called *kyōdō*, between NPOs and the government in policy making has been a fashionable administrative technique in Japan since the enactment of the 1998 NPO Law, as it promises to facilitate successful, effective policy implementation while achieving cost cutting. It is realized through the entrustment of projects to NPOs by the government. An NPO, for instance, might provide specific social services to the public in place of the government, which then promotes the NPO. In the case I present, SLG serves as an actual provider of lifelong learning opportunities to local residents with the funding of the municipal government. Here in this chapter, I introduce as an example an entrustment case that failed, however. I argue that power sharing is often problematic, as power tends to be tipped toward the government by its hold over policy development. At the same time, I observed resistance from the NPO. SLG members tried to insert meaning into the entrustment project, and their actions went beyond the rational, purposive function of the assignment defined by the government. This chapter demonstrates that due to tensions between disparate rationalities, NPOs in real public administration have left many grassroots participants disillusioned. Further, this chapter intends to enhance anthropological understanding of public administration (e.g., Rhodes 2005)—a currently emerging field.

Chapter 6 examines the meaning of civil society in contemporary Japan, combining ethnographic evidence on the emerging NPO sector with rich "civil society" (*shimin shakai*) arguments from Japanese literature in intellectual history, political science, sociology, and economics in the World War II and postwar eras. I specifically shed light on grassroots constituents of civil society—people called *shimin* or citizens—in order to keep my grounded analysis strategy, and I aim to reframe the Japanese civil society literature especially from the perspective of *shimin*. In Japanese social movements, there were people called *shimin*—for instance, in citizens' movements (*shimin undō*) in the 1950s and 1960s. Such individuals had contentious relationships with the state. Meanwhile, I argue *shimin* under the NPO system have internalized a coercive volunteer subjectivity, and they are expected to be apolitical and to collaborate with authority. In my view, this type of *shimin* supporting the NPO did not suddenly appear in modern Japanese history; I argue the emergence of such *shimin* can be traced to the political subjectivity supporting World War II as total war. I argue this by taking a groundbreaking approach presented in the more recent reinterpretation made by Nakano Toshio (2001) of the works by Ōtsuka Hisao and Maruyama Masao, two eminent scholars in postwar Japan. Furthermore, I maintain that through the mobilization of such *shimin*, the NPO, or "civil society," has been a key form of agency in neoliberalism since the 1980s in Japan. The institutionalization of NPOs is an inevitable expansion of neoliberal policy that has reorganized the Japanese public sphere. It is part of a calculated, strategic reorganization geared toward establishing small government in the post-Keynesian welfare state. Today, *shimin* organized under the NPO are a cultural product, systematically produced through state-supervised education in order to achieve the neoliberal state's goal. Further, this chapter presents *shimin* as an ideal national subjectivity. However, my ethnography captures strong grassroots disagreement with the state's deliberate efforts to institutionalize "civil society." The conflicts within the ongoing process of NPO construction contain powerful narratives regarding state behaviors.

Chapter 7 presents, as an epilogue, a reflexive account of my fieldwork experience at SLG. I have been employing AR, an action-minded social research strategy. After hearing about a great deal of frustration over the organization from SLG volunteers during the initial stage of my fieldwork, I stepped in to facilitate several problem-solving processes. In so doing, I explored the following questions: What did they want to change? What changes could they generate? Meanwhile, I kept in view several self-reflexive questions about my own role: Who am I in this organization? What kind of role do the SLG people expect me to play? How do I define myself? Why am I doing this research? How do I interact with people in my field site during my fieldwork? This chapter examines possibilities for and meanings of doing research as a native anthropologist.

Chapter 2

Kawazoe

Landscape

My field site was located in Kawazoe (pseudonym), an old district in Tokyo that people call *shitamachi*. One- and two-story Japanese houses and mom-and-pop shops of various kinds dot the urban landscape, spreading out from clusters around a couple of Japan Railway (JR) and metro lines. In this crowded area, the streets are very narrow, and there is little space between homes and buildings. Cars are not a convenient means of transportation; pedestrians and cyclists come and go through the streets. When one walks into the back alleys, one often hears regular muffled industrial sounds, which come from somewhere or another. These are mainly coming from nearby family-run factories that manufacture small metal parts. These alleys used to offer splendid play areas for children, but nowadays one rarely sees youngsters here. For me, the scenery has a nostalgic feel. It is the sort of neighborhood that could have been seen in any Japanese urban area.

Geographically, Kawazoe is located on the eastern side of Tokyo or, more specifically, in the Kōtō delta region, which itself is formed by major two rivers, Sumidagawa and Arakawa, which empty into Tokyo Bay. Four meters above sea level at its highest point, Kawazoe occupies about fourteen square kilometers. It is located in the sixth smallest municipality in the twenty-three wards of the Tokyo Metropolitan Government, with a population of some 220,000 and a density of about 16,000 persons per square kilometer (SWG 2006).

Recently, people have come to call the neighborhood *kawanote,* which translates roughly to "riverside" or "waterfront." The term *kawanote* is often used in contrast to *yamanote,* which signifies the upper western residential areas of Tokyo, instead of the term *shitamachi*, which has negative connotations. *Shita* originally meant "down" (antonym of "up" or *ue*) in Japanese. The term *kawanote* seems to have been coined in order to combat the negative image associated with the term *shitamachi*.[1]

Picture 2.1 A Kawazoe neighborhood, December 2006

I often found this term *kawanote* in documents produced by the municipal government. In addition, I saw it in several advertisements for newly developed condominiums in the district. High-rise condo construction has been booming in Tokyo since the late 1990s; these projects, led by major construction companies, are often conceived as part of revitalization schemes to boost the local economy. Presenting the phrase *kawanote no kurashi* (life in Kawanote) with images of panoramic night views of Tokyo taken from the condominiums, the advertisements try to sell a chic lifestyle along the urban waterfront. These tower condos have been defining a new Tokyo skyline. Further, in March 2006, a plan was announced for the construction of a second Tokyo tower in this area, which, if completed, would be the tallest freestanding tower (610 meters) in the world and the tallest man-made structure in Japan (*Nihon Keizai Shimbun*, March 25, 2006). Kawazoe is changing fast.

It seems, however, that local people have not adopted this new way of life; they continue to enjoy their old routines. One thing that impressed me was the way in which residents closely associated their daily lives with the Sumidagawa River. The river plays a significant cultural and social role in the local community throughout the year. In spring, residents enjoy the fantastic display of about 500 blossoming cherry trees on the riverbanks. I was told that Tokugawa Yoshimune, the eighth Tokugawa *shogun*, originally planted 100 cherry blossom trees around this place during the Kyouho era (1716–1736), and trees were replanted several times following floods and the Great Kanto Earthquake of 1923, expanding the number (see SWG 1978c; Rom International 2004, 151–54). Among local people, the riverbank is popularly called *bokutei* (*boku* is a Chinese-style reading of the *sumi* character in Sumidagawa in an older way of its writing, and *tei* is a Chinese-style reading of tsutsumi in Japanese, which means embankment). Nowadays, in early April, one can see beautiful cherry blossoms in full bloom, which look like a white cloud trail under the Tokyo metropolitan expressway, when one stands at the river embankment near the Kototoi Bridge.

These cherry blossoms inspired a popular Japanese song titled *Hana* (*Flowers*) or *Near the River in the Spring*. This song was one of the pieces I learned in music class in junior high school. Its lyrics are as follows:

Picture 2.2 Tokyo skyline and Sumidagawa River pouring into Tokyo Bay (top), February 2005 (Reproduced with permission from Mainichi Shimbun)

Near the river in the spring
Beautiful is the sight
Golden ripples glistening
In the April light
Have you seen the color green
That only spring can bring?
Have you heard a hummingbird
When it starts to sing?

Near the river in the spring
Beautiful is the dawn
Cherry trees are blossoming
Lovers on the lawn
Have you seen the willow tree
Whose branches hang so low
Rustling in the shadows there
Of love's afterglow?

Lyrics by Takeshima Hagoromo,
translated by Greg Irwin (1998)

In mid-April, the cherry blossoms flutter over a regatta as Waseda and Keio, two prestigious colleges in Tokyo, make their way from Ryōgoku Bridge up toward the Sakura Bridge. At the spring children's festival held this time of year, youngsters can enter a sumo tournament, go fishing, and ride a mini-steam locomotive. The last Saturday of July features a large fireworks show on the riverbanks near Asakusa, a city center in downtown Tokyo. The fireworks attract nearly 1 million people. It becomes an annual competition, with each pyrotechnic group trying to outdo the previous year's display. The result is an incredible variety of some 20,000 fireworks—not only works of diverse colors and patterns but also complicated shapes and characters. The fireworks, a tradition originating in 1733, started as part of a ritual for the dead when the country suffered from famine and disease (SWG 1978c). The fireworks continued every year, although they ceased during World War II and resumed in 1978. In early August, it is time again for a regatta. This time, the races are for local adults and junior high school students. This regatta occurs in conjunction with a summer evening festival in a riverside garden formerly owned by the regional lord Yasuda Zenjiro, founder of Yasuda *zaibatsu* (a conglomerate). An outdoor tea ceremony, a concert featuring traditional instruments, and a *haiku* (Japanese-style poetry) composition party take place in the garden. In fall, people spend a great deal of time gazing at the beautiful foliage on the riverbank; then they wait for spring to come again.

Crisscrossing the neighborhood is a number of smallish waterways, and many local places have been named after something related to rivers or water. There are several riverside parks in the neighborhood. Located between two small rivers—the Ōyokogawa and the Yokojukkengawa—one riverside park features golf courses, tennis courts, and a croquet playing field. Local life is perpetually touched by these rivers. My field site was located at a metro station named Hikifune, meaning "pull-boats." One local resident told me that the neighborhood used to have a small river called Hikufunegawa, which was buried a couple of decades ago due to the readjustment of town lots. This river was about four meters wide. On this waterway, people enjoyed boating on vessels that were pulled up from the land by laborers.

Kawazoe is a very old neighborhood that people began inhabiting hundreds of years ago. Due to the abundant water resources, and therefore fertile land, the local history book complied by the municipal government (SWG 1978c) mentions that Kawazoe was originally developed as a major source of farm products in urban Edo (an older name for Tokyo), and

Picture 2.3 Sumidagawa River as viewed from below the Tokyo metropolitan expressway near Ryōgoku boat dock; Komagata Bridge is seen crossing the river, December 2006

lots of farmers populated this area, although nowadays one cannot see or even imagine this rural scenery. Furthermore, the district was traditionally an important place for water (or river) traffic, entering from and to Edo. Indeed, Sumidagawa River was mentioned in several pieces of Japanese medieval travel literature, including *Ise monogatari* (The Tales of Ise) of the tenth century (see SKBS 2000). This work is known as a collection of poems or *waka* (a Japanese poetic form) with brief prose introductions. In the story, Section Nine is about one man (identified as Ariwara no Narihiara, one of the six saints of Japanese poetry) traveling with his followers from Heian-kyō (present-day Kyoto), the capital at that time, to the east. An episode follows (translation by Vos 1957, 173):

> When they still went along further and further, there was a very big river between the provinces of Musashi and Shimōsa. That [river] is called Sumidagawa. When they stood in a group on the bank of that river and reflected [upon their long journey], they were all worrying, thinking: "How endlessly far we have come!" But then the ferryman called: "Come quickly on board, it is already getting dark!" When they had gone aboard and were about to cross [the river], all were very sad, [for] each of them had someone he loved in the capital. At that very moment a white bird with red beak and legs and of the size of a snipe was eating fish while sporting on the water. As it was a bird which is not seen in the capital, none of them knew [it]. When they asked the ferryman, he said: "This is the capital-bird!" Upon hearing this [one of them] recited:
>
>> If you are true to your name
>>> Well, let me ask you something,
>> Capital-bird:
>>> Is the one I love
>> Alive or dead:
>
> So that all in the boat burst into tears.

Local people often talked proudly about their hometown being mentioned in such a famous Japanese classic. I myself remember reading this story when I took a Japanese classics course in high school, and I finally realized that my field site was actually the place that I had read about.

Kawazoe is without doubt historically and culturally rich. Several Japanese modern writers, including the well-known Mori Ogai, Akutagawa Ryunosuke, Koda Rohan, and Hori Tatsuo, lived in this neighborhood (SWTL 1990). Nagai Kafū, a novelist and playwright in the early 1900s (mostly Taisho and Showa eras), wrote the novel *Bokutō kitan* ([1937] 1969, roughly translated as *A Strange Tale from the East Side of the River*). The river in the title represents Sumidagawa River, and Nagai, who was influenced by French naturalism, vividly described ordinary life in the early Showa period, using an affair with a novelist and a prostitute for his subject matter. The story was actually developed in an abolished red-light district on the east side of the Sumidagawa River, currently a part of Mukōjima—a well-known district where numerous *ryōtei* (first-class Japanese restaurants) are clustered and *geisha* girls remain in business. Following the collapse of the asset-inflated, so-called "bubble" economy of the late 1980s through the early 1990s, many *ryōtei* closed; currently, only some twenty *ryōtei* remain in business, although most ordinary residents of the area have almost nothing to do with these expensive restaurants. Meanwhile, another well-known site in Kawazoe is Ryōgoku, a place where sumo-wrestling bouts are held throughout the year. As a landmark of the town, there is a Sumo Hall (Ryōgoku kokugikan), where three of the six grand Sumo tournaments are held in January, May, and September; the other tournaments are held in major cities—Osaka, Nagoya, and Fukuoka. Near the JR Ryōgoku station, you can easily see Sumo wrestlers hanging around. They grow hair in order to form a topknot, like the old *samurai*, casually wearing traditional Japanese *yukata* robes.

My field site Kawazoe reminds many Japanese of two major disasters of the last century. According to the local history book (SWG 1978c), the first was the Great Kanto Earthquake of September 1923, which took the lives of 91,344 people—almost half from this area—along with 13,275 missing people (SWG 1978c, 806; see also Tokyoto Irei Kyōkai 2005a). The second was the heavy bombardment by the United States in March 1945 during World War II, in which 83,793 civilians were killed, and 267,171 homes were destroyed, with more than 1 million people affected (SWG 1978c, 1076; see also Tokyoto Irei Kyōkai 2005b). The totally devastated Kawazoe was, however, vigorously revived in the early postwar era, when Japan experienced high economic growth triggered by the procurement demand generated by the Korean War. In 1950 and 1951, the number of factories, mostly small/medium-size family-run, in Kawazoe, jumped by about 50 percent, from 3,295 to 4,898 (6,807 in the prewar period), the number of factory workers increased by about 40 percent, from 34,712 to 48,868, and the total amount of shipments on an annual basis from 1.67 million yen to 5.01 million yen, led not only by clothes (mostly four times) and papers (triple) but also metals (double), machines (double), and precision instruments (triple) (SWG 1978a, 87–88). Those small/medium-size factories solidly supported the miraculous economic development over the next couple of decades, in the mid 1950s, 1960s, and early 1970s.

Nowadays, Kawazoe has gained more attention as a major production site for Japanese traditional goods, such as alloy casting, glassware, textiles, paper crafts, paper folded screens (*byōbu*), paper umbrellas, handmade woodwork, tortoiseshell, dolls, battledore (*hagoita*), and so on. In order to galvanize the local economy, the municipal government implemented a unique policy—locally manufactured products would be presented in museum settings (SWG 1985, 260–61). Dozens of very small museums exhibit such historically significant products, and artisans directly sell their products, while telling their means of production. Some of these museums are attached to factories, while others occupy small, open spaces in remodeled houses. For example, one museum exhibits the history of baseball equipment, such as wooden bats, balls, and gloves, and how they are manufactured. Others include a museum making various fortune seals (*senja-fuda*), which people use to print their own name cards and paste them on temple and shrine poles as pilgrimage commemoratives. One display shows the entire procedure used in casting, from the pouring of the molten metal into a mold to the finishing steps of the product. Another focuses on paulownia (*kiri*) wood products, in particular, the casting of chests of drawers made of paulownia, popular among Japanese, and tools needed in the manufacturing process (SWG 1997, 86–91). Since its inception in 1984, this industry-promotion policy has been successful in informing residents about the industries and products in their neighborhood.

Lastly, I should mention one social problem that Kawazoe faces: a decreasing population and accelerating aging society. According to the local history book (SWG 1978a), the population of this area was 77,595 in November 1945, shortly after World War II ended. Compared to the national census conducted in 1940, this figure showed that 85 percent of the local population was lost. However, the population gradually recovered in the early postwar era, with the annual increase rates more than 30 percent during the period 1946–1949 and nearly 7 percent during the period 1950–1954; it peaked at 326,000 in May 1963 in tandem with the economic development of Japanese society. The population at that time was almost equivalent to the peak population before the war in 1925. Since then, however, the total population figures have been declining. The history book attributes the decline to three causes (SWG 1978a, 27–28). First, there was the change of supply-demand balance in the Japanese labor market in the 1960s; in other words, the number of job hunters exceeded job openings around that time. Laborers, in particular young people, preferred jobs at bigger companies outside of Kawazoe, which provided better benefits, rather than working at small/medium-size companies in Kawazoe with low wages and long working hours. Second, people started to move to outside districts—those more convenient for commuting to their workplaces in western Tokyo, Chiba, and Saitama. Those areas provided better living conditions than Kawazoe. In fact, expanding pollution amid the national economic growth, including smog, noise, and bad smell, also accelerated the trend. Third, several factories themselves moved to suburban areas, looking for wider land opportunities and a potential labor force. Since 1963, the local population has been decreasing, primarily led by young men; meanwhile, the aging population is steadily increasing. The elderly population (sixty-five years of age or older) nearly doubled, from 10,535 people in 1960 to 20,751 in 1978 (SWG 1978a, 48), and it continues to increase. As of June 1, 2006, 20.6 percent of the total population was elderly, ahead of the national average (SWG 2006).[2] Under the circumstances, my field site, SLG, an NPO promoting lifelong learning, plays a significant role in providing learning opportunities to this expanding aged population. In fact, SLG successfully absorbs the local aged population as course takers and even mobilizes these residents as volunteers. These details will be discussed further in chapters 3 and 4.

Associational Life in Kawazoe

Kawazoe, a Tokyo neighborhood, is home to many voluntary third-sector groups. A wide array of social groups and social networks is active at the local level, including neighborhood associations, foundations, citizens' groups, and a local NGO. These groups have solidly established themselves in the neighborhood and have supported local associational life. In this section, I briefly introduce these groups individually. My field site, SLG, a new third-sector group, was generated within this active, rich, local associational landscape.

Neighborhood Associations

There are 164 neighborhood associations, or *chōkai*, in Kawazoe.[3] The neighborhood association, also known as *chōnaikai* or *jichikai*, is a major community- or territory-based social organization in Japanese society. The term *jichikai* is used more often in certain official settings, but I employ the term *chōkai* because this is the term that people at my field site preferred to use, and I believe it is more popular among ordinary people. Neighborhood associations are organized as volunteer-based groups that aim to achieve self-governance and mutual assistance. Primarily, they function as grassroots administrative entities; *chōkai* collect garbage for recycling, organize seasonal festivals (*matsuri*), take the national census, prevent juvenile delinquency, and deliver disaster relief in emergencies.

My field site is located in the area of Kawazoe 2-*chōme chōkai*. Regarding the purpose of the organization's activities, one of the *chōkai* members told me that members aim to help each other and promote mutual friendship for the betterment of the community. At the time of my fieldwork, there were about 660 households in the neighborhood, 540 of which (about 80 percent) joined the *chōkai*. Anybody living or working in the neighborhood can join. Many people living in apartment houses, such as students and young couples, do not join as individuals; instead, these residents join as a group, typically as an apartment unit. Members were required to pay a monthly fee of 500 yen (approximately $4.50). These funds were used for buying such items as shared cleaning equipment and decorations for the summer festival. In addition, the municipal government provided 100,000 yen (approximately $900) annually for activities. The government's aid was specifically used for paying electric bills for crime-prevention lights that *chōkai* managed in the neighborhood.

The Kawazoe 2-chōme *chōkai* has a president (*kaichō*), a vice president (*fuku-kaichō*), and a person in charge of accounting (*kaikei*), and collectively they are called *sanyaku*—three key officials who are elected (but mostly nominated by predecessors) from members every other year. Further, the association organizes age-based subgroups, such as associations for children (*kodomo-kai*), young men (*seinen-bu*), and the elderly (*rōjin-kai*). Women, mostly housewives, also have organized a group (*josei-bu* or *fujin-bu*). Although *chōkai* involves voluntary activities, I have the sense that participation in the age-based groups is largely compulsory if they are members. Further, the *chōkai* has special sections: general affairs; crime prevention (*bōhan*) and traffic control, both of which are closely linked to the local police department; firefighting linked to the local fire department; and disaster relief. One member of each household, usually the male householder, is assigned to one of these special sections, which often has nothing to do with the individual's interests. Asked why they registered for the *chōkai*, one member told me that there were several merits: it is easier to get information on the neighborhood, since the members would receive the circular notice (*kairanban*); one can participate in *chōkai*-sponsored events such as festivals; and residents can generate a stronger voice as a group than as individuals when they need to make a request of the municipal government. In fact, each *chōkai* makes a federation (*rengōkai*) with other neighborhood associations in

order to form a stronger opinion to the government and business entities as an associational group. In Kawazoe, the member told me that
chōkai stands as one of the most trusted social organizations within the
local population.

PTAs

The PTA, or Parent-Teacher Association, is another major associational
group in Kawazoe. I gained the impression that the PTA is almost equivalent to the neighborhood association in terms of power and eminence in
the community. There are forty-two PTAs (thirty for elementary schools
and twelve for junior high schools) in the district. One PTA, based at a
junior high school in Kawazoe, has one president, one vice president, and
eleven administrative staff, including teachers and parents, for example.
The voluntary activities organized by PTAs include helping at school
athletic meets (*undōkai*) and cultural festivals (*bunkasai*), participating in
cleaning in the school district, and arranging thank-you parties for the
teachers (*shaonkai*) at graduation time. Members' primary goals are to
link the family and the school and to promote the sound development of
children. Each local PTA belongs to a national organization, the National
Congress of the Parent-Teacher Association of Japan, and an equivalent
at the prefectural level. Those upper organizations are categorized as an
incorporated association (*shadan hōjin*), a key type of third-sector entity
in Japanese society, which I will explain later in this chapter.

A similar organization is called the Youth Development Committee (*seishōnen ikusei iinkai*). This group has a broader membership—most
members are drawn from PTAs, but schoolteachers and members of
neighborhood associations, juvenile welfare institutions (*jidōkan*), and
amateur sports associations also are represented. This group is particularly interested in preventing juvenile delinquency. Members, whose
objective is to encourage delinquency prevention at the grassroots level,
conduct regular patrols in the community. Further, the group appoints
junior high school and senior high school students as Junior Leaders.
Participation in this group is completely voluntary, and the number of
youth participants is quite low. In Kawazoe, I heard that only around
thirty junior high school students (and no high school students) had
registered for the group's activities out of a total estimated population
of 10,000 junior high and high school students. The junior high school
students in this group are expected to play an important role in local
activities; in particular, they are charged with leading the children's
associations affiliated with the neighborhood associations and helping
children participate in local social life.

Culture-Promoting Foundation

Certain groups in Kawazoe patronize a music hall near a JR station, which is one of the major public facilities in the district. A national symphony orchestra is based in this hall, where local residents can enjoy classical music at special discounted prices. The group that is in charge of the hall is the Culture-Promoting Foundation (*bunka shinkō zaidan*). The major activities of the foundation are organizing music concerts, public relations, and managing the facility. Those businesses are entrusted to it by the municipal government.

This group takes the organizational form of the incorporated foundation (*zaidan hōjin*)—a major third-sector entity incorporated under Article 34 of the 1898 Civil Code. As I mentioned in the previous chapter, there are two kinds of public interest corporations: incorporated foundations (*zaidan hōjin*) and incorporated associations (*shadan hōjin*). In Japan, as of October 1, 2005, there were 25,263 public interest corporations, 12,586 of which were incorporated foundations (MIAC 2006). According to Civil Code Article 34, the objective of an incorporated foundation or association must be charity, worship, religion, education, art, and other activities for public interest, and not for profit. Further, a group certified as an incorporated foundation is generally required to provide proof of an endowment of at least 300 million yen (approximately $2.7 million) as a "sound financial base" and an annual budget of 30 million yen (approximately $270,000). Related to this point, as Robert Pekkanen and Karla Simon (2003, 80) put it, the major difference between an incorporated foundation (*zaidan*) and an incorporated association (*shadan*) is that the latter is "formed around a group of members," while the former is "formed around an amount of money." In other words, zaidan requires money up front to establish the organizational entity, while there are no such requirements for *shadan*.

The municipal government in Kawazoe established this Culture-Promoting Foundation in March 1996 by providing 5,000 million yen (approximately $45 million) when the music hall opened; since then, the government has been supportive of the organization's activities, entrusting all aspects of facility management to the foundation. For the fiscal year 2003, the foundation received about 660 million yen (approximately $6.3 million) from the government as aid money, according to the foundation's annual report (SBSZ 2003). The size of the allowance accounted for almost 76 percent of the total annual revenue of 870 million yen (approximately $8.4 million). Nearly 450 million yen (approximately $4.2 million) were used for facility operational costs, while 230 million yen (approximately $2.1 million) were used for business expenses. This financial dependency makes the foundation act as a quasi-government organization, like many other third-sector groups in Japan. The foundation does not have members but is governed by a board of directors in accordance with basic rules laid out by its founders in its charter. The annual report revealed that the board of the Culture-Promoting Foundation was comprised of sixteen directors. The secretariat was composed of fifteen staff, including three part timers.

Amateur Sports Association

The Amateur Sports Association (*taiiku kyōkai*) is another major incorporated foundation. This association is organized by thirty-two clubs with some 2,000 local people devoted to local sports such as volleyball, tennis, baseball, soccer, karate, swimming, and golf. According to a leader of the Kawazoe tennis club, the Amateur Sports Association, established shortly after World War II in 1951, encourages everyone in Kawazoe to enjoy sports and provides support for the proper and safe conduct of sporting activities. Asked to identify the most important work of the association, the man told me that member clubs devote the greatest effort to sending players to the National Sports Festivals (*kokutai*), the largest amateur sports festivals in Japan. Thus the major task is to organize athletic competitions at the municipal level and to select the best athletes for competitions at the prefectural level. The national festivals, which occur every year, allow prefectures to compete against one another; traditionally, the prefecture hosting the festival is supposed to win the championship. Fostering junior sports clubs is another important area of the Amateur Sports Association's work. Of Kawazoe's thirty-two local sports clubs, twelve have junior sports clubs. The local association is part of the Tokyo Amateur Athletic Association and the Japan Amateur Sports Association, both of which are legally registered as incorporated foundations. The local association receives the financial resources necessary for the further promotion of sports from these upper organizations and, in turn, it distributes subsidies to grassroots organizations for their daily activities. The secretariat was housed in the city hall. However, there were no regular secretariat staff members at the Kawazoe branch; the leader I talked to, and a couple of helpers, voluntarily performed the administrative work. In addition, the staff of the municipality answered the telephones when necessary.

A similar group is called the Cultural Groups Federation (*bunka dantai rengō*), which is organized by local cultural groups in Kawazoe. The groups can be characterized as independent gatherings for hobby clubs by people who like Japanese traditional music such as *minyō* and *shigin*, instruments including *koto* and *shakuhachi*, painting (*nihonga*), tea ceremony (*sadō*), flower arrangement (*kadō*), and calligraphy (*shodō*). It was not as well organized as its sports counterpart, however. In fact, the cultural group does not have a corporate status like the Amateur Sports Association. It should be included as a citizens group, which I will explain later.

Senior Citizens' Manpower Center

As mentioned earlier, there is another type of public interest legal person: the incorporated association (*shadan hōjin*). There are several incorporated associations in Kawazoe, including the Senior Citizens' Manpower Center (*kōreisha jinzai sentā*), Workers' Welfare Service Center (*kinrōsha fukushi sentā*), Medical Association (*ishi-kai*), Dental Association (*shikaishi-kai*), and Association for Pharmacists (*yakuzaishi-kai*). In Japan, as of October 1, 2005, there were 12,677 incorporated associations (MIAC 2006). Actually, this type of organizational entity is very familiar to me. Before returning to graduate school, I worked for an incorporated association, Kyodo News, a wire news service. This news agency had chosen this nonprofit status in order to pursue free expression as a journalistic institution without being burdened by economic motives. Kyodo News is made up of various member organizations across Japan, including national and local newspapers, television stations, and radio stations, all of which pay membership fees (the amount of which depends on the size of the company and the number of readers). It is operated under a charter of association and is governed by a general assembly of all members, who elect a board of directors to oversee the day-to-day activities of the organization.

In Kawazoe, the Senior Citizens' Manpower Center is one of the major incorporated associations. The center, established in 1979, looks for and creates job opportunities, mostly on a part-time basis, for retired persons. Advocating "active aging," one secretariat staff member told me that the center primarily helps the elderly positively join in their communities, putting in circulation their experienced knowledge, skills, and free time. The jobs mostly include handyman-type activities, including cleaning and weeding, carpentry, and facility management for parking lots and buildings, most of which were paid on an hourly basis. For example, cleaning earned 850 yen (approximately $8), weeding was 1,000 yen (approximately $9), and carpentry was 1,700 yen (approximately $15). Anyone who is over sixty years of age and living in Kawazoe is eligible to become a member and to gain access to the job information that the center offers. Each member pays 1,000 yen as an annual fee.

The business was originally and is continuously funded by the national government as a policy amid ongoing demographic change—aging—in Japanese society. Each municipal government was expected to set up a workforce center for senior citizens in the 1950s, and the centers were later reincorporated as incorporated associations. The local centers are under control of the national and prefectural equivalents and have a strong link to the municipal government's local commerce and industry division. Administered by nine (four regular and five part-time) secretariat staff members, the Kawazoe center had 1,737 registered members (1,082 men and 655 women) as of September 2006 (telephone inquiry with an official of the center, September 22, 2006).

Social Welfare Council

The Social Welfare Council (*shakai fukushi kyōgikai* or *shakyō*) is well known among local people as a major source of traditional volunteer opportunities, such as assisting the elderly, the physically disabled, children, and migrant workers. People looking for volunteer opportunities in the area of nursing the aged or *kaigo* usually go to this council first. In fact, the council is now being reorganized into volunteering promotion centers at the prefecture and municipal levels. Instead of *shakyō, borantia sentā* or *borasen* (the designation of "volunteer center") seems to be becoming more popular among the residents. The council is campaigning for volunteering, introducing lots of volunteer opportunities for local residents in the monthly newsletter and on the Internet. The opportunities include help for the aged—changing sheets and serving lunch—and support handicapped persons' participation in the municipal sports festival. The council also organizes volunteers. To my knowledge, sixty-five local volunteer circles were affiliated with this council. Volunteers with the council have performed Braille translation, learned sign language, given rides and haircuts to the aged, and so on. Among them, I observed that volunteers from the Red Cross (*sekijūji*) were very active at this social welfare facility. Further, the council plays a significant role in supporting single-mother families in the municipality by providing dormitories, sending presents to people who turn 100, and providing money to volunteer groups organized primarily for helping the handicapped.

In legal terms, this entity is registered as a social welfare services corporation (*shakai fukushi hōjin*), placing it within the wider category of public interest corporations, which is defined in Article 34 of the Civil Code but authorized by the Social Welfare Services Law. The Social Welfare Council is organized by a unit of the municipality, and the total number of councils was about 3,400 across the country and sixty-three in Tokyo (Tokyo Council of Social Welfare 2006). The Kawazoe Social Welfare Council was established in May 1960 by the municipal government and was approved as a social welfare services corporation in 1962. The council was administered by twenty-six staff members, and their salaries were fully financed by the municipal government's social welfare budget. I have a sense that the social welfare council works as an actual service provider for the government's social welfare policy.

Citizens' Groups

Associational life in Kawazoe is characterized by a flourishing of small, independent, community-based citizens' groups (*shimin dantai* or *shimin gurūpu*). Some groups do not even have names; they are merely referred to as gatherings. In this category, women's groups promoting international exchange (*kokusai kōryū*) and community development (*machizukuri*) groups are very active in the neighborhood. The women's group promoting international exchange is an independently organized association for women who have participated in international exchange missions dispatched by the municipal government. There were about thirty women, mostly housewives, and the group was positively involved in Japanese education as teachers for migrant workers and the families in Kawazoe. Meanwhile, I observed that one community development group was active in revitalizing the area of Mukōjima, a traditional Tokyo neighborhood. The key member was a landowner in the area, and the members included owners of mom-and-pop shops and family-oriented factories, and *salaryman* (white-collar workers). Focusing on old-style Japanese architecture in the neighborhood, the group invited artists, architects, designers, and college students majoring in architecture and design and created active discussion space for thinking about community revitalization from the perspective of art and architecture.

In legal terms, citizens' groups are categorized as *nin'i dantai*—informal private groups. Such organizations are neither controlled nor protected by Japanese law. According to a survey conducted by the Cabinet Office (2001), the estimated number of third-sector entities in Japanese society, including both registered and nonregistered groups but excluding neighborhood associations, is 87,928. Among them, 204 NPOs were incorporated under the 1998 NPO Law when the survey was announced in September 2000, and about 26,000 were structured as public interest corporations such as incorporated foundations and associations. Of the remaining entities, it has been estimated that more than 60,000 groups fall into the category "citizens' group."[4]

Environmental NGO

Kawazoe is home to one environmental NGO. It is one that promotes the use (i.e., recycling) of rainwater. This environmental NGO aims to build a self-sustaining society through rainwater utilization in the local community and beyond. It was originally established as part of a community revitalization project in Kawazoe; in particular, it was intended to provide relief preparation for disasters. As noted earlier, the Kawazoe district was totally destroyed by the Great Kanto Earthquake of 1923. Members of this environmental group are campaigning to set up a tank for each household for the storage of rainwater so that residents can secure independent water resources. Nowadays, around the district, these water-collection containers often can be seen outside of homes, although people usually use collected rainwater for watering flowers and flushing their toilets in daily life.

According to its members, this Kawazoe-based NGO is trying to construct a loose network with some 300 people across the country from Osaka, Ehime, and Okinawa, exchanging water-utilization information and technologies. Further, the group aims to contribute to the development of irrigation systems that effectively use rainwater in the Asia-Pacific region. As part of this transnational effort, the NGO held an international conference on rainwater utilization in the summer of 2005. The conference, co-organized by the municipal government in Kawazoe, and supported by Japanese state agencies, local corporations, and the United Nations Environmental Program, attracted some 2,000 individuals from both Japan and foreign countries interested in environmental issues, including activists, researchers, journalists, and businesspersons.

I have classified this group as an NGO. In the Japanese context, NGOs are categorized as groups that are active on international issues. Some pursue development, while others are involved in peace, the environment, human rights, and so on. Currently, some internationally active NGOs, such as the Japan NGO Center for International Cooperation and Peace Winds Japan, have NPO status under the 1998 NPO Law. This Kawazoe-based group also received the official corporate status in August 2006.

Co-ops

The Japan Consumers' Co-operative Union, known as Co-op (*seikyō*), is another active associational group. The union is a social movement pursuing a more human lifestyle and sustainable society through the concerted efforts of individual citizens (see Japan Consumers' Co-operative

Union 2002, 2006c; Tanaka 2005). Historically, co-op movements existed in Japan prior to World War II, but they were banned under the militaristic government during the war. The current co-op movement was legalized when the Consumers' Livelihood Co-operative Society Law was passed and enacted in 1948, and the Japan Consumers' Co-operative Union was officially established in 1951. During the period of high economic growth in the 1960s and 1970s, the co-op movement gained full force as economic growth brought with it environmental destruction and contaminated products due to insufficient quality control. Consumers, mostly concerned housewives, threatened by these economic, social, and environmental problems, sought to exercise their rights by joining co-ops rooted in their local communities. The co-op movement stimulated a consumer movement, one of the new social movements in Japan in the 1970s and 1980s. Some of the movement's activists formally developed their activities as a political party, *Seikatsusha* Network, later (see LeBlanc 1999). Shedding light on social welfare, environment, gender, and peace, primarily from the perspective of women and children, the party regularly won several seats at local assemblies, mostly in the urban Tokyo area (Seikatsusha Network 2006).

Consumer co-op activities include retail co-ops (166 of 572 member societies), university co-ops (148), medical co-ops (118), schoolteacher co-ops (44), institutional co-ops (77), and so on (Japan Consumers' Co-operative Union 2006b). Meanwhile, if asked about co-ops or *seikyō*, I believe many Japanese people would comment on their original strategy for food safety. Co-op members organize study groups to learn about food safety and to sample and review co-op brand products, including organic rice, fruits, meat, milk, and so on. Today, co-ops are an integral part of communities, with 30 percent of all households in Japan belonging to one (Japan Consumers' Co-operative Union 2006a). In Kawazoe, there were two co-op outlets, and members could purchase the co-op brand products at discounted prices or by catalogue mail orders.

Red Cross

A local branch of the Japanese Red Cross Society (*sekijūji*) has been active in Kawazoe. The Red Cross is well known in Japanese society for its global emergency-relief operations, nationwide hospitals, and nursing education. Local residents in Kawazoe know the Red Cross because they often see the organization's blood-donation campaign around the JR station every weekend and at festival sites. As mentioned earlier, I often encountered volunteers from the Red Cross who were very active in supporting local social welfare facilities. They conduct activities on a nonpaid basis as volunteers. At SLG, I met one very active Red Cross volunteer. She was a leader of a local Red Cross volunteer group, and I had the impression that she was always a strong advocator of the virtue of volunteerism among local residents whenever provided an opportunity to do so. In fact, the Japanese Red Cross Society has been built on a grassroots foundation of organized volunteerism in Japan. According to a source (Japanese Red Cross Society 2006, 7), when most of Japan's infrastructure had been destroyed and required reconstruction after World War II, the delegates of the American Red Cross introduced the concept of "volunteering" to Japanese society. The first Japanese Red Cross Volunteer Corps was established in 1948, and in 1950, the network of the Corps was expanded through the country. The regulations of the Corps stipulate the missions as: (1) disaster relief, (2) health and sanitation, (3) social welfare, and (4) dissemination of the Red Cross Principles.

In legal terms, the Japanese Red Cross Society is a special corporation (*tokushu hōjin*) established under the Japanese Red Cross Law. The Red Cross is nationally organized by its own members. Any individual can become a member by paying an annual membership fee of 500 yen (approximately $4) or more, and nearly 13 million individuals were registered as individual members and some 190,000 corporations as corporate members as of January 2006 (Japanese Red Cross Society 2006, 6). They have the right to vote to elect the Board of Representatives. In addition, as I mentioned earlier, volunteers play significant roles in implementing the Red Cross program at the grassroots level. Red Cross volunteers are organized into three different types of groups: community volunteers, youth (student) volunteers, and special volunteers who have skills or experience for disaster-relief activities. Specialized volunteers undertake a variety of activities, including radio communications, first aid, water safety, acupuncture, massage, Braille transcription, and language services. What we often observe in everyday life is the first type: community volunteers who are active in social welfare institutions and hospital. As of March 31, 2005, there were 3,245,351 people (2,803 Corps) registered as community volunteers across the country (Japanese Red Cross Society 2006, 7). In Kawazoe, seventy people, mostly housewives, registered as community volunteers for the local Red Cross volunteer group as of March 31, 2002 (telephone inquiry with a Red Cross official, September 26, 2006).

Business Exchange

Several independent groups have been organized by small business owners. Kawazoe Business Exchange (*igyōshu kōryūkai*) is one such entity. This group was organized by a dozen self-employed persons—business and factory owners in the district, including an accountant, a brass-processing manufacturer, a paper-box manufacturer, a bottle-cap manufacturer, and a plumber. The group's primary purposes are to facilitate the exchange of information, to expand members' networks beyond their existing businesses sectors, and to contribute to community development in Kawazoe. One member of the Kawazoe Business Exchange told me that they established this exchange in order to galvanize the local economy, since the economic conditions in Kawazoe, made up of small, family-oriented businesses, largely depend on the information exchange. Many of these groups were created during the "bubble" economy of the late 1980s through the early 1990s. However, he said to me privately, after the burst of the economy, their activities lost momentum. In fact, many members could not afford to join volunteer activities, as the economic downturn directly hit the small, family-run factories in Kawazoe from which members came. Some members even teetered on the edge of bankruptcy. Thus the activities of the organization largely depend on the economic climate.

Most of the members originally came from the Kawazoe branch of the Tokyo Junior Chamber (*seinen kaigisho*, usually called JC). According to its fiftieth anniversary commemoration book (Tokyo Junior Chamber 1999, 4–5), the group was established by young local and business leaders under forty years of age in 1949 and aimed to contribute to the sound reconstruction of a new Japan after World War II. The group was helped by the Tokyo Chamber of Commerce and Industry (a special corporation created under the Chamber of Commerce and Industry Law) from the start. The JC is not a club of financiers, nor a body simply involved in delivering social services; it is a movement of young leaders with ideals and concrete, integrated policies that consistently challenge the way forward. It is the major young businesspersons' organization in Japan, with more than 700 members (Tokyo Junior Chamber 2006). The organization is affiliated with the Junior Chamber International Japan, which is legally classified as an incorporated association.

Media

The media is a key actor in associational life. Here in Kawazoe, popular media include daily newspapers, television, radio, and magazines. Cable television, which primarily specializes in local news and community-based programs, is one of the major information sources for residents. The local television also provides radio programs and the broadband network for the Internet. For instance, *Weekly Kawazoe*, a popular channel for residents, offers broad information on public events, meetings, entertainment, and notices from the municipal government on a weekly basis. *Special Channel* presents classical music concerts sponsored by the Culture-Promoting Foundation, choral performances by local mothers' groups and elementary school students, and traditional folk song (*minyō*) performances by local enthusiasts. Originally the cable television was jointly established by the municipal government and local businesses in 1990 but was later acquired by one of the major cable television providers due to a sluggish business environment. Although the subscription rate in Kawazoe has remained at about 11 percent or 105,000 households over the past decade, the new company aims to increase the subscription rate to some 20 percent, an average subscription rate in the Japanese cable television industry (SCT 2006). The cable television market is gradually expanding, and local people take advantage of getting information for their social lives.

Local Shrines and Temples

Japan is a secular society. Even so, local people regularly go to temples and shrines. On the initial days of the New Year, each temple and shrine is crowded with visitors. People usually visit family graves during the equinoctial week (*ohigan*) and the Bon festival. In Kawazoe, there are thirty-one major shrines and temples as well as five Christian churches across town. In the Japanese third sector, there is a classification for religious corporations (*shūkyō hōjin*), as I introduced in the previous chapter. For example, shrines in Kawazoe are under the control of the Tokyo Shrine Agency, a religious corporation comprised of all of the 1,398 shrines in Tokyo (Tokyo Shrine Agency 2006). Further, some 78,000 shrines across the country are controlled by the Association of Shrines (*Jinja honchō*), a religious corporation, located next to Meiji Jingū in Tokyo.[5] Meanwhile, it seems that traditional temples are not as strictly controlled as shrines. There were new religious cults in Kawazoe (I confirmed two), and one was registered as a religious corporation.

During my fieldwork, I had a sense that local temples and shrines play significant roles as associational actors. I met a Buddhist monk who actively participated in and organized volunteer activities at his temple, including voluntary cleaning activities in the community. He came to my field site NPO as a volunteer too. I had a chance to ask him directly why he was so active in volunteering. He told me that his volunteer activities offered a good chance to get to know people in his community. "I came to know what local people wanted and what I could do for them. Knowing people's wishes and responding to them is one of my important jobs," he said. Actually, his comments and behavior made me realize later an important reality—volunteers overlap with their associational activities in Kawazoe, which I will argue in the following section.

SLG's Entry into the Associational Landscape

One autumn afternoon shortly after I started my fieldwork, I had an opportunity to visit small shops in the local community with two secretariat staff members, Mr. Kawade and Mr. Kose, from my field site, SLG. We brought 1,000 posters and 1,000 tickets to advertise a lecture organized by SLG; we asked people at the local mom-and-pop shops to sell these tickets on behalf of the organization. We went to two liquor shops, a bookstore, a Japanese-style bar (*izakaya*), Japanese noodle shops (*sobaya*), a Japanese public bath (*sentō*), and other establishments. I heard from Mr. Kawade that SLG was taking advantage of the network of one of its directors, who had influence in local business circles. As we visited these businesses, I felt that I was given a good opportunity to become acquainted with the landscape in which SLG was situated. I had never been to this part of downtown Tokyo before. We had an interesting conversation about NPOs with the owner of a rice-cracker shop. In a conversation with us, he said this:

> Honestly speaking, I don't know very much about NPOs. I don't know what they are doing. However, right now I often think about what I should do after retirement. I am now over fifty. Eventually, I wonder if I may also be involved with these kinds of activities. Some day maybe I will come to understand what NPO activities are.

We had another intriguing exchange with the wife of a local metal-parts manufacturer:

The wife:	What's SLG? I believe that I was asked by my friend to cooperate to sell tickets, but . . .
Mr. Kawade:	SLG is an NPO.
The wife:	Huh? *NPO*? Recently, I have heard that term many times. . . . But I don't know exactly what it is. . . .
[Silence]	
Mr. Kawade:	SLG is registered with the Tokyo Metropolitan Government.
The wife:	Oh, I am relieved to hear that. I think this kind of thing should always be confirmed. . . .

This was one of the most common statements I heard from people about the emerging NPO phenomenon in this society. At the ordinary grassroots level, the NPO, a newly institutionalized third-sector organization, was something totally unknown.

Thus my initial question in my fieldwork was as follows: What were the ways in which SLG had joined in the dense existing associational landscape in Kawazoe, described earlier? On this point, one of the symbolic incidents I experienced at SLG was a discussion about how to increase volunteer participation by achieving linkage with neighborhood associations (*chōkai*). During my fieldwork, I attended biweekly meetings of SLG's recruitment department. The agenda one day was how to increase the number of volunteers. Setting a quantitative target for the year, the attendees decided to recruit twenty new volunteers. Mr. Koba, the director in charge of this division, spoke to the attendees:

> In order to achieve the target, I think it is important that we take some actions. Until now, we were just waiting for new people to come to SLG. I think SLG could enter into the local community through the *chōkai* network. Why don't we link SLG with the neighborhood more? Many of the people in our neighborhood still don't know SLG or even our activities well. Why don't we directly visit homes and distribute our advertisements? However, I believe that one of the key points in the advertisement is that we are not just volunteers. We are volunteers for an "NPO." NPOs are front-runners in society. Try to let neighborhood people think about the meaning of volunteering for an NPO.

Following this remark, they discussed making posters that introduced SLG activities, which they would bring to *chōkai*, requesting that they be posted on bulletin boards. As I introduced earlier in this chapter, *chōkai* are widely considered the most reliable and trustworthy institutions in the local community. They also are tightly connected to the municipal government and local businesses. They further discussed how to connect with PTAs and other associational groups in Kawazoe. By establishing a relationship with existing associational groups such as *chōkai*, SLG probably would be able to easily win the trust of local people by upholding the associational landscape. In fact, this was one method for newcomers such as SLG to gain "social trust" (*shakaiteki shinyō*) in the existing social and political milieu. Social trust was indeed a key word in the Japanese NPO world. The primary reason to obtain NPO status is, as Figure 2.1

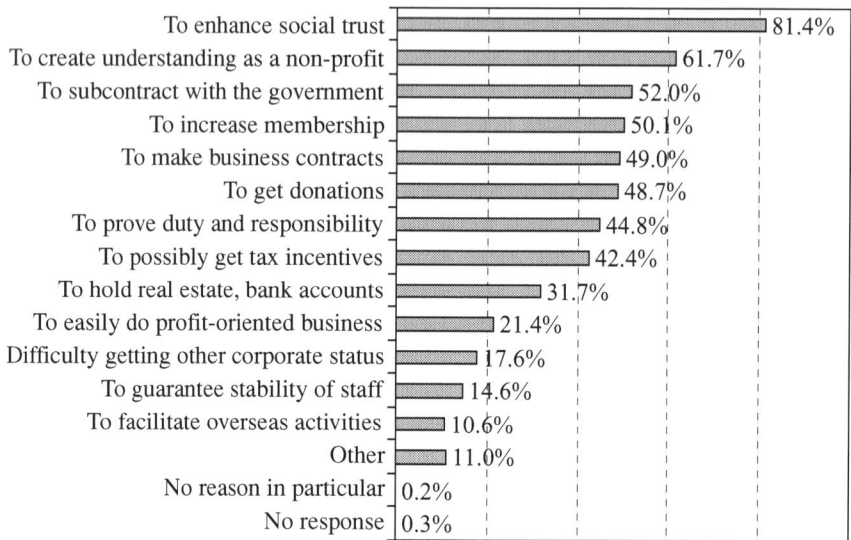

To enhance social trust — 81.4%
To create understanding as a non-profit — 61.7%
To subcontract with the government — 52.0%
To increase membership — 50.1%
To make business contracts — 49.0%
To get donations — 48.7%
To prove duty and responsibility — 44.8%
To possibly get tax incentives — 42.4%
To hold real estate, bank accounts — 31.7%
To easily do profit-oriented business — 21.4%
Difficulty getting other corporate status — 17.6%
To guarantee stability of staff — 14.6%
To facilitate overseas activities — 10.6%
Other — 11.0%
No reason in particular — 0.2%
No response — 0.3%

(Economic Planning Agency 2000, 134)

Figure 2.1 Reasons to Incorporate as an NPO

shows, to enhance social trust as an organization, according to a government survey (Economic Planning Agency 2000, 134).

As time went by at SLG, I gradually noticed a distinctive characteristic of the volunteers: people from the conventional associational groups, such as neighborhood associations and PTAs, were concurrently very active at SLG as well. I formed the impression that these people's support of SLG overlapped with their associational activities, as shown in Figure 2.2. These individuals all played significant roles in organizing and operating SLG activities, bringing their established knowledge and experiences to this newly institutionalized third-sector organization. Mr. Koba was a leader in the neighborhood associations, and Mr. Harada was a leader of a local PTA and organized a community development group. Ms. Katō, who had worked for an incorporated association as a director for three decades, was active in training and organizing volunteers. Mr. Ito, a leader of a local amateur sports association, helped organize several lifelong learning courses on sports. Ms. Tajima and Ms. Kunimatsu came from a local women's group promoting international exchange. Ms. Kaneko was organizing a local environmental NGO and serving as vice president at SLG. Ms. Asaoka, originally from the Red

Cross, often instructed other volunteers, especially young people, about the normative role of volunteers. Mr. Nakamoto was an active member of the local lawyers' association. Ms. Yokota was a member in the co-op movement. Mr. Aota was a producer at the cable television company. Mr. Tomoda was a Buddhist monk at a local temple. Ms. Murase and Ms. Andō had a friend working at the secretariat of the Culture-Promoting Foundation, who often jointly planned courses on classical music with local orchestra members. Mr. Kawade, originally from a business exchange circle in Kawazoe, participated in SLG as a secretariat staff member. SLG, an NPO, looked new, however, it was deeply supported by traditional associational power. Developing crossed social networks, SLG came to build solid social trust as a new associational group in Kawazoe.

In a sense, I believe that the emergence of NPOs has forged in an unprecedented direction in Japan. NPOs have created networks in a manner that has never been seen in conventional Japanese society. Ueno Chizuko (1994, 281–301) argues that traditional Japanese society is based on three types of networks: kinship, or *ketsu-en*, territorial

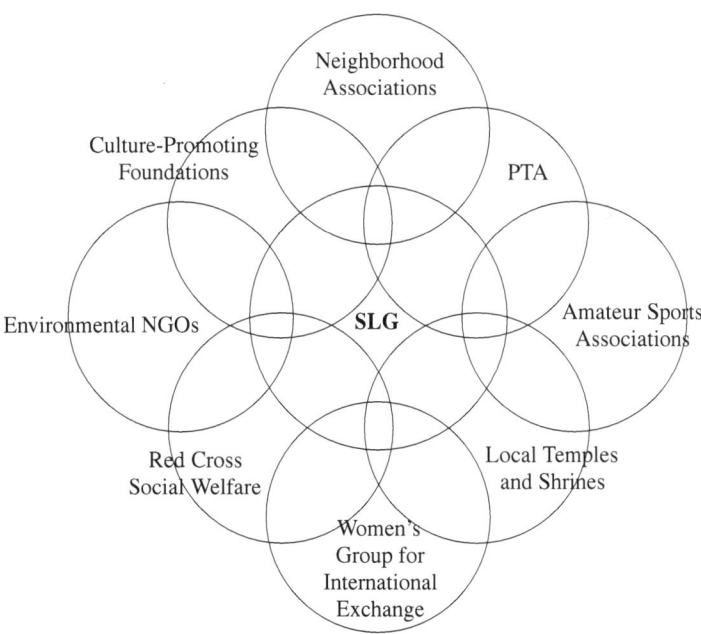

Figure 2.2 Conceptual Map of Local Associational Landscape in Kawazoe

bonds, or *chi-en*, and the corporate network, or *sha-en*. Japanese people are now beginning to bond through particular symbols; instead of making connections through conventional kinship, territorial bonds, or the corporate network, they can now choose to network with others on the basis of common values. Ueno termed this type of network *sentaku-en*, or the relation that people can choose. Networks involving NPOs seem to conform to Ueno's concept of sentaku-en. What I often heard at SLG—and what I myself experienced—was that people who would never have met in the traditional Japanese system are now interacting in the framework of NPOs. Meeting people in this way is a very different experience from any other I have had in my life. For a man like me, in his early thirties, associates ordinarily would be limited to people from work, school, and family. However, involvement with an NPO brought new encounters beyond my current networks. While involved with SLG, I met people from local associational groups. I had the experience of expanding horizontal and flexible social networks instead of walling myself within traditional vertical relationships in Japanese society. Further, I also confirmed this in a conversation with Ms. Andō. She told me, "I have met many wonderful people that I would have never met at other places. They have enhanced the quality of my life through discussions in course planning and meetings with SLG course takers. Without this, I would have only been a housewife." The NPO is indeed perceived as a catalyst for social change.

Social Capital Argument

Before moving to the next chapter, I would like to mention a key concept—social capital. The local associational groups and networks introduced earlier often are presented in the context of social capital in contemporary civil society scholarship, as I introduced in chapter 1.

Is Japanese social capital rich or poor? It also is that Japan is a "high social trust" nation characterized by communitarian capitalism (Vogel 1987; Thurow 1996). It is also said that Japan has a vibrant associational life with roots that go back to the rich capital stores of prewar Japan, and that the dense social networks of the prewar era are still used to mobilize the conservative vote (Hastings 1995). Meanwhile, Japanese political scientists, influenced by Robert Putnam (1993, 1995, 2000), have conducted quantitative research on social capital in Japan (e.g., Inoguchi 2000, 2002). One extensive study available on this topic, conducted by the Japanese Cabinet Office, was announced in June 2003. According to this study (Cabinet Office 2003), regions where volunteering is active show relatively low crime rates, low unemployment rates, and high birth rates. If we locate these findings within the concept of social capital, as the researchers did, then we would conclude that active volunteering activities enrich social linkage through human networks in local communities, which in turn results in the accumulation of social capital. From this perspective, volunteer activities definitely lead to a desirable result: peaceful, safe, and stable communities. Returning to the question I raised at the beginning of the paragraph, the research suggests that urban areas such as Tokyo and Osaka are social-capital poor, while regional areas are social-capital rich, due to the urbanization process.

Further, I am interested in how this seemingly new concept—social capital—has been introduced, argued, and even justified in contemporary Japanese society.[6] In particular, how are NPOs located in the social-capital argument? In fact, the research project described earlier encourages the government to pursue collaborative policies to build strong social capital in Japan. The researchers' key stance is that the government can build social capital through policies that build volunteering activities. According to the research report (Cabinet Office 2003, 101–102), such policies should cover a wide range, as the significance of social capital is not limited to any particular area. The government has been implementing various kinds of policies and programs related to community development, including community support and revitalization programs. The government also is given the following recommendations: create more policies to encourage participation in volunteer activities and activate existing volunteering programs. These policies will lead to greater social capital, as they play a significant role in creating human relationships among volunteers based on the norm of reciprocity. In this sense, volunteer-based NPO activities act as a seedbed for the cultivation of social capital. As highly recommended in the study, the government can take advantage of existing social capital for new policy implementation. By thus invoking social capital, the government is justifying a strategic reorganization of the existing social and political systems that will suit it. Social capital is available to the government to reduce its administrative costs by removing activities from the domain of the state. In fact, the report argues that social capital makes it possible to save taxpayers money through the devolution process as work moves from the state to the volunteer-based NPO sector. It is about the community successfully achieving progress toward solving social ills.

I would say that my field site, SLG, can be located squarely in this macro-discourse on social capital. In the next chapter, citing the case of SLG, I illuminate how this social capital argument in the policy recommendation documents was embodied at the local grassroots level, even though the term *social capital* was never used at my field site, and people at my field site seemed not to be familiar with the concept. I provide a detailed account of the ways in which one NPO was generated and operated in a local community in collaboration with the local government.

Chapter 3

NPO: A New Third Sector

SLG: An NPO Promoting Lifelong Learning

Mr. Endō registered for a course at SLG in the spring of 2002. He selected a class on the local history of Kawazoe. While working weekdays in Ōtemachi, a bustling business district in Tokyo, he wanted to study something, having graduated from college with an economics degree almost ten years earlier. A few months prior to his enrollment, he saw an advertisement for a Kawazoe history course in an insert in the daily newspaper to which he subscribed. Instead of the conventional subjects of lifelong learning[1] (e.g., foreign languages and liberal arts), he was looking to study something unique. The course he registered for at SLG was one of the most popular courses, Kawazoe Studies. The class served to introduce local residents to the history and culture of Kawazoe. For the upcoming spring semester, SLG prepared a Kawazoe Studies course focusing on the bridges over the Sumidagawa River. The course picked five bridges in the municipality from a total of eighteen bridges over the river, presenting local stories, related history and literature, and engineering and design. The course instructor was a university professor of engineering who had written a book on these bridges. During discussion time, many of the senior course participants were asked to share their memories of the bridges from childhood. The class met six times, every other Saturday morning, from April through June 2002. On the final class day, participants enjoyed a cruise on the river guided by their instructor. Along with Mr. Endō, seven men and thirteen women took the course.

Among the Kawazoe Studies offerings, a course for training tour guides was popular in the fall of 2002. Nine men and twenty-three women attended this class. One of the course participants, Ms. Nakamura, a housewife in her late thirties, commented, "Everything I

51

Picture 3.1 Tour guide course by a local historical statue of Katsu Kaishu, a political leader in the late Edo and Meiji periods; Katsu was born in Honjo, Tokyo, part of the neighborhood

heard during the course was new. I was trained as a local tour guide. However, the course meant more than that to me. Many of the places we visited were ones I had never visited. The course provided a good opportunity for new residents to become familiar with the area, since most of the participants, including me, were newcomers to Kawazoe." The course was presented with the cooperation of the local culture and tourist association, an affiliate of the municipal government. Over the eight sessions, which featured lectures and field trips, the participants learned detailed information regarding historic sites in Kawazoe. After finishing the course, participants were eligible to register as volunteer tour guides at the local culture and tourist association. All of them registered for this volunteer opportunity. Meanwhile, another popular course that was repeatedly offered at SLG focused on composing auto-biographies. In the fall of 2001, eight senior citizens (two men and six women) enrolled in the course wrote personal "ending notes" for family members to read upon their deaths. Reflecting upon their own lives, the participants enjoyed chronicling their experiences, many of which were unknown even to their children. They wrote narratives every week and read them aloud in class, with the instructor suggesting improvements. The instructor's motto was "the most important thing is, above all, enjoying writing." After finishing the three-month course at SLG, the members of this group formed an independent learning circle and continued to write their autobiographies.

Like these courses, SLG offered a variety of lifelong learning opportunities to local residents. As shown in Figure 3.1 (further details are in Appendix 1), the organization offered a total of nearly 200 individual courses over two years, from 2001 to 2003. The course list represented the concept of lifelong learning at SLG. It included activities in various areas—not just culture and hobbies but also career development, foreign languages, dance, and sports. An individual could take many of these classes on his or her own initiative to enrich and improve his or her life. SLG classified its courses in eight categories: area/community studies (i.e., Kawazoe Studies), career development (computer, bookkeeping, English, etc.), languages, children's courses (English for kids, rhythmics, storytelling, etc.), liberal arts (literature, history, art history, etc.), hobbies (drawing, ceramic arts, cooking, etc.), sports and refreshment, and special events and lectures. Liberal arts subjects, including Japanese literature, world history, and foreign language (English and Chinese in particular), as well as drawing, are most popular. These courses had solid demand from local residents, and applications for the courses always came pouring in as soon as they were advertised via a monthly newsletter published by SLG. Most courses had sessions every week or every other week and lasted three to six months. SLG offered these courses to local residents as well as nonresidents who worked in the municipality. During the fiscal year 2003 (from April 2003 through March 2004), 1,814 local people registered for SLG courses. Course participants spanned all generations, from minors to seniors (see Figure 3.2). However, the majority of participants—65 percent—was over fifty years of age, and 78 percent (1,411) of the total of 1,814 participants were women.

In addition to the regular courses, SLG organized several special one-day events and lectures each year. On the first day of summer vacation in July, SLG held a summer festival targeting local children. Several activities were prepared to introduce traditional Japanese handcrafts and toys such as *koma* (tops), *kendama* (cups and balls), *kusabue* (grass reed), *takeuma* (stilts), and *origami* (paper folding). On this occasion, local seniors invited from neighborhood associations and PTAs served as instructors, teaching the children how to make the toys and play with them.

Furthermore, SLG offered special lectures, hosting well-known persons such as writers and actors to speak. The lectures included what

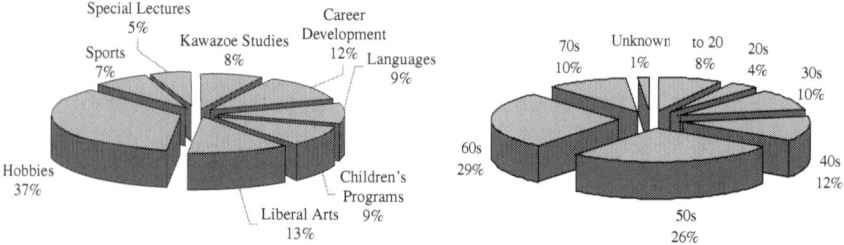

Figure 3.1: Courses Offered at SLG   Figure 3.2: Course Participants
at SLG

they called *Trend Seminar*, planned twice a year, which let local people learn more about something that was newsworthy or trendy. Shortly after I started my fieldwork, I joined the organizing committee for the lecture. At the first series that year, SLG had invited a lawyer. The man was well known in Japan, since he was the prosecutor in investigating the Lockheed-Marubeni scandal a couple of decades earlier. In the early 1990s, he started up an incorporated foundation in social welfare, organizing volunteers interested in elderly care, and since then he was

Picture 3.2 Chinese language and culture course

Picture 3.3 Drawing course on still life

Picture 3.4 Summer kids' festival at SLG

regarded in the mass media as a strong advocator of volunteerism in Japanese society. As I describe in detail in the next section of this chapter, local people were participating in SLG activities as volunteers, so they were eager to listen to all kinds of stories on volunteering, in this case, social welfare volunteers—the most popular category in the NPO incorporation. For the second series, meanwhile, the committee was considering another key topic for SLG—community. The seminar in the fall featured the widow of a famous Japanese comic storyteller (*rakugoka*). A native of Honjo, a Kawazoe neighborhood, she told a story entitled *Life in Shitamachi* (downtown Tokyo), which covered her sad experiences during wartime as well as her postwar life. During World War II, she was separated from her parents when she and her brother were evacuated from Tokyo. She then lost her parents in the heavy U.S. bombardment of Tokyo in March 1945, in which more than 80,000 civilians perished. Hearing her experiences as a war orphan reminded the audience of the tragedies, of the conflicts, and of how people in Kawazoe helped each other survive in the postwar period. After the second lecture, one audience member sent a comment to SLG remarking on the importance of the talk and the need to transmit such experiences to the next generation. In this way, SLG played an important role in passing on traditional local culture. Over a year, thousands of local people came to these events and lectures.

Tuition for SLG courses was set at a very low price due to the nonprofit characteristics of the organization. The tuition for one course was generally around 6,000–8,000 yen (approximately $55–$75)—almost half or a quarter of the cost of classes at other lifelong learning providers. The money earned as tuition primarily went to instructors as gratuities (with the amount of compensation varying with teaching experience), while some went to facility fees. SLG generated no major profits through its course offerings. This brings up an interesting question: How did SLG finance itself as an organization? The money SLG required to function, including personnel fees for administrative staff and other facility maintenance fees, actually came from the municipal government. For the fiscal year 2004, for example, the money from the government was 86.3 percent of the total annual budget, some 155 million yen (approximately $1.3 million); meanwhile, only 3.9 percent (706,750 yen, or approximately $6,100) came from membership fees and 13.3 percent (24 million yen, or approximately $210,000) from their own businesses—mostly earned from one-day special events and lectures. There were no donations from individuals and corporations.[2] Given this situation, some have wondered whether SLG is a third-sector NPO that should be associated neither with the government nor with businesses. During the fieldwork, this also occurred to me. This financial structure explicitly reflects how SLG was originally established. I argue the historical development later in this chapter.

Activities Organized by Volunteers

Some might say that the kinds of lifelong learning opportunities that SLG offered could probably be provided by university extension (non-degree) programs, language schools, and culture centers (*karuchā sentā* in Japanese, most of which are operated by newspaper publishers and department stores). This is true. Many lifelong learning opportunities are available in Japanese society (see Thomas 1985; Ogawa 1991; Kawanobe 1994; Thomas et al. 1997; Sasai 1998; Gordon 1998; K. Sato 1998; Wilson 2001; Rausch 2003, 2004; Watanabe 2005; Ogawa 2005). However, what made SLG stand out among these offerings (and what impressed me throughout my fieldwork) was that the organization's operation was primarily performed by ordinary local resident volunteers within the framework of an NPO. These individuals' activities were conducted on a nonpaid, voluntary basis. Volunteer participants planned and implemented courses, distributed information on lifelong learning in the community, and promoted the virtue of lifelong learning.

As of March 31, 2003, SLG had a total of 102 registered volunteers, 68 percent of whom were women and 32 percent of whom were men. As Figures 3.3 and 3.4 show, more than half of the volunteers were over fifty years of age, and housewives were the most active volunteer participants. Volunteer activities at SLG, as of April 2004, were organized into five departments: course planning, volunteer recruitment and training, public relations, learning support, and planetarium operations. All

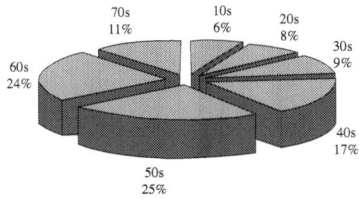

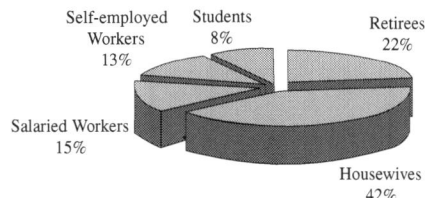

Figure 3.3 Volunteers' Ages at SLG

Figure 3.4 Volunteers' Occupations at SLG

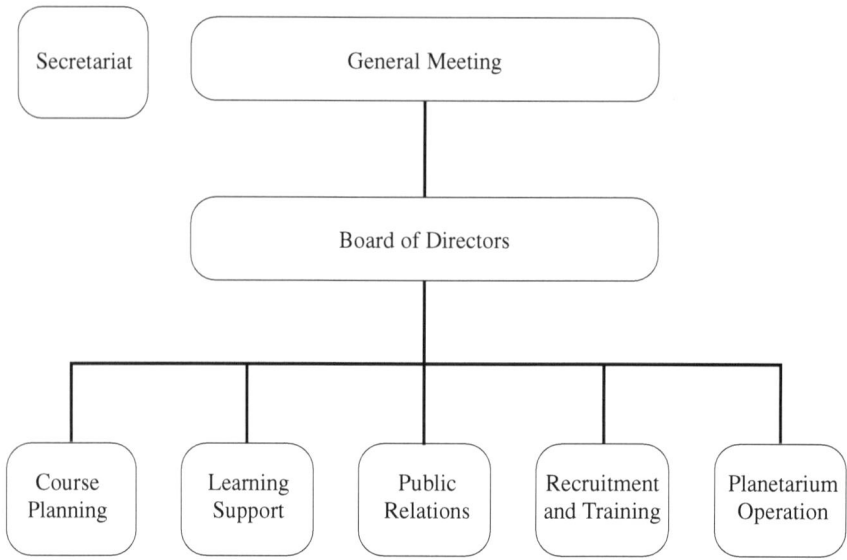

Figure 3.5 Organizational Structure of SLG

of the registered volunteers were expected to belong to one department based on their interests. Among the five departments, course planning drew the most volunteers.

Course Planning

Every other Tuesday night, around 7 p.m., volunteers in the course planning department went to a regular meeting. Some men and women came directly from their workplaces, and housewife volunteers ran up after finishing dinner preparations. Meanwhile, secretariat staff members unlocked the doors of the meeting room and started organizing hand-outs and materials for the day's discussion. On one day in November, the discussion was going to be on regular lifelong learning courses, a special one-day event and lecture, and what SLG would offer the next spring (and beyond). It was a free two-hour discussion. Ms. Kunimatsu, a local business owner and leader of the course planning night team, facilitated the series of discussions. Ten other volunteers attended that night, in addition to two secretariat staff members. The thirty-six regis-tered volunteers in the course planning department divided themselves into a couple of subgroups based on their availability for attending meetings (afternoon or night), and they aimed to jointly produce feasible course plans.

On that night the group started by outlining the course selections following requests from the local residents. The course planning process usually started with the volunteers considering requests from local residents in Kawazoe. SLG prepared *yume shīto*, or dream sheets, on which local residents could request what they wanted to learn. These sheets were readily available at any public place in the municipality—city hall, libraries, and other public facilities. Some residents brought filled-out sheets to the secretariat, and others faxed them. The sheets also were distributed on the last day of SLG courses, along with a course evaluation survey. Based on such requests, SLG provided lifelong learning courses. But, most practically, volunteers registered in the course planning department were expected to seek instructors through their networks in Kawazoe and beyond and to negotiate the course content and schedule with them. The instructors included college professors, retired high school teachers, local historians, traditional craftsmen, and SLG volunteers themselves.

Ms. Kunimatsu had some thirty *yume shīto* submitted by the local residents. The requests covered a variety of new course ideas, including

Picture 3.5 Volunteers' discussion scene for course planning

a reading course for the best-selling novel, *Harry Potter*, in English, a preparation course for the newly created Test of English for International Communication (TOEIC) Bridge test, a cooking course for men, wine tasting, aqua fitness for working women, making silver clay, accessories with beads, and so on. Ms. Kunimatsu also had a couple of requests from recent course takers asking for advanced courses in Chinese and bookkeeping. One interesting request from a local resident was a course on *Tetsuwan Atomu*, a popular cartoon robot character known as *Astro Boy* in English. It originated as a *manga* comic series started in 1952 by a well-known cartoonist, Tezuka Osamu, and broadcasted on Japanese television in the early 1960s. Many Japanese people, mostly adults in their forties and fifties, had some sense of comfort when they talked about the robot character. The anonymous local resident mentioned that since this year (2002) would be the fiftieth anniversary of the cartoon appearing as a manga comic series, it might be a good opportunity to create a course to reflect Japan's postwar history as well as Japanese manga industry. Ms. Tajima, a housewife volunteer, said, "I was wondering why we might focus not only on the comic itself but also on robots. I was thinking that lots of factories in Kawazoe, even though they are small and family oriented, are currently introducing some robots in their production processes. That perspective would even give a chance to reexamine our community." Ms. Andō responded, "Also, kids might be interested in robots, I mean, science as a whole. Why don't we expand our focus more into science and technology?" Several volunteers who were interested in the course design created a subgroup and continued this sort of discussion in a very constructive manner. They discussed the course purpose and content, target population, and course fee, while looking for a teacher. The request finally took the shape of a special lecture the following fall. Inviting a son of Tezuka Osamu as a speaker, it focused on the historical development of the comic series in postwar Japan, while slides of the works were projected on a screen. The talk also referred to the introduction of robots in our daily as well as future lives. Nearly 100 local residents, including elementary and junior high school students, in addition to SLG volunteers, participated in the lecture.

Another request that drew the volunteers' attention was about the tale of Forty-Seven *Rōnin* (masterless *samurai*), popularly known as the *Chūshingura* (translatable as the treasury of loyal retainers). This is a true story about the valor and ideal of Japan's *samurai*. Forty-seven *samurai* avenged the disgrace and forced *seppuku* (ritual suicide) of their master, Lord Asano, by assassinating Lord Kira, the official responsible for his death. After a year of debate at all levels of society, the *rōnin* (masterless samurai) committed *seppuku* as they had been ordered.[3] This story was well known as the honorable fulfillment of revenge, especially for an admirable leader, embodying the virtue of loyalty in *bushidō*. The forty-seven *samurai* are memorialized in a play (originally in *Kabuki* and *Jōruri* and now in television dramas and movies) called *Chūshingura*. The Kira's mansion, which the *samurai* attacked at that time, was located in Honjo, a part of my field site Kawazoe. This incident happened in 1703, and the request was submitted since the following year would be the 300th anniversary. Ms. Kunimatsu responded, "This is very interesting. We can freely and creatively think about courses related to *Chūshingura*." Ms. Yokota, a housewife volunteer, responded, "Yes, we can think about a course on history, literature, fine arts, traditional culture, and so on." The request was actualized in the following years in a variety of ways, including a Kawazoe studies course focusing on *rakugo*, or Japanese traditional comic storytelling, on *Chūshingura*, and on history and literature courses in the liberal arts category.

In their course planning, it seemed to me that course planning discussions emphasized three things. The first was the Kawazoe Studies program, which was presented through regular courses, special lectures, and events. In the eyes of the people at SLG, their program development made the organization different from other lifelong learning providers. For both course takers and course planners, the program implemented at SLG generated reflective thoughts on the community and fostered community development sensitivity through lifelong learning activities. The second point was the idea that course contents should mirror the times. The course planning volunteers were very sensitive to what residents should know about the rapidly changing social, political, and economic environment. As shown in Appendix 1, courses offered by SLG addressed such timely topics as Middle Eastern history and culture following the start of the Iraq War in March 2003, for example. Third, what I was primarily impressed with during my fieldwork was that SLG volunteers recognized their involvement in the process of course planning and implementation as part of their own experience of lifelong learning. Ms. Minami, a piano instructor in her early forties, designed an introductory course on opera after volunteering for one year in the course planning department. She shared her own experiences with some newly joined volunteers. "I planned a course on opera, responding to a request from a local resident. Currently I am happy to help with the course. Every week I became obsessed with the course preparation, though. While making use of my job as a piano teacher, I was wondering how much I could help course participants understand opera music with an instructor. I believe in being involved in this process; I make efforts to achieve something that is definitely a part of my own lifelong learn-

Picture 3.6 A housewife volunteer assisting in a children's craft course

ing. I appreciate volunteering at SLG. It gives me a chance to enhance myself in such a way." When courses started at SLG, volunteers were allowed to sit in on courses for free, and most did so. Meanwhile, they were expected to help facilitate the courses. Volunteers' responsibilities included locking and unlocking classrooms, preparing handouts, and taking attendance. Further, in fine arts and craft-making courses, volunteers were asked to help course takers make products. Volunteers from all other departments at SLG were welcome to join in this final process of course implementation. Many told me that such participations in the courses were the happiest moments of their time as volunteers.

Learning Support

The learning support department, composed of twenty-three volunteers, mostly seniors, sponsored opportunities twice a year (usually in the spring and fall) for course takers finishing SLG courses to present what they had learned over the past months. Collaborating with volunteers in the course planning department, learning support volunteers encouraged course takers to participate in the presentations. The course participants, given fifteen to twenty minutes, presented the results of their courses over the past three to six months—songs, dances, storytelling for children—on the stage of the lifelong learning center where SLG was housed. Picture 3.7 is a snapshot of a presentation by those who took a popular course on *dodoitsu*—Japanese storytelling from the late Edo period, combining *shamisen* sound with narration to present a unique (mostly comical) monologue on love and work. The presentation was held over a weekend, with some ten groups taking the stage. Further, there were exhibits by those who took such courses as ceramic arts, Japanese paper crafts, Chinese embroidery, and patchwork. Course takers would be expected to present their pieces of work for one week.

The department also was in charge of encouraging course takers to form independent learning circles after finishing SLG's regular courses so that they could continue to learn with others. The autobiography learning circle, which I profiled earlier in this chapter, is an example of this department's efforts. The department realized that sixty-five such groups were active, and volunteers in the department also tried to network with them, encouraging information exchanges among various

Picture 3.7 *Dodoitsu* (Japanese traditional storytelling) presentation; coursetakers enjoy presenting old love and work stories with *shamisen* sounds

circle participants. In the fall of 2005, it organized the first conference of that kind, and twenty-two people from ten circles shared their experiences. Further, helped by SLG secretariat staff members, volunteers in the department were asking lifelong learning and hobby clubs in the municipality to register their activities into a database they were building. The database was designed to link clubs to local residents who wished to join their activities and to forge networks among people who share interests. I heard there was information on some 600 items registered, including their activities' contents and instructors' contact information; this number was gradually increasing through their efforts.

Public Relations

The public relations department, which aimed to provide information on lifelong learning, attracted many young volunteers. Thirty-one volunteers comprised this department—most of whom were in their twenties and thirties and some of whom were in their fifties and sixties—divided into three groups. The first group published a monthly newsletter titled *Mirai* (the future), widely informing the public about SLG activities, upcoming courses, and events and volunteer opportunities. Ms. Horie, an editor and a housewife volunteer, said, "We want to advertise our activities to as many people as possible in an easily understandable way. We try to write clearly with pictures and illustrations. Simply saying, 'these are our activities and our roles within SLG.'" She added, "We don't get money for writing or taking pictures. We are amateurs. But I believe we are doing something public, thus we have a responsibility to write our activities clearly and accurately to the local residents. We are trying to be as professional as possible." For this purpose, there was a column titled *Kaze* (winds) written by volunteers. It was composed of a series of 100-word writings in Japanese, and volunteers took advantage of this column to practice writing. This A-3 size four-page publication was distributed to each of the some 82,000 households in the municipality as an insert in the local daily newspaper. Mr. Endō, whom I mentioned at the beginning of this chapter, was drawn to SLG by this publication. The second group was in charge of developing the SLG Web site, which mostly reflected the monthly publication's contents and was updated once a month. This group was actually started by graduates of a course on how to create a homepage. Twenty-five people joined this group since its establishment and continued its activities. As of December 2006, the number of pages on the homepage had increased to nearly 150 pages, three times the initial number. Mr. Yamamura, a *salaryman*, joined the group in February 2004. He expressed his honest thought with a laugh: "I never had experience

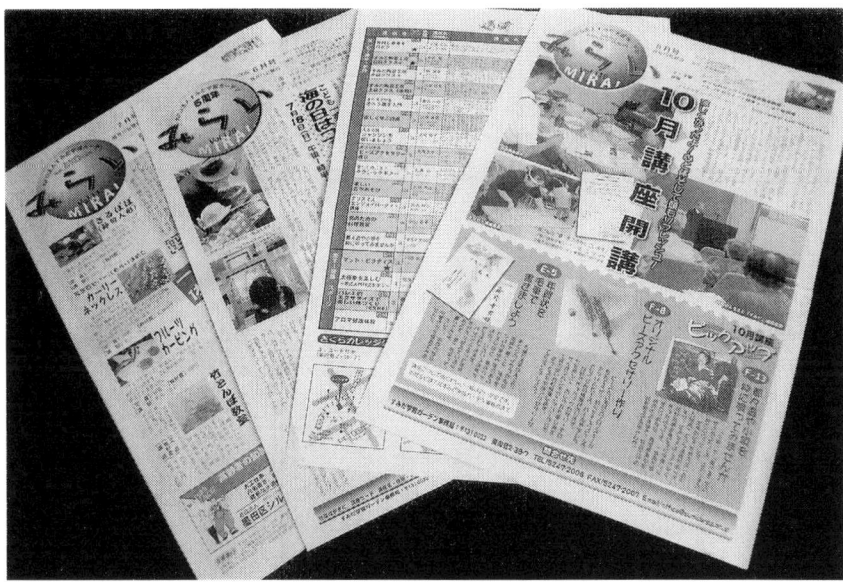

Picture 3.8 Monthly newsletter *Mirai,* published by SLG, introducing its courses and activities to local residents

making a homepage. I was just interested in making one. When I first attended a meeting of the group, I was very impressed with what they were doing. It seemed like a lot of work (for 'unpaid' volunteers)." After learning technical skills from senior members, he is able to upload two pages a month. Members of the group usually did their assigned jobs at home, brought what they made to the meetings every other week, and combined them with what they accomplished at the meeting. Meanwhile, the third group produced a short TV program introducing SLG activities, including current popular courses and upcoming events, for the local cable television station. This twenty-minute program was aired once every other month on cable television in Kawazoe. Volunteers in this group actually appeared on cable television; they reported on SLG's regular lifelong learning courses and special one-day lectures and events, interviewed course participants, and took pictures for the television camera. This team was aided by a producer from the local cable television, whom I mentioned in chapter 2. They usually got together every Saturday afternoon to produce the program.

Volunteer Recruitment and Training

The volunteer recruitment and training department was interested in expanding SLG membership and the training system. People with some professional background in planning and human resources seemed to be attracted to this department, where their experience could be utilized. Among the twelve volunteers registered to the department, Mr. Kondō, a leader in the department, had taken early retirement from a position in charge of planning at a tool-and-dye company, and Ms. Katō, an assistant leader, was a retired director of an incorporated association.

The department provided many opportunities for volunteers to share with each other their stories of serving at SLG. For example, they produced a monthly A-4 size newsletter for members, with the aim of exchanging information as well as sharing some self-reflections on their daily activities. Further, the department held open houses twice a year for local people interested in SLG and its volunteer activities, followed by a three-month training program for newly enrolled volunteers. The recruitment methodology employed at SLG was, simply put, that volunteers recruited volunteers and then trained them. An introductory comment made by Mr. Kondō in the three-month training program illustrates this recruitment effort:

> I want to tell you what we are doing here at SLG. Maybe I should say something about what volunteerism is, or what NPOs are. But I would rather use this opportunity to say more specific things. We realize ourselves as volunteers promoting lifelong learning. The word "volunteers" probably conjures up images of social welfare assistants or disaster-relief workers. However, we are volunteers promoting lifelong learning for local residents. It is about offering places for learning, providing information on learning, and supporting continued learning. To start, I really want to ask you to come to our meetings. Please look at the white board. You can find a schedule of meetings. We will always welcome you with coffee and snacks. I believe, from my experience, doing volunteer activities here at SLG will lead to your own lifelong learning, which was often said here. Furthermore, I feel some satisfaction when course takers enjoy courses with which I am involved. I believe you will too.

One day at an open house, a couple of questions followed this introductory comment, although the listeners were generally calm. A man who participated in the open house said, "My job is irregular. Is it a problem?" A senior volunteer, Mr. Iwata, responded, "No, you participate in our activities when you have time." Ms. Andō, a housewife volunteer attending the open house on that day, added, "You might have no idea about what you will do as a volunteer. At the beginning I had no idea what I could do here either. So I started with what I could do—that was housekeeping for a course, as many of you may think of it. Start gradually. Don't be in a hurry." Listening to Ms. Ando's suggestion, another woman commented, "Actually I took several courses here at SLG, and last year I took a magic course. I was impressed with the woman who helped with the course offering. Thanks to her efforts, the course ran very smoothly and well. I heard that she was helping the course as a volunteer. I also wanted to help courses like her. That's why I came here today."

The three-month training I witnessed started with a session where senior volunteers introduced SLG activities. Volunteers in the department then conducted intensive interviews with newly registered volunteers, asking them about their interests and motivations and determining which department they wanted to join. Afterward, the new volunteers were paired with current volunteers who shared their interests. The senior volunteers were expected to take care of the new volunteers, largely by bringing them to activities and helping them participate. Additionally, senior volunteers told their experiences to junior volunteers and helped them solve problems they faced. After the three-month training period, the new volunteers formally registered at SLG. At this stage, they had a chance to switch departments if they wished to do so. In addition to this main workload, the department organized, when necessary, in-house training seminars for registered volunteers. They invited researchers on lifelong learning and volunteerism for professional enhancement.

As part of training, furthermore, volunteers in this department were starting to network with other volunteers in active lifelong learning facilities beyond Kawazoe, mostly neighboring groups in and around Tokyo. They went out or invited over their counterparts a couple of times a year and exchanged information on their activities. Mr. Iwata, a *salaryman* in his thirties and a volunteer of this department, told me that by networking with other volunteers in different lifelong learning organizations, he came to objectify his own activities at SLG and understood which points they should improve and which points they were stronger on than others. He wrote a New Year's resolution in a monthly newsletter, which the recruitment and training department published—"I was thinking that I would like to tell our SLG activities to our colleagues across the country. I would like to expand my networking with other lifelong learning groups. It would be the best if I could have more friends." I observed his activities during my fieldwork, and I was impressed that he gradually empowered himself as an individual, or a citizen, not just only a volunteer, through networking and knowing people and their activities. I was thinking that he confirmed that what he was doing at SLG was meaningful through this networking.

Planetarium Operation

The planetarium operation department, established in April 2004 after I left the field site, was in charge of creating programs for the planetarium attached to the building in which SLG was housed. Operations of the planetarium, a facility originally managed by the municipal government, were partially entrusted to SLG in April 2002. This planetarium was one of the few public planetarium facilities left in central Tokyo, and third-grade students in Kawazoe and its neighborhood municipalities regularly visited it as part of their science classes. Volunteers in the department, along with planetarium engineers, participated in the content operation of the planetarium.

Board of Directors

SLG had a board of directors (*riji-kai*) to discuss the strategic issues of the organization. It met once a month on every fourth Saturday morning. Each of the five departments elected two or three representatives to the board; usually a leader and assistant leaders took the director (*riji*) positions. The board also functioned as an intermediary network for other associational groups in Kawazoe. Leaders from a variety of local groups, which I introduced in chapter 2, also were invited to join the board as directors and sometimes as observers. From the directors, a president (*rijichō*) and a couple of vice presidents (*fuku-rijichō*) were nominated; the president expedited the proceedings at the monthly meeting.

Based on the demographic data, indicating that housewives were the most active participants at SLG, which I introduced earlier in this chapter, some would argue that gender dynamics in the traditionally male-dominated Japanese society are now changing through NPOs. This conclusion is, however, difficult for me to support. At my field site, I did observe that women were active as grassroots volunteers. However, the management of the organization led by the board of directors was dominated by men. As of March 31, 2003, twenty-five men and only four women sat on SLG's board of directors. In my observations, most female participants at SLG were relatively distant from the NPO's management and key decision-making processes, even though they were actively involved with grassroots activities, especially course planning and implementation. A similar phenomenon is reported by Joan Pynes (2000), who examined the representation of women as chief executive officers and board members in nonprofit organizations in the United States. Her findings suggest that more women than men serve as chief executive officers and fiscal officers of nonprofits, but that these organizations have more men than women as board presidents and treasurers. Likewise, at my field site, men dominated the board. Women did serve, however, as financial and administrative officers at the secretariat.

General Meeting

The general meeting (*sōkai*) was held once a year, as required under the NPO Law. Here at SLG it usually was held in May and functioned as the highest level decision-making institution at SLG. This meeting was led by the board of directors. All of the volunteers were expected to attend, and high-ranking government officials and members of the board of education in Kawazoe were invited. The ostensible purpose of the meeting was to discuss and approve all of the current year's activities and the next year's plan, including the budget. However, in the two times I attended this meeting during my fieldwork, it was rare to see active discussions between ordinarily volunteers and board members on the meeting agenda. The meeting took approximately thirty minutes, with the SLG head simply reading the agenda items to the floor. The meeting, in other words, was not dynamic. It is possible that there was a reluctance to reveal inside conflicts in front of government officials. Traditionally in Japan, nothing is supposed to happen at this kind of meeting. There is a ridiculing term for this type of meeting, called *shan shan sōkai*—referring to the hand-clapping sounds of attendees only participating in the closing hand-clapping ceremony known as *tejime*. If something happens, for example, if somebody raises a question, then it dampens the perception of achievement of the current management and even destroys harmony. I felt that attending these meetings was one of the most boring parts of my fieldwork.

Secretariat

Lastly, within the organization, all administrative work stemming from the volunteer activities outlined earlier was supported by the paid staff of the secretariat (*jimu kyoku*). This work primarily consisted of collecting tuitions, arranging classrooms, and controlling information regarding course takers and instructors. During my fieldwork, from 2001 to 2003, SLG was dramatically expanding its staff. When I started in September

2001, the organization had seven full-time staff members (including me as nonpaid, full-time staff researcher) and six part timers, headed by the secretary general (*jimu kyokuchō*). In April 2004, there were fifteen regular staff members and eight part timers engaged in expanding the business. However, consistently, the majority of secretariat staff members were women. At that time, twenty out of twenty-three staff members were female.

When I was working at the secretariat, one of my interests was the NPO as a new workplace in Japanese society. NPOs have created a new style of occupation in contemporary Japan, as careers in these organizations differ from conventional "*salaryman*" and "*OL*" (office lady) jobs. At SLG, several young people on the secretariat staff joined the NPO after working in a different sector. I asked one of these new staff members, Mr. Honda, why he had chosen an NPO as his new workplace. A native of Kawazoe, Mr. Honda was thirty-one years old. He had worked as a salesman for a housing materials company listed on the Tokyo Stock Exchange for nine years after graduating from college. While eating lunch, I asked, "Why did you choose to work at an NPO?" He replied, "I wanted to work for my community. When I was working at my previous company, I was in western Japan for seven years. I never had a chance to come back to Tokyo, to my hometown. Why do I have to work such a way? I was looking for another way of my life."

This type of narrative was not unique to people working at SLG but also could be read in the popular press. The *Asahi Shimbun* (June 7, 2003) newspaper reported a survey on NPOs conducted by the Hakuhodo Institute of Life and Living, a think tank affiliated with a major advertising company. The survey asked 1,000 men and women what they thought of NPOs. According to the survey, 31 percent of respondents intended to create NPOs or to work for NPOs. The creators of the survey interpreted the NPO as something to discover when one is searching for personal meaning in life. A weekly business magazine, *Shūkan Tōyō Keizai* (March 29, 2003 issue), targeting *salaryman* between the ages of forty and sixty, encouraged its readers to think about NPO involvement as a new lifestyle. The magazine presents comments from people in its target demographic who participate in NPO activities. For instance, *Tōyō Keizai* printed the following remarks from the former director of a Tokyo bank, "In the morning I go to work at 7:30. I try to finish at 6 as often as possible. After 6, it is time for my NPO activity. On Saturday and Sunday, I do it, too. . . . I can make a contribution at my workplace. But I also want to contribute something to this society. I can do this by participating in an NPO." In an *Asahi Shimbun* newspaper article, December 19, 2002, entitled "Let's make an NPO. Solving ordinary problems with friends," a bureaucrat in his thirties who had joined several kinds of NPOs expressed his view that "NPOs play a significant role because they can act in a very flexible manner. In my work in public administration, I am involved in the macro process of law making. However, it is difficult to be involved with something on a case-by-case basis." The article also described a female advertising professional in her thirties who had established an NPO focusing on public relations. Prior to founding the NPO, she had been assisting international development NGOs by creating introductory pamphlets and posters as a volunteer. As she had found it difficult to balance her job and her volunteer work, she decided to create an NPO that would embrace both dimensions of her life and that would ensure that her work continued. In her words, "Even if I can't do this activity, somebody will take it over if it is an NPO. The organizational mission will never fade away." Indeed, working at or making an NPO represents a new way of life.

Encouraged by these social trends, universities have established both undergraduate and graduate training programs in nonprofit sector management in which summer internships at NPOs are required. For example, in 1994, Osaka University, one of the core national universities in Japan, started a graduate program offering theoretical and practical training to professionals in the nonprofit sector. Waseda University in Tokyo established a similar graduate program in 2003. Rikkyo University in Tokyo created a graduate program in nonprofit management in 2002. Meiji University in Tokyo created an undergraduate program in nonprofit management in its business department in 2003. These programs were established in response to the growing need of NPOs to secure staff with both practical and academic knowledge as well as proficiency in law and management theory.

Historical Background

SLG did not suddenly appear in the local associational landscape of Kawazoe. The new third-sector organization solidly emerged from existing associational life in downtown Tokyo. In 1994, a municipal government entity in downtown Tokyo opened a public facility for promoting lifelong learning in the local community. This facility was located where SLG is now housed. It represented the first attempt to build such a facility in a Tokyo metropolitan municipality. This move in Kawazoe was made in direct response to the national enactment of the Law for the Promotion of Lifelong Learning in 1990. This law prescribed measures such as the establishment of a Lifelong Learning Council at the national and prefectural levels for the local promotion of lifelong learning, provisions for the development of lifelong learning in designated communities, and surveys for assessing the learning demands and needs of prefecture residents (see Kawanobe 1994). Lifelong learning responsibilities at the prefectural level include collecting and providing information about learning opportunities, training local supervisors and instructors, developing lifelong learning programs appropriate to the needs of residents, investigating the demand for learning, evaluating the results of learning, and administering lifelong learning programs. As Kawanobe (1994, 489–90) indicates, the framework for lifelong learning at the local municipal level, in contrast to the prefectural level, depends on each municipality's particular environment.

As I mentioned earlier, there are several lifelong learning opportunities in Japan, including university extension programs, language schools, and cultural centers. Japan is unquestionably a society that highly values lifelong learning. The Social Education Law of 1949 created a solid foundation for social education in Japan. The law articulated the idea that social education is a legal right of the Japanese people. According to Article 3 of the Social Education Law, both the national and municipal governments must make every effort to set up and operate public facilities for lifelong learning to allow everyone in the population to take advantage of opportunities to enhance their lives by cultivating themselves. According to Article 7 of the law, furthermore, the state and local public bodies shall endeavor to attain the aim of education by the establishment of such institutions as libraries, museums, and citizens' public halls (*kōminkan*) by the utilization of school institutions and other appropriate methods.

In Kawazoe, where there were no higher education institutions such as traditional colleges or universities, one of the chief wishes of local residents and municipal government officials was, for many years, to establish a place where residents could continue to learn at a very low cost. Following the enactment of the 1949 Social Education Law, the government provided a few learning opportunities. They were very limited, however. In urban Tokyo communities like Kawazoe, there were no public facilities called *kōminkan*, which often were seen in rural Japan. Instead, youth halls, or *seinenkan*, and public gyms, or *taiikukan*, provided some programs equivalent to those that *kōminkan* provided (SWG 1978b, 990–1013; see also SWBE 1986). Moreover, for a place like Kawazoe, with a rapidly aging populace, as I introduced in chapter 2, it was extremely important to consider individuals' demands to achieve worthwhile lives through learning activities.

The municipal government started a discussion on developing comprehensive lifelong learning opportunities in the municipality in the early

1980s. During this time, the concept of lifelong learning was regarded as an extremely important idea on a national scale (Sato 1998, 86–95). In 1981, amid rapid changes in Japanese social life following advances in science and technology and the progress of internationalization, the Central Council for Education, an authoritative advisory body to the Education Minister, submitted a report stating that Japanese people needed to explore possibilities for creating a society based on lifelong education (Central Council for Education 1981). In 1984, the Ad Hoc Council on Education, which pursued the vision presented in the Central Council for Education's 1981 report, was established as an advisory committee to Prime Minister Nakasone Yasuhiro. The following year, the council emphasized that "education in the future should have 'lifelong learning' as its basic premise" and encouraged a transition from a conventional system divided into two categories—school education and social education—to a lifelong learning system (Ad Hoc Council on Education 1987; see also Hood 2001 for Nakasone's legacy in educational reform).

In September 1987, following these national initiatives, the municipal government in Kawazoe stepped in to establish a task force on lifelong learning under the direct guidance of the mayor. The next year, the task force recommended that the municipal government set up a nondegree-oriented "community college" for adults in the municipality (SWG 1990). The task force report, which articulated an ideal style of lifelong learning in Kawazoe, in fact described what my field site, SLG, would later provide to local residents. Specifically, the report recommended that a newly created lifelong learning program should offer courses that directly and broadly reflected local residents' needs, should actively provide lifelong learning information, should regularly prepare presentation opportunities for learners, and should form networks with other associational groups. The program, the report said, also should extend opportunities to learn about the traditional culture of Kawazoe and aim to transmit cultural information to the next generation.

In February 1990, the government officially announced that it would build a public facility to sponsor lifelong learning opportunities. This project was bolstered by the euphoric mood of the "bubble" economy of the late 1980s to early 1990s. By the time the lifelong learning center was completed in 1994, however, the government faced huge fiscal difficulties against the backdrop of a deadlocked Japanese society and economy, primarily due to the decline of tax revenues following the collapse of the "bubble" economy. At that moment, it occurred to the government to make a local residents' group operate the center. The government recruited local residents as volunteers and assigned them the task of creating lifelong learning courses, thereby delegating an active role of the government as defined by the education laws. In fact, the group would generate no additional cost to the government while still perfectly fulfilling its objective. Ultimately, this group would become my field site when it changed its organizational form to that of an NPO, a new third-sector citizens' organization. The original group was nominally labeled a "citizens' group," according to the classifications I outlined in chapter 2. Despite this categorization, in actuality, the citizens' group was strictly controlled by the municipal government. That is, the government dispatched its staff to help but more precisely to oversee volunteers' work, and it funded the operation, as part of its "citizens' group" support policy.

"NPO-ization" Led by the Government

Why did the "citizens' group" become an NPO? Why did the group choose to get NPO status? Answering these questions was one of the research agenda items for my fieldwork. I pointedly asked many people why SLG chose to become an NPO. To understand the transition, I had a lot of conversations with the participants of the original founding group and local government officials, while digging up meeting records and archives from hundreds of boxes in an underground storage space of the public lifelong learning center. After sifting through the seemingly discarded and uncared-for materials for almost half a month, I found a document titled "Toward Incorporating the Resident-based Lifelong Learning Organization by Local Residents" (SWG 1999b). It was a seven-page proposal prepared by the municipal government. Actually, the government had enlisted a private think tank to make the proposal, and specialists hired by the government played a significant role in directing the discussion of the agenda with the government and local volunteers. This document was one of the most crucial findings of my research exploring why SLG had become an NPO. A summary of the document (full translation is available as Appendix 2) follows:

Government Proposal toward "NPO-ization"

1. From Volunteers' Groups to NPO

The Government and NPOs

> In this country, we believe that solving social problems is a
> mission of the government. We believe that social services
> should be provided by the government. Social services have

been based on key political principles of equality and fairness, however, it is doubtful nowadays that social services are responding to complicated new social problems and the diversified values of citizens. The government was expected to respond to such problems and values in a prompt manner and on an individual basis, however, if the government does this, its cost will increase.

On the other hand, NPOs make it possible to respond to such problems promptly and individually, taking advantage of volunteers and their contributions meanwhile achieving cost cutting to the government by providing the services. Social activities generated by NPOs, whatever they are, will make people realize the importance of independent, spontaneous activities for human beings and society. The expected role of NPOs will further increase in the twenty-first century, when the government tightens its budget.

The relationship between the government and NPOs is complementary. Both the government and NPOs are expected to respond to various social needs while making use of their characteristics. NPOs have strong images of providing nonprofit, volunteer-based social activities.

2. The Meaning of Incorporation as an NPO

Lifelong learning activities must be in line with the NPO Law.

In the NPO Law, twelve areas, including social welfare, social education, and community development are mentioned.[4] Promoting lifelong learning can surely be categorized as social education. Lifelong learning activities promoted by local residents provide learning opportunities as one of the basic social services and contribute to the development of lifelong learning in the local community. They offer independent, spontaneous learning activities that contribute to the betterment of society, deserving of NPO status. By achieving NPO status, the group can expand its activities. This also will make it possible to form collaborative relationships with the government and other private-sector companies as an equal partner.

3. The Agenda for Incorporation

> In order to achieve this, the current group needs to
> (1) strengthen organizational power as a business entity;
> (2) secure human resources for NPO operation; and
> (3) secure stable financial resources.

After finding this proposal, I set up an informal meeting at a drinking establishment with a senior official who was the director of the lifelong learning policy in the municipal government at that time. She told me this:

> I was involved with SLG before the group got NPO status. The former organization was operated under direct initiatives of the municipal government. Under the circumstances, it seemed that members had lost direction. They never found any shared meaning and purpose among them. Due to the lack of unified consensus, there were many trivial conflicts among the members. Many people, including me, were frustrated with the situation. Around the same time, Japanese society saw the emergence of NPOs as the NPO Law passed the Diet. Thus, *I* proposed the organizational form of NPO to the original group. I believed that people would rally behind a mission that an NPO would define. If we created and defined a mission, we could avoid petty conflicts because people could share in the mission—the meaning of their activities as an organization: promoting lifelong learning in Kawazoe. (emphasis added)

Indeed, what I heard through conversations with grassroots volunteers at that time was the same: the former group had lost direction as an organization. They told me that the situation primarily stemmed from the government's policy in running the group. The government actually paid the volunteers 1,000 yen (approximately $9) a day as reimbursement for transportation costs. However, the money was somewhat unnecessary, as many people came to the organization by bicycle or on foot from their homes in the neighborhood, thus incurring little or no cost. If the volunteers worked throughout an entire day, 500 yen (approximately $4.50) was further provided as a lunch allowance. In a month, some volunteers earned more than 30,000 yen (approximately $270). Under this situation, the group began to lose sight of its purpose—promoting lifelong learning in the local community. Some volunteers apparently came to make pocket money. There were many conflicts among volunteers.

In early 1999, shortly after the enactment of the NPO Law in December 1998, the government organized a special "advisory committee" to discuss the "NPO-ization" of the group. The committee appointed twenty-two people, including eight government officials, six specialists on lifelong learning, and eight resident volunteers. The specialists in the area of lifelong learning were directly appointed by the government, and a couple of them were heavily involved with writing the proposal I introduced earlier. Meetings were held eight times (once a month) from January through August 1999, although the committee spent only its last two meetings on "NPO-ization." I obtained and read all of the documented meeting records, but I gained the impression that the meeting records of the first six gatherings were not succinct. At the first six meetings, they merely confirmed the lifelong learning policy of the municipality over the past two decades, which I reviewed earlier. My goal here is to answer my original question: Why was the NPO created? I will thus exclusively focus on the last two discussions by examining how the government introduced the new organizational and social form of the NPO and explained it to the local resident volunteers, as well as how the volunteers responded to the government's proposal. Amid the government-led, top-down process of "NPO-ization," what did the volunteers feel and experience? In the following section, I analyze the minutes of the proceedings based on findings from meeting records, combined with interviews with the participants at that time, aiming to capturing grassroots voices on the "NPO-ization" as much as possible.

Response to the Government Proposal

In July 1999, the government submitted to this committee the proposal that I found. In response to the proposal, the committee members engaged in discussion. The government led the discussion, introducing this new type of organization called the NPO to the volunteers. It seemed that the government actually "taught" the group what NPOs were.

The director of the lifelong learning policy in the municipal government started the discussion.

Director (Government):

The proposal we gave to you is only an ideal model. We understand that the reality is not so easy. My concern is how to integrate the current system into the new one. How do we create a decision-making system? Who holds the power of decision making within the NPO? Who operates the organization in a real sense? We need to discuss the details thoroughly. In particular, what will be the organizational form?

While the government tried to proceed with the process of "NPO-ization," volunteers got lost.

Volunteer (housewife):

Wait. . . . I understand the direction. However, why become an NPO? At this stage, we want to talk more about the merits and demerits of getting NPO status. Speaking of demerits, for example, the accounting requirement under the NPO Law sounds like it could be a burden.

The volunteers focused on the pros and cons of getting NPO status. Why do we have to be "NPO-ized"? What are the merits for us? Is there any meaning in becoming an NPO? Will this be a burden for us? Specialists hired by the municipal government prepared the answers to their questions. Of course, all of them were pro-NPO scholars.

Specialist:

The status itself is easy to get. Thinking about what you are doing, because there are no religious and political activities, getting the NPO status should be an automatic process if you apply for the status. The NPO Law clearly prohibits NPOs that are involved with any religious or political activities. You are required to submit certain kinds of documents in the process of information disclosure. The law defines the submission as a duty for all NPOs recognized under the law. The duty leads to social trust of NPOs in society. However, making documents available might take a lot of time, and it might be a burden and have demerits. As to merits, you can formally situate your activities in society. For example, you would like to create collaborative partnerships with the Board of Education in the municipal government. In the current situation, it is difficult for the government to create such a relationship with a citizens' group. Legally speaking, you are an informal private group. However, incorporated status means that your group legally and formally is accepted by society. Furthermore, you may ease people's minds. If you can get NPO status, it means that the things you have been doing so far will be understood as socially beneficial activities.

Other volunteers inquired further.

Volunteer (former junior high school principal):

In order to get the status, it seems to me that it will be a lot of trouble to prepare such documents as accounting reports. What is really going on at NPOs that have already received the status?

Specialist:

It has only been less than one year since the law was created. Thus, we don't have any reports on it. We need to wait for a couple more years to make that determination. Anyway, I believe that we need to have solid determination among you to make a not-for-profit company. Otherwise, it is just going to fail.

Following these responses, the volunteers came to understand that obtaining NPO status would increase the social trust of the group. It seemed that this was a plus in their minds. However, their concern was: Who would incorporate it? Who would control the application process? Who was going to take leadership in the process? To get incorporation, they needed a founder. Who was it going to be? The government responded to them.

Vice Director (government):

We plan to reorganize the current group and start it as a new organization next April (April 2000). We are going to specifically pursue the process of incorporation following the advice of these meetings. We are also considering asking local residents to join in the discussion.

At this stage, several volunteers who participated in the discussion claimed that they gradually noticed that everything had already been prepared and organized by the government. It seemed obvious that the current group was supposed to become an NPO. The government would establish an NPO and strongly support it. They also knew that the government would allocate 50 million yen (approximately $450,000) to the new organization each year for the time being. Money was indeed a key issue; it would decide whether the activities continued or stopped, although the government implied that the amount of the funding might be decreased because it expected the new organization to eventually become independent of the government.

Volunteer (former junior high school principal):

> If the money is suddenly cut, I believe that our activities will be seriously restricted. Our activities might have to cease. Thus, we had better seriously consider the funding issue.

Specialist:

> Why don't we stop talking in this manner? What we are talking about is the incorporation of an NPO. We are now moving toward becoming independent of the government. What are we expected to do? What we are going to do is what the government did, but did not do so well. Under the name of an NPO, I would like to emphasize that you, the residents, are going to take strong leadership in promoting lifelong learning in our community.

Volunteer (former junior high school principal):

> I know what you mean. However, look at the reality. Look at us. We are so dependent on the government. I remember when the current group was started. At that time, the government entrusted some work to us, in a sense. However, remember what happened over the last five years. We didn't do anything without the government's help.

Specialist:

> If you understand it, why don't you become more independent? You know well the situation surrounding us. If so, why don't you become independent when you go to the next step of becoming an NPO?

Volunteer (former junior high school principal):

> I am not sure how to do that. But, we need to be separated from the government and become more independent.

Volunteer (college professor):

> Fifty million yen is really a lot of money. Indeed, we need money to do our activities. More importantly, however, what we need to think about, I believe, is what kind of relationship we should pursue with the local government.

The volunteers were in fact puzzled over what was going on—a hasty move in which they were involved. They expressed their honest concerns regarding the move.

Volunteer (housewife):

> Over the past five years, the current group has played a significant role in the community. I think it is more realistic if we discuss reorganizing the current organization as an NPO over the upcoming five years. I just heard that next April is the date by which we will be reorganized as an NPO. I think there is no need to be hasty, however. This is because the management of an NPO is not so easy. With the current stagnant economy, the other day I heard that some famous NPOs couldn't even pay their personnel fees. Donations from businesses and individuals are not so easily collected either. What I want to say is that it is impossible to incorporate an NPO if organizations are really not needed by the local community. Why do we need to incorporate as an NPO? We can operate the NPO only when we have a shared vision among people. We are going to be able to overcome the difficulties we may face only when we have a solid shared vision of what lifelong learning is. We need to create a vision about why we reorganized this group and incorporated it as an NPO.

The other added her opinion.

Volunteer (housewife):

> I just want to say one thing: Who will take the leadership role in incorporating the NPO? In fact, if we don't have a certain number of people among us volunteers who think that this should be done, we can't establish the NPO. We are only members of an advisory group organized by the government. We could say, "You had better do it." We can't

say, "We will do it," however. That would not work in this volunteer-based organization.

Chair (government-hired specialist):

I appreciate everybody's opinions. Since we are just an advisory group, probably the best expression is, "It is desirable to reorganize the current organization as an NPO." I hope nobody has any objections with this conclusion.

When I read this meeting record and then conducted a series of interviews, I got the feeling that the government had played a considerable role in the "NPO-ization" while strategically mobilizing both specialists and local residents as volunteers to be aligned with its logic. The volunteers expressed honest concerns regarding "NPO-ization." However, it was clear that everything was already decided. The record even gave me the impression that the meeting itself was perfunctory. Volunteers were there just because they needed to be present as token participants. The "NPO-ization" was a project prepared by the government.

At the end of August 1999, the "advisory committee" submitted the result of the discussion to the municipal government's board of education as a proposal. At this stage, the government's board customarily would accept the proposal on "NPO-ization" and automatically put it into practice. The proposal was developed as a report titled "On Creating an Organization Promoting Lifelong Learning by Local Residents" (SWG 1999a). The proposal's first main point was that the municipal government would continue its generous support for creating the residents' organization. The government would offer as much financial and human resources support as possible. Instead of suggesting that the organization be an administrative arm of the municipal government, the proposal confirmed that the main actors of the activities would be local residents. The proposal stated that the new organization should have a decision-making system led by the residents, including an annual meeting as a top decision-making forum, a monthly directors' meeting, and volunteers' meetings. The government would not intervene in any of these decision-making processes. In addition, the proposal stated that the new organization would have a board of directors headed by a president and a couple of vice presidents. It would also have a secretariat. The volunteers would be divided into four groups based on their interests: course planning, learning support, public relations, and volunteer recruiting. Finally, the proposal recommended that the residents' organization apply for NPO status in order to build some positive collaborative relationships with the municipal government and local businesses.

Following the proposal, the municipal government proactively led the group's transition to an NPO, targeting April 2000 (April is the first month of the Japanese fiscal year), as originally planned, as the new organization's incorporation date. In order to meet this deadline, the government organized a preparation committee to facilitate the transition to the new organization. The municipal government nominated the committee members. The committee was organized with six current volunteers and eight leaders from local associational groups. The first task of the committee was to determine the organization's name. Volunteers felt that the group's current name sounded excessively bureaucratic. After accepting ideas from volunteers, the new organizational name—SLG (pseudonym)—was selected. The real name in Japanese connotes the activation of lifelong learning activities in the local community through an analogy to several kinds of flowers blooming in a garden. Second, the government named a local lawyer as president to guide the new organization. He was expected to facilitate all of the legal procedures required to obtain NPO status. Preparing documents for the process was not hard, however, laypeople found the legal terms of incorporation difficult to understand. In the end, the lawyer wrote the entire articles of association (*teikan*) by himself, which later led to problems related to power concentration at the head of the organization and causes of frustration among volunteers (I introduced several narratives of their frustration in chapter 7). At the same time, the organization stopped providing all volunteers with the 1,000 yen (approximately $9) a day remuneration. Instead, the organization introduced a membership system. There are two types of membership: regular membership (*sei-kaiin*) and supporting membership (*kōen-kaiin*). Regular members were compelled to pay a 3,000-yen (approximately $27) membership fee to become registered. The regular membership gave them the right to vote in the general meeting, a top decision-making body at SLG. Meanwhile, supporting members donated a membership fee, usually more than 10,000 yen (approximately $90), but did not participate in the actual activities. Most of the supporting members were from local mom-and-pop shops and family-oriented small businesses. It seemed that they were directly asked by members of the board of directors to purchase a membership.

On the Transition

In what way were the volunteers told about the transition to an NPO? I obtained a memo on a series of lecture and discussion sessions on the "NPO-ization" held in February 2000. The lecture series was entitled "What Are NPOs?" The series lecturer, a well-known NPO practitioner in Japan, was invited by the municipal government. According to a memo taken by a lecture participant, the first item on the agenda was the difference between volunteer and NPO activities. Volunteering was presented as the activities of individuals. In contrast, NPO programs were described as institutionalized citizens' activities. According to the lecture, participation in NPOs is voluntary and is based on individual free will. However, NPOs are organizations promoting projects and aiming to achieve certain results. The lecturer told them this:

> Many NPOs are primarily supported by volunteers who are motivated by individual, spontaneous will. However, activities done by volunteers and activities done by NPOs have different characteristics. If an organization has NPO status under the NPO Law, it should move beyond volunteerism. Your NPO activities should be "continuous (*keizokuteki*)" to produce certain results.

This speech implied that an NPO is not allowed to stop its activities for individual reasons. The message I got from him was that once an organization is recognized under the NPO Law, it has a responsibility to continue its activities. Otherwise, the activities of the organization should not be recognized as those of an NPO. The second agenda item concerned "what has changed and what has not changed" in the transition to NPO status. What had not changed was that volunteers supported lifelong learning for local residents. This would be the most crucial aspect of the new organization. Meanwhile, one major change was that the new organization intended to expand its business. The former group had been limited to offering lifelong learning courses in the locality. Under the name of an NPO, the new organization would even provide other services beyond lifelong learning to local residents by constructing collaborative relationships with the municipal government and local businesses. The lecturer emphasized that NPOs can do anything they want. NPOs are in the private sector. The former group had been under the direct control of the government, whereas the new organization would not be part of the government. One of the strongest advantages of the change in organizational form would be flexibility. In the framework of the government, many constraints had limited the group's activities. NPOs can make money, as long as the earnings are not distributed among the members but are specifically used for the continuation of business, as defined by the NPO Law. In this context, the new organization expected that training and enhancing the skills of volunteers would be another important element of the new structure. Such training would be necessary to enhance the NPO's capacity as an organization. The third item on the agenda was a statement that the new organization would consciously target two kinds of "customers." One group of customers would be local people who took lifelong learning courses. The new organization would be expected to understand their expectations for learning. The second type of customers would include volunteers who paid membership fees. They would be an important financial resource for operating activities as an NPO. Thus recruiting new volunteers or expanding the membership would be another key to enhancing the capacity of the new NPO.

After these lecture sessions, discussions between the preparation committee members and ordinary volunteers were opened.[5]

Volunteer 1: Is this decision of becoming an NPO decided? Or are we still considering it?

Committee: We are still discussing this, although it has basically been decided. If you want to say something, please bring your opinion to the secretariat of the current group. Indeed, we have to admit that the government intervened a lot in the process of NPO-ization. However, the important thing is that we can become independent of the government soon by getting NPO status.

Volunteer 2: Today, I heard about the membership fee for the first time. I was never informed of it. If we set the membership fee, only people who can afford to participate in the new organization will be involved. I don't mean that the actual amount of the membership fee is big or small. It's just the principle of it.

Committee: In its current form, this group is financed 100 percent by the municipal government. If this continues, we won't be able to avoid feeling that we are just helping the government. We are doing the government's work, instead of government officials doing it. However, if we pay something for our own activities, our consciousness will be different. We can develop the consciousness that we can be independent of the government. Under the name of an NPO, we will be reorganized. We are going to become an equal partner with the government.

Volunteer 3: Why do we need to be incorporated as an NPO? I am not sure why people who are voluntarily participating in this activity have to pay money to volunteer.

Committee: Paying a membership fee is a verification of our motivation to conduct our own activities independently of the government. Realistically speaking, it would be impossible to operate the new organization with only the membership fee. The membership fee is a matter of our consciousness that we wish to be independent of the government. Actually, the membership fee will be used for the members themselves. For example, the money will be used for a lecture series specifically targeting members. Members will benefit from the money they pay.

Volunteer 3: To operate an NPO, we need human beings, information, and money. I understand that becoming an NPO means pushing self-actualization among our volunteers. I was wondering, however, whether the intention of this move is cost cutting, due to the severe financial situation of the municipal government. . . .

Three months after this discussion was held, in May 2000, the preparation committee sponsored a general meeting to reorganize the original group. The newly established organization formally changed its name to SLG. Shortly after the general meeting, SLG applied for NPO status with the Tokyo Metropolitan Government.

At that time, nearly eighty people were registered as volunteers. When the former group was reorganized as an NPO, I heard that at least twenty volunteers had left the group. However, honestly, I was not able to obtain the exact information on how many volunteers were registered at the last stage of the former entity, as the materials of the former group were, to an amazing and a rather surprising extent, disorganized. I had the opportunity to conduct interviews with a couple of people who left the group at that time. Their stories were very impressive and informed my way of thinking about my field site. One of the volunteers, Mr. Mizouchi, in his seventies, told me this:

I was getting frustrated because the group was becoming more focused on how to *manage* people when it pursued NPO status. I was an engineer of construction equipment. Affiliated with a trading company as a consultant, I worked all over the world. I was in Nigeria, Malaysia, Indonesia, South Korea, China, Guam, and the United States. In my life, diversity was usual. I learned that differences were common. However, I even felt that SLG did not accept any diversity. I even felt that we were all expected to feel and behave the same way. Thus, I would say that tadpoles are getting together there. I could not see any positive development. . . . Anyway, I was thinking that SLG should pay people who are doing "duty-like" activities, even though they call the activities *volunteering*. (emphasis added)

Mr. Nomura, a man in his fifties who ran a grocery store in the community, offered an insightful perspective on NPOs. He spent five years as a volunteer for course planning.

When we were organizing courses, what was important was how each planner saw and felt experiences in daily life. I can even say that whether a course was successful or not depended on the "personality" of the planner. Do the current people at SLG realize the importance of the "personality" issue? An NPO might be an organizational form under which we can pursue effective management. But how many people now think about the meaning of lifelong learning? Probably the outward appearance as an organization looks good because of its NPO status. I was not against the group getting NPO status. However, it seems to me that people are just driven by the new organizational concept—NPO. I would say SLG lost something important. Lifelong learning is a very deep concept. It is hard to fully understand it. But SLG is an organization promoting lifelong learning in this community. Thus people in the new organization should first of all show their vision of lifelong learning to the residents. Their role is to lead residents' learning activities. Many local people are watching SLG.

In spite of these concerns, SLG was granted NPO status by the Tokyo Metropolitan Government on September 30, 2000, without incident.

Proper NPOs?

I entered my field site in September 2001. At that time, it had been almost a year since the original group had received NPO status. While attending every meeting of volunteers as a secretariat staff-researcher at SLG, I gradually noticed that many people, regardless of whether they were directors, volunteers, or secretariat staff, were very frustrated with the current situation. I realized that the frustrations were directly related to the new organizational style, the NPO. It seemed to me that the volunteers and staff did not fully digest the concept of the NPO. They struggled with the following questions: What are NPOs? What should we do as members of NPOs? Indeed, it might be reasonable that they had such questions, as the municipal government had introduced the concept of NPOs rather suddenly. In fact, the term *NPO* was largely unfamiliar to many Japanese people, including me. Even though it had been more than one year since NPO status had been conferred, people in my field site were still very annoyed by the organizational form in which they had become involved. Throughout my fieldwork, I was looking for how SLG people understood *NPO*. I often heard extensive discussions on the topic. I had a chance to observe a directors' meeting that involved intensive conversation about the meaning of NPOs. The SLG head proposed a discussion on the topic:

Head: We have never formally discussed what NPOs are. What are "proper" NPOs? We know some say that SLG is not a proper NPO. Indeed, the government was intentionally involved with creating this NPO.

Vice Head 1: I think an organization like SLG emerged in order to fill a gap between conventional institutions.

Head: I really want to ask you guys to study more about NPOs. What I want is for you all not to make arguments based on your own experiences, but to know what a normative NPO is. What I imagine is that Doctors without Borders is a proper NPO.

Vice Head 1: I am still not sure why volunteer-based organizations need to get NPO status. . . .

Head: It's for collecting money. That is my understanding.

Vice Head 2: What we need are real, specific measures about what we should do here at SLG. We are often told that SLG is not a proper NPO. If so, I want SLG to become a proper NPO. We should make serious efforts to become a proper NPO. I want to ask why it is not a proper NPO and which parts are not proper.... What is proper? What is not proper? Are there any models of proper NPOs?

Director 1: I understand that not-proper NPOs lack passion generated from a shared vision.

Vice Head 2: I want to get rid of the "not-proper" parts of SLG as an NPO.

Vice Head 1: As a board member in charge of course planning, I have always thought about what we can do here. Usually, I understand that we should have a goal as an educational institution. As a lifelong learning NPO, what can we pursue as a goal? What is our shared goal?

Honestly speaking, I was annoyed with this reality—lots of confusion at the grassroots level following the government-led creation of a "third"-sector organization.

At the initial stage of my fieldwork, I thought that I was looking at one peculiar, nontypical NPO. SLG might be too unique. However, through conducting my fieldwork, I came to believe that NPOs such as SLG are not so uncommon in this country. At an NPO I visited for my research, I heard an interesting story. The director, in her fifties, offered the following motivation for receiving NPO status:

We are promoting "listening volunteering." This is well known in the United States as "peer counseling." I learned it there. The term *peer counseling* is currently often heard. However, ten years ago, it was not.... A couple of years ago, we started to be asked frequently by the municipal government to have seminars teaching peer counseling. The funding seemed to come from the social welfare budget. One day, we were asked by a government official to get NPO status. The official said, "It is easier to make a contract with an NPO, instead of a non-authorized, informal group." At that time, we were expecting to establish a solid relationship with the government.

> We wanted to get entrustment contracts from the government. That's why we got NPO status.

I heard a similar narrative one Saturday morning on an NHK television program featuring a Japanese NPO (NHK 2002).

> I volunteer to read for kids. I started this activity because I wanted to do something for society. I wanted to contribute something to my community. Currently, our activities are done after school. However, if we get NPO status, we can go into schools between classes or at lunchtime. Moreover, what is attractive for us is that we can easily get funding from the government if we are doing our activities as an NPO.

I came to have the impression that government-led NPO creation is not unusual, and gradually I became sure that SLG might be one of the typical NPOs in this society. In fact, I observed that SLG was treated as a prototype community-oriented lifelong learning provider, especially among government officials in charge of lifelong learning policy. SLG often welcomed inspecting parties from across the country.

Meanwhile, on a grassroots level at SLG, annoyance about what NPOs should be was persistently heard among the volunteers. On the way home from a course planning meeting one night, Ms. Kunimatsu, introduced earlier in this chapter as a facilitator of the course planning discussion, expressed her disappointment about a conversation that had taken place. The discussion of the night had indeed been messy. Nobody had controlled the discussion, and to make the matter worse, the discussion materials were not well prepared by the secretariat. Many people had been confused and had complained about this. Sometimes these complaints served to destroy constructive arguments that others were trying to make. Ms. Kunimatsu said:

> I think again tonight that this group is difficult. We repeated the same things over and over again. We haven't learned anything from past experiences. . . . I am very tired. I was wondering if we have reached our limit. As you know, this organization was not generated by citizens' voluntary power. The municipal government played a key role in generating this organization. I have fully known its limits and weaknesses since its establishment. I don't believe that it is in a state to be an NPO. Today I felt this again. When we moved to an NPO, I hoped we could have the same ideal under the framework of an NPO. However, today I again confirmed

that everybody looks toward different things and has different ideals. What kind of lifelong learning do we want to pursue as an organization? We should have deepened the argument on that point before becoming the NPO.

A couple of months later, Ms. Kunimatsu left the organization very much disappointed with it.

As the annoyance at the grassroots level grew, I heard another impressive comment from Ms. Asaoka, a veteran volunteer from the local Red Cross. At a biweekly meeting, the recruitment and training department discussed the necessity of creating a shared vision among volunteers. Constructing a shared vision as an NPO was a crucial item on the long-term agenda of volunteers in the department. They believed that a shared vision would be developed under the NPO structure. This persistent goal was never achieved, however. In fact, the inability to set a shared vision exhausted the volunteers. This resulted in some of the volunteers leaving the organization. Ms. Asaoka said:

> The reason we can't set a shared vision is, I believe, that this NPO was established in a very unnatural fashion. We are not an NPO in the proper sense. I understand NPOs should be spontaneously developed from the bottom up. That's how we understood it when we studied applying for NPO status. Actually, everybody was upset about the way it was done by the government, remember? Thus, we volunteers are still struggling to understand this new type of organization. We are still in the middle of a transition. We need to overcome the difficulties by ourselves.

Ms. Katō, an assistant leader, responded:

> For the past year, I have been repeating that we need *a mission*. The discussion itself was our learning process. I believe we were creating our shared vision. However, since becoming an NPO, the main theme of the discussion has always been driven by the theory of organization—NPO. But this was not what we wanted, right? We have even lost sight of our most important mission as a lifelong learning promoter. What does lifelong learning mean to us? (emphasis added)

That term *mission* was mentioned as a key word on the "NPO-ization" by the director of lifelong learning policy in a meeting, as I documented earlier in this chapter. The government tried to unify the volunteers with a mission in the process of "NPO-ization." However, SLG volunteers faced difficulties in setting up a mission in terms of the kind of lifelong learning they sought to pursue. There were no organization-wide discussions on this issue beyond the departments and among all of the SLG volunteers about which lifelong learning activities members wanted to pursue jointly and what they would do to provide lifelong learning opportunities to the Kawazoe community. In my view, SLG members could not democratize the top-down style of lifelong learning led by the government nor democratize their own organizational life. Furthermore, the deadlocked situation explicitly presented that the hasty top-down institutionalization of SLG was not easily accepted by grassroots volunteers and only accelerated annoyance among them. I end this chapter with a comment by Ms. Asaoka responding to the earlier comment from Ms. Katō:

> This organization is contradictory. We didn't even need to get
> NPO status to just promote lifelong learning.

I believe this comment honestly represents a grassroots volunteer's voice.

Even with such frustration, however, volunteers were involved in SLG activities. In the next chapter, I explore why they participate in the activities, focusing on a volunteer mobilization technique employed by the local government in Tokyo. Further, in the following chapters, I locate my detailed, culturally specific data collected through fieldwork into the macro-discourse or theoretical and historical literature, both in and outside of Japan, on volunteerism (chapter 4), associative democracy (chapter 5), and social movements (chapter 6). I thus squarely connect my ethnographic data on Japan to the global scholarship on civil society—a topic that is nowadays central in social science research.

Chapter 4

Invited by the State

You Can Volunteer with a Single Finger!

A person in a wheelchair is at a loss in an elevator hall since the button is in an awkward position. Another person briskly moves toward the elevator and pushes the button.

Man in wheelchair: "Thank you."

Narration: "Why don't you start to volunteer? You can volunteer with a single finger. . . . Think about something you can do for someone else."

This was a vignette from a nationwide television commercial that aired when I was doing fieldwork in Kawazoe. There was a paper advertisement with the same content, shown on the next page. The sponsor was the Japan Advertising Council, known as AC, a public interest corporation that promotes serving the common good through public service campaigns. The novel phrase—*You can volunteer with a single finger!* (*Yubi ippon de dekiru borantia*)—has permeated the thoughts and behaviors of Japanese people.

In this chapter, I argue that such Foucauldian, coercive, self-disciplined subjectivity—what I call volunteer subjectivity—is being intentionally produced and reproduced under the name of volunteerism in contemporary Japanese society. The process of promoting this volunteer subjectivity, which has pierced the very basis of consciousness, is resulting in the institutionalization of a new relationship between the state and the individual. During the course of ethnographic fieldwork focusing on volunteerism stemming from the 1998 NPO Law, I looked at the mobilization of volunteer subjects[1] in Japanese society, and I gradually came to realize that the agent is surely the state. In fact, the Japanese

93

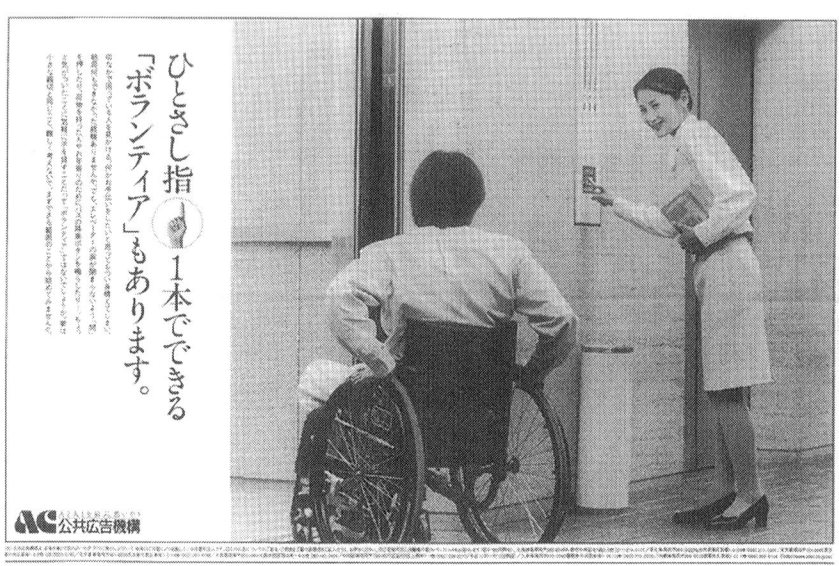

Picture 4.1 An advertisement of *You Can Volunteer with a Single Finger!* (Reproduced with permission from the Japan Advertising Council)

government at various levels plays a significant role in mobilizing these volunteer subjects. At the practical level, the municipal government *invites* residents to become volunteers to provide specific social services in the local community such as in lifelong learning program planning in the community, where I did fieldwork, museum operation, and elderly care services. The government then organizes the residents into the NPO incorporated under the NPO Law.

The motivation for this is not simply to augment social services offered by the state. I found that the volunteer activities organized under NPOs actually replace the government's provision of these services. The primary purpose of this NPO policy is cutting costs in public administration, a key agenda in globally dominant neoliberal politics. Meanwhile, the volunteer subjectivity that supports NPO activities has been systematically produced and reproduced. The Japanese government was trying to revise the Fundamental Law of Education, a basic charter defining the direction of state-supervised education, in order to situate *borantia,* or volunteering, as one of the core courses in the Japanese school system. The revision was approved by the National Diet in December 2006. It aimed to generate a subjectivity focused toward civic engagement, in which people can spontaneously participate in problem-solving processes in public affairs.

I started this fieldwork with these key questions: Why have Japanese recently been hearing the term *borantia* so often? Who actually sets up this emerging discourse of borantia? What exactly happens in volunteerism under the NPO Law? It seems to me that such actions as portrayed in the vignette could practically be termed as everyday kindness (*shinsetsu*), but I began to observe that acts such as these were now consciously being labeled *borantia.* In fact, even though no Western, Judeo-Christian tradition is deeply rooted among its people, Japanese society is not a complete stranger to the concept of volunteerism. Japan has a tradition of neighbors helping each other, symbolized by the term *otagaisama* (for each other), which represents a sensitivity to mutual aid. Japanese society has such a set of rules for daily life, rooted in the local community. Its members have traditionally forged close ties based on mutual aid. One typical example was the form of cooperative labor known as *yui* (literally, tying), through which community members would help each other plant and harvest fields, rebuild homes, thatch roofs, and engage in other activities that could best be done by a group (Hoshino 2000). In today's society as well, if one of their neighbors is having a funeral, the Japanese go along to help out; in areas with heavy snowfall, neighbors of households without able-bodied adults willingly help with snow shoveling. In every case, helpers accept no payment, because members of the local community help and support each other, as part of the spirit of otagaisama.

Thus why is contemporary Japanese society now intentionally choosing to define activities that are not particularly noteworthy, such as pushing an elevator button and picking up trash, as volunteering? Who is participating in this social trend? What are ordinary people experiencing, and what do they think of this phenomenon? In this chapter, I explore the implication of this emerging form of volunteerism.

Discourses of "Borantia"

In a popular vocabulary encyclopedia (*Gendai yōgo no kiso chishiki*), the term *borantia* first appeared in the 1960 volume. However, at that point it was only explained in the foreign loan words section, referring to a volunteer soldier in the military. In 1968, the meaning was expanded into a conventional social welfare term, with both of these definitions continuing to be in use today. In 1979, borantia was first introduced as a way to participate in society, particularly for women. The encyclopedia explained that borantia is a sort of spirit, whereby the residents of a community have a consciousness as members of society to spontaneously participate in social and political life and to make voluntary efforts for the common good. The embodiment of this spirit is called "volunteer activity," the definition explained. Beyond social welfare, the term *borantia* is now recognized as applying to a wide range of spontaneous activities in social and political life. Interestingly, Ichikawa Fusae, one of the first women in the Diet in Japan's postwar politics to advocate the improvements of women's status, wrote the explanation. She was a leader in the women's suffrage league and played a significant role in obtaining women's suffrage in Japan. Currently the vocabulary encyclopedia has expanded the itemization of the term *borantia* to more than twenty definitions.

The aforementioned explanation describes the popular discourse of volunteerism. From Japanese academia, meanwhile, Kaneko Ikuyou (1992) sets forth a new meaning of volunteering in contemporary Japan, introducing the key term *tsunagari,* or social networking. Volunteering, he writes, represents a relationality in society—when a person sees that other people face problems, he or she tries to solve the problems jointly with those people. Kaneko argues that *tsunagari* generated from volunteer activities makes society diversified and enriched. Volunteering is a principle of behavior for people who want to find new perspectives and senses of value. It could even be a window for seeing beyond the deadlocked situation of society, he writes (Kaneko 1992, 69).

I believe that there are two possible answers as to why volunteering is in such vogue in Japan at present. The general perception of emerging borantia took root in the wake of the Great Hanshin-Awaji Earthquake that devastated Hyogo and Osaka Prefectures in western Japan on January 17, 1995, and claimed 6,401 lives. A total of 1,377,300 people joined volunteer activities from January 1995 through January 1996 from all over Japan, dedicating themselves to rescue and reconstructive work (Economic Planning Agency 2000, 7). Faced with the sudden emergence of a huge number of volunteers in 1995, some members of the mass media called this "The First Year of Volunteerism." Several Japan-based scholars, primarily sociologists, did extensive research on the impact of the post-Hanshin volunteering on political, economic, and social institutions (e.g., Yamashita and Suga 2002; see also Fujii 2002). Their work pointed out the inability of traditional government bureaucracy to deal with the tragic aftermath of the earthquake, in contrast to the impressive work done by the volunteers, and dramatized the need for a social and political structure that recognizes the valuable contributions of volunteer-based civic groups and NPOs to society. Furthermore, they argued that the earthquake changed the way that people at the "grassroots" level comprehended the meaning and reality of society.

Aside from the earthquake and the massive response from volunteers that it evoked, the emergence of volunteers in Japan may reflect a convergence of domestic and global developments. As I briefly introduced in chapter 1, Lester Salamon (1994) argues that the development of volunteerism is indicative of a global associational revolution, a movement characterized by a massive array of self-governing, voluntary, private organizations pursuing public purposes outside of the formal apparatus of the state. This expansion of associational groups could permanently alter the relationship between states and citizens, Salamon argues. Think-tank specialists see the ongoing proliferation of volunteerism as evidence of Japan's evolving "civil society," a term that refers to more direct participation by the citizenry in addressing social needs (Yamamoto 1996). This was the eventual result of Japanese postwar economic prosperity, which generated a sizable urban middle class (10–11). Furthermore, the prolonged malaise of the Japanese economy since the 1990s challenged the validity of the ideals of material achievement that shaped Japan in the decades after World War II. The system of lifetime employment, once the pride of Japan's companies, was showing cracks. In this increasingly uncertain environment, getting a job with a company no longer meant the guarantee of a stable future. Rather, people in Japan began shifting their priorities to pursue something they could truly support. In this context, volunteerism gave ordinary people a chance to strategically choose to develop meaning in their lives, described by Lynne Nakano as a lifestyle choice for establishing self-identities (Nakano 2000, 2005). Volunteering was advocated as a conscious, self-motivated action for enriching one's life amidst socioeconomic uncertainty.

But these explanations do not seem sufficient. They do not answer some of my original questions: Who has defined the macro-discourse of volunteering in Japanese society? Who has defined one particular activity as appropriate and desirable and called it "volunteering"? Who actually benefits from this emerging phenomenon of volunteering? In order to answer these questions, allow me to introduce a volunteer mobilization project by the state—a municipal government—that I observed and experienced.

Volunteers Invited by the State

Ms. Tajima, a housewife in her fifties, was an active woman in the local community, playing key roles in the women's section of the neighborhood association and in her daughters' school PTA, as well as in organizing a summer camp for children. After finishing child rearing some ten years ago, Ms. Tajima started looking for "something new in life." One day an advertisement in a local newspaper caught her eye. The advertisement was recruiting on behalf of a woman's group for an international exchange program. The group, which was affiliated with the municipal government, planned to visit Hungary and the Czech Republic. Ms. Tajima had a strong interest in the music of Central and Eastern Europe, which motivated her to apply, although she told me that she did not exactly understand the purpose of the mission. Ms. Tajima thought that she deserved to apply for the mission in light of her contribution to the community as a neighborhood association and PTA member. She wrote an essay entitled "Challenge to the Unknown World," mentioning her rich experiences in the community and her own interest in exploring something new in her life. She was then chosen as a member of the delegation to Eastern Europe. This was her first involvement with the government.

In May 1994, Ms. Tajima received a call from a municipal government official asking for her help after she returned from the three-week international exchange mission. The call was from a director of a newly created public facility for promoting lifelong learning in the municipality. The director asked for her to become a volunteer in curriculum planning and in the operation of the facility. She describes her impression of the call:

> For a long time, I was a traditional Japanese housewife—
> *ryōsai-kenbo* ("good wife and wise mother"). I graduated from a
> private girls' school—from its junior high through college—one
> famous for *ryōsai-kenbo* education. I served and still serve
> my husband, and I fully took care of my two daughters. As
> my hobby, I enjoyed baking cakes. I felt fully satisfied
> when my family enjoyed my homemade cakes. But on the other
> hand, I wanted to start something new while my mother-in-
> law (who lives in her household) was still healthy. Someday
> I will have to take care of her. When I was thinking about
> the rest of my life, I thought, "I want to be more involved
> with society." Actually, at that time, I have to admit that I
> was looking for a place I could go. When I got the call from
> the municipal government officer, I thought this was maybe
> a last chance to explore another road in my life. I thought
> I would participate in the community more and more. The
> director expected me to play such an important role in the
> community, right? The call really confirmed my reason for

being in this community. Thus I decided to accept the offer from the government and join the lifelong learning project for the community as a volunteer. I really have enjoyed volunteering here. However, I never imagined that I would be involved in promoting lifelong learning in such an active manner. That was new territory for me.

Around the same time, Mr. Koba, another person I met at SLG, also was asked for his help by the director of lifelong learning policy in the municipal government. He was a leader of a neighborhood association in his community and was appointed as a member of a task force to promote administrative reform in the municipal government. He talked to me about why he became involved in this volunteering activity:

> When I was a leader of my neighborhood association nearly ten years ago, I came to know Ms. Saeki, director of lifelong learning policy at the municipal government. At that time, she was in the community development division. I was directly asked by her to help this community-oriented lifelong learning project. I was never reluctant to do it. As a disposition shared by us in downtown Tokyo, if somebody we know well wants to do something but needs help, we gladly help out. That follows our feeling of *otagaisama*.

When he talked to me about this, it seemed that he was very proud of this story. This was partly because this episode revealed that he had a relationship with a high-ranking official in the municipal government. Furthermore, the direct call for help verified that the government trusted him. The government, frankly, tickled his pride.

The municipal government also publicly recruited people who spontaneously responded to their request for volunteers for the project. Everywhere in the community, including public libraries, hospitals, banks, subway stations, and the municipal government head office, along with its branches, there appeared B-5-size notices. These notices, undecorated and written in black ink on blue paper, had a simple message:

> "Why don't you join us?" The municipal government is now recruiting volunteers to do planning and operations for education activities at a newly created lifelong learning center in the community. The center opens this coming December. The only requirement for eligibility is to be a resident or worker in the municipality.

The notice impressively ended with a couple of poem-like sentences:

> You can do something!
> You might want to do something!
> Why don't you step into a new life?
> You can start through this volunteer activity.

Meanwhile, I examined the government's internal documents on this volunteer-mobilization project, which demonstrated the justification for organizing local residents as volunteers to implement lifelong learning policy. A paper entitled "On Learning Activities and Volunteering" is one of the few documents available mentioning the vision of the municipal government for this project (cf. NCLL 1992):

> The basic principle . . . of the lifelong learning policy . . . should be self-learning by residents themselves. The learning activities should be operated through the residents' spontaneous will. However, such opportunity for learning could be strategically arranged and intentionally organized by the municipal government. In this project, the residents can be both students and teachers. They can learn from each other. The residents are expected to not only acquire new knowledge and skills but also to enhance themselves and improve the quality of their lives through involvement in this project. Thus, the proposed project of lifelong learning can be "hand-made" by the volunteer-residents.

The paper further argues:

> Lifelong learning is a positive learning activity in a community, one where independent residents build their own learning promotion system and provide learning opportunities for the residents. That is, lifelong learning is independent, self-directed volunteering activities by the residents themselves.

While building this policy, the main concern of the government was that of who could be mobilized for this community-oriented lifelong learning project. The government actually pointed to the residents' mobilization for this project as the highest priority. The government indeed needed to open to the public the volunteering opportunity. However, in order to maintain a level of control, it decided to issue select invitations to volunteer. In fact, a number of seats were to be filled by some chosen people, all highly educated; most had college degrees and high profiles in their local communities. By sharing the vision of the project, such *invited* volunteers were strongly expected to play significant roles in operating the project, instead of the municipal government itself.

By the opening of the lifelong learning center, forty-seven residents, including thirty-four *invited* volunteers, such as Ms. Tajima and Mr. Koba, had responded to the government's recruitment. Meanwhile, there were thirteen purely voluntary participants. In total, there were thirty-two women and fifteen men. Among the thirty-four *invited* people, all directly appointed by the government, were former teachers from a university, a high school, and an elementary school, women who had participated in the government-sponsored international exchange program, leaders of the neighborhood association, PTA leaders, Red Cross volunteers, local NGO practitioners, co-op members, local amateur sports association leaders, and local women's groups. All were leaders of local associational groups that I introduced in chapter 2. The municipal government organized all of the forty-seven volunteers into a citizens' group, which would be finally reorganized as SLG, an NPO organized under the 1998 NPO Law, for promoting lifelong learning in the local community. The thirty-four *invited* volunteers were, as planned, assigned to central positions in the project, such as planning lifelong learning courses in literature, foreign languages, pottery, and calligraphy, for example, and publishing a newsletter on lifelong learning activities in the community. The other voluntary participants were primarily expected to help the *invited* volunteers.

This deliberate distinction of volunteers' roles created by the municipal government resulted in lasting frustration among the purely voluntary volunteers. Despite this, the number of people who voluntarily joined this lifelong learning project increased each year. While doing my fieldwork, the number of volunteers amounted to more than 100. However, the *invited* volunteers continuously tried to influence all things regarding the operation, feeling some sense of duty to do so since they were directly asked by the government. They sustained a solid belief that what they were doing was fully supported by the government. "I don't want to fail," Ms. Tajima often said to me when I asked her why she was working so eagerly. It was like a duty and a regular job. The only difference was that she was not being paid, and what she was doing was termed *borantia*.

Volunteering as Potential for Individualization?

Throughout my fieldwork, I was surprised by one point shared by almost all of the volunteers. It was their answers to my very simple questions: "Why are you volunteering here? Why did you choose volunteering for promoting lifelong learning?" Answers were never on the tips of their tongues. The thirty-four *invited* volunteers could simply say that they were asked to volunteer. However, even the 100-plus people who eventually registered as *pure* volunteers generally seemed not to have any particular reasons for volunteering in activities specifically related to promoting lifelong learning. Why did they choose this particular type of volunteering activity for supporting lifelong learning? Why did they not choose another kind of volunteering? Each gave their own particular reasons for volunteering.

Mr. Iwata, a businessman in his early thirties, told me that meeting people was his motivation:

> I am not from this area. I wanted to meet local people. I often have to move due to my job. For the past seven years, I have moved eleven times. However, I never had a chance to meet local people in these places. Now I have met many, many people. That is one of the main reasons I am volunteering here.

Mr. Matsuda, a college professor in his forties, talked to me in the same way about why he joined this activity:

> I wanted to be more involved in my community. I moved here three years ago. I bought a house. However, I didn't know anybody in this community. Therefore, volunteering here is a precious chance to get to know people.

Along the same lines, Mr. Takahashi, the oldest volunteer, in his seventies, formerly a toy factory owner, said:

> I am volunteering here for networking in case of an emergency. Think about the possibility of a huge earthquake happening here in downtown Tokyo. In that case, we need to know each other to survive the disaster by helping each other. Volunteering here offers me a chance to know who is who in the community.

Ms. Hayashi, in her late forties, also told me why she was volunteering:

> I took advantage of this volunteering opportunity for my career development. Many years ago, I wanted to be a writer. Instead, I got married and had two kids. I did not have enough time. About five years ago, I saw an advertisement for recruiting

some volunteer writers for a newsletter informing people
about lifelong learning opportunities in the local community.
The ad reminded me of my dream, that I wanted to learn
how to write articles professionally. Fortunately, there were
some professional editors the municipal government hired.
I learned a lot from them. Actually, the editors even helped
me make a network for publishing. Through the network,
now I earn money by writing some short articles. It is a great
achievement for me, even if the articles are short.

Indeed, as earlier noted, most of the volunteers did not specifically seek
volunteering opportunities with lifelong learning. Rather, they were looking for something to satisfy their own individual needs. These volunteers
have their own reasons for wanting to engage in volunteer service, which
was, only by chance, promoting lifelong learning in the local community,
an opportunity prepared by the municipal government.

Nakano Toshio (1999) discusses the phenomenon of volunteering by
introducing the idea of *individualization*, or self-actualization.[2] "Who am
I? What do I want to do? What can I do? In what way shall I construct
my identity?" Alberto Melucci (1989) points out that in contemporary
society, individualization is realized in the context of a reflexively
ordered environment. In fact, the process of individualization requires
a self-reflexive form of action. Our life-political environment is not a
one-dimensional hierarchical power structure. It is expressed by multiple
values generated by affluent information resources and reinforced by
social conflicts. Such an environment makes it possible for us to negotiate
and intentionally choose another identity, a reflexive production of self in
the life-political arenas from which social identities are constructed. No
fixed identities are confirmed. Conventional social divisions, by means
of which membership in class, family, gender, or nation-state is defined,
are now becoming increasingly flexible, and their boundary lines are
becoming more diffused. New kinds of social identities are connoted by
such figurations as "nomads of the present." The volunteers in my field
site abstractly expressed what they might want to do, or said that they
simply wanted to do something in general. The vehicle for volunteering
did not matter much. While these people were looking for something,
the municipal government offered a place for volunteering in a timely
manner. People happened to encounter chances for volunteer work in
the area of lifelong learning. They justified the situation by saying that
they encountered what they were looking for, and then they realized
that they finally found new meaning in their lives.

Actually, I myself experienced this. I did not have a strong interest in volunteering. I had never had a volunteer experience in my life

prior to starting this project. However, I had thought that if I had the chance, I wanted to be involved in society as a volunteer; I believed that my involvement could contribute positively to society. I had no idea, though, about what kind of volunteering activities I wanted to engage in. One day I happened to help a children's class as a volunteer because the assigned volunteer had suddenly become sick. That day I wrote in my field notes what I felt:

> Today I helped in a course for kids as a volunteer. As part of the coursework, kids made their own illustrated books—writing stories, drawing pictures, and binding the pages. There were about twenty kids in the course. Today was the final session. We volunteers helped in the bookbinding process. I had several conversations with the kids. One young girl told me while I helped her, "I wanted this book to be a present to myself. Actually, September 1 is my birthday. I really enjoyed this course. I want to take a course like this again." Another child told me, "I have come to this (lifelong learning) center since I was in my first year of elementary school. I took many fine arts courses here. I like these courses." I felt a feeling of satisfaction and happiness when I heard such comments from the kids. Probably the feeling I felt was a kind of joy in being a volunteer. The volunteers who find meaning in doing volunteer work here must have this type of feeling I felt today.

I was not so interested in children's courses, or in promoting lifelong learning activities. However, from the bottom of my heart, I was very much moved by my own first "volunteer" experience. I felt joy run through my body and mind. I even thought that I found a new aspect of myself. At the same time, however, I thought that this feeling could be dangerous. Somebody, including an authority such as the government, could take advantage of this kind of feeling for achieving its own purposes, while mobilizing people under the beautiful name "volunteerism." In fact, Melucci warns of the possibility that the process of individualization faces a sort of blockade when we abandon the serious self-reflexive form of action and blindly believe in existing power. In such cases, one falls into a dependence on authority. Melucci writes, "The process of individualization involves, on the one hand, the potential for individual control over the conditions and levels of action; yet, on the other, it entails the expropriation of these self-reflexive and self-productive resources by society itself" (1989, 48; also cited by Nakano, 1999, 85). Given volunteer opportunities by the government, people simply felt joy as a part of self-actualization while they were volunteering. They wanted to repeat the same experience again, as I did. We only considered the pure feeling that we were helping, bettering society.

However, all of us were, on another level, only reacting to the government's appeal. This meant that volunteers subconsciously became enablers of the system, not fully aware that they were recruited and manipulated by the government into becoming a part of the existing social structure in order to compensate for the government's insufficiencies. While mobilizing the local residents as volunteers, the fiscally constrained, conservative municipal government actually shrank its staff in its lifelong learning division. It abolished the position of director of lifelong learning policy under the name of administrative structural reform in 2000, the year my field site SLG gained NPO status. It occurred to me that the government could conveniently mobilize people as volunteers, particularly if the ideas of the volunteer recruits were naïve.

Reproduction of Volunteer Subjectivity through Education

Even though volunteering is part of self-individualization, examples of lifelong learning volunteers in my fieldwork verify that it is quite controllable by others. In the process of education reform, the Japanese government has been making serious efforts to institutionalize the expression of voluntary will in the existing society in an effective, strategic manner (MEXT 2002). At a practical level, the institutionalization of volunteer subjectivity is encouraged through the national education program. In Japan, the Education Ministry strictly supervises the content of education. Through education as a national project, such subjectivity is recognized as important and ideal for society, and justified as a desirable social identity for supporting the currently existing society. In particular, students are expected to absorb volunteer subjectivity as something necessary for good citizenship. In contemporary discourse, the volunteer subjectivity organized under NPOs is even expected to revive the deadlocked economy and society, as Japan lost direction after the burst of the "bubble" economy of the late 1980s through the early 1990s.

On March 20, 2003, the Japanese government received an epoch-making proposal, one that aimed to revise the Fundamental Law of Education, from the Central Council for Education, an authoritative advisory body to the Education Minister (see Okada 2002 for detailed studies on the revision). The education law has defined the basic concept of the Japanese educational system since 1947, controlled textbook content, and defined the daily school regimen as its guiding principles.

Based on reflections of Japan's nationalist education before and during World War II, and with the aim of building a democratic and peaceful society, the concept of individualism has been prominent in Japanese educational philosophy. Actually, the law, which often is dubbed an "education constitution," is the only law among several fundamental laws enacted during the Allied Forces' occupation after World War II, that has not yet been revised, although some politicians have tried.[3] The latest attempt to revise the law was initiated in November 2001 by the Education Minister at the time, Tōyama Atsuko. Minister Tōyama told the council that a study of revisions to the law was necessary to deal with "changes we are facing" by nurturing creativity and fostering respect for tradition and culture—"qualities," she said, that are required for the nation's citizens (*Asahi Shimbun*, November 27, 2001).

In this groundbreaking proposal by the Central Council for Education, the key slogan of education called for an agenda toward education in the new millennium—"the nurturing of spiritually rich and strong Japanese people who will generate new ground for the 21st century." More specific to the revisions, the proposal recommended that seven principles be added to the current Fundamental Law of Education:

1. Establishment of reliable school education

2. Promotion of university reforms to lead a knowledge-oriented era

3. Restoration of the ability of the home to educate children and promote cooperation and collaboration of schools, homes, and communities

4. Promotion of a sense of civic engagement for proactively participating in public life

5. Fostering of respect for Japan's traditions and culture, patriotic spirit for the homeland and country, as well as the consciousness of being a member of the international community

6. Realization of a lifelong learning society

7. Establishment of a basic promotional plan for education

(Central Council for Education 2003)

The proposal promotes the cultivation of a sense of civic responsibility while maintaining an underlying tone of patriotic emphasis on nationalistic identity formation. This idea stresses the importance of nurturing awareness and a positive attitude toward becoming actively involved in public forums supportive of the state and the individual.

Furthermore, in the proposal, a new term, *New Public* (*atarashii kōkyō*), is introduced, while the meaning of "public" has been tactically reconceptualized. In Japanese society, "public" has usually meant the state or something related to the state. However, this new statement is redefining the public sphere by institutionalizing volunteer subjectivity. The concept of public has been expanded. It includes an area of civic engagement for supporting a *New Public*. It is a sphere in which people in general or people who are interested in a cause can voluntarily participate. The proposal aims to establish a foundation of solidarity for good citizens to promote a better society, defined as increased civic engagement, which in itself would help society.

> The creation of a *New Public* . . . aims to encourage the proactive participation of volunteering subjects for the state and society in the 21st century. . . . It is the responsibility of people living in a democratic country to be proactively involved in matters of the state and society. The situation of the state and society depends on the people's will to seek something better. However, so far, we Japanese have tended to depend on somebody else's action regarding these issues. We believe it is someone else's responsibility. But that is not good. Instead, we need to cultivate a sense of public awareness. Through the volunteers' work just after the Great Hanshin-Awaji Earthquake, we confirmed that we have a tradition of mutual aid. Now we are stepping into a new era in which we are supporting a sense of values that we now call a *New Public*. That is, we try to solve the social problems we face by ourselves, including life improvement issues in the daily lives of the local community as well as matters of the global environment and human rights. It is expected that one will try to use one's abilities and time for others, for the local community, and for society, based on one's own will. For supporting a *New Public*, what one needs is self-awareness as an active participant in the making of state and society, bravery for practicing social justice, and an attitude of respect for Japanese traditional social norms. (Central Council for Education 2003)

Here, in other words, in the *New Public* sphere, Japanese people are expected to spontaneously do what they feel they need to do by themselves, instead of waiting for something to be provided by the government. That, in theory, is the civic engagement that the Education Ministry expects to institutionalize as volunteer subjectivity.

A reality in Japan is that volunteering often sounds like it is mandatory. In the educational philosophy promulgated by the Central Council for Education, volunteering to support the *New Public* is expected to officially be established in school education as something compulsory. In fact, the council recommended introducing volunteerism as a part of the core curriculum, such as in moral education (*dōtoku*) and social studies courses. In another proposal on volunteer promotion by the Central Council for Education, its basic stance on promoting volunteerism is that

> [v]olunteering should be considered a key for solving social problems we are now facing. Volunteering provides an opportunity for the social participation of independent, autonomous individuals. Such individuals are expected to contribute to generating and supporting the new "public."[4] In other words, learning volunteering plays a dominant role in supporting the concept of the "public." It will become crucial to support a rich civil society. (Central Council for Education 2002)

In a further example, the proposal mentions how to introduce volunteering to children at the elementary, secondary, and college levels:

> For youth in the growth phase, both schools and local communities should intentionally and strategically introduce volunteer activities. Considering their educational value, we urge youth to have various kinds of "direct" volunteer experiences. . . . Learning to volunteer provides an opportunity for spontaneous learning and activity, and generates people who are considerate. Volunteering will give students a chance to enhance the meaning of their lives throughout their lifetimes. Furthermore, doing so will create a solid foundation for becoming a spontaneous, independent person who can always contribute to society through everyday activities. (Central Council for Education 2002)

In fact, the council urged students from elementary schools to universities to participate in volunteering, as these activities could be an important factor in high school and college admissions, and could be counted as credit. To generate real-life volunteer experience, it was reported that Waseda University, one of the prestigious private universities in Tokyo, planned to dispatch its 250 students into elementary and junior high schools in the Shinjuku ward of central Tokyo as teaching assistants for computer science and club activities (*Nihon Keizai Shimbun,* June 14, 2002). This is definitely becoming a trend in Japanese university education. Moreover, the council proposed establishing a "young volunteer passport" system, under which students who volunteer may be given discounts on entrance fees to public facilities (Central Council for Education 2002). This document would be a record of individual volunteer activities and would apply toward school credit, entrance examinations, and employment recruitment evaluations.

Meanwhile, some critics point out that forcing students to participate in volunteer activities and offering rewards as incentives will distort the original spirit of volunteerism. The *Asahi Shimbun* newspaper, on April 9, 2002, editorialized:

> The important thing in volunteer activities is not simply the number of hours put in. What counts is how one uses one's physical and mental resources to learn, care, and understand what it is like to help other people. Helping out at nursing homes and similar institutions is not the only form of volunteer work. Active volunteerism involves identifying problems and working out solutions, as was the case for the young people who helped address the issue of HIV-tainted blood products, for example. Moreover, it ought to be more amply rewarded. One can gain joy when his action makes a difference, no matter how modest.

It is indeed possible that "overnight volunteers" might suddenly become popular in schools because volunteers would receive merit points for their volunteer activities, which would be recorded in their teachers' reports to schools to which they plan to apply. The meaning of "volunteer" will change if and when it becomes virtually compulsory in schools.

Interestingly enough, the proposal on volunteer promotion by the Central Council for Education (2002) never used the English-loan word *borantia* for its definition of "volunteering." "Volunteering" was instead translated as *hōshi* in Japanese, which literally means "service" in English. The Japanese term—*hōshi*—actually has a nuance that implies supporting society or even sacrificing oneself for the public welfare. The proposal justified the usage of the term *hōshi* because it correctly expressed the broad meaning of volunteering. It stated:

> Both *hōshi* and *borantia* commonly mean activities for someone else and society as a whole, providing time without expectation of material reward. . . . What we pursue here is contribution to

the *New Public,* which is supported by each individual providing his or her time and ability. That is, more specifically, we
pursue activities for someone else as well as for oneself, and
for society as a whole, not expecting any reward. In this sense,
we broadly define these activities as *hōshi.* . . . From this point
of view, our traditional community services such as neighborhood associations, youth groups, firefighting, and festivals are
all based on *hōshi.* (Central Council for Education 2002)

However, I have never perceived that the volunteers in my field site see
their activities as *hōshi.* They were actually very sensitive to the term
and never used it for describing their activities. One volunteer at SLG
said this in a meeting:

I don't think that volunteerism is *hōshi.* We volunteers are
not building a relationship between people who give services
and people who receive services. We primarily try to enhance
ourselves through volunteering. I believe that we are now
in a transition from a money-based society to a heart-based
society. Volunteering offers us a clue to the meaning in life.
We are not doing it for others but doing it for ourselves and
for our own lives.

Another said the following:

I believe that there is no ideal type of volunteering. Each
organization or group has its own style. I think it is possible
to have various styles of volunteering.

While listening to these opinions, I felt that the argument made by the
Education Ministry in its macro-discourse is far from the reality of volunteering as actually practiced.

It seems contradictory that the government can ignore such reality
at the grassroots level, since education is situated as the first step for
effectively making routine the creation of this coercive social consciousness (e.g., Illich 1972; Foucault 1977; Miller 2002). This occurs through
forms of educational practice that shape volunteering as supporting the
New Public. Education controlled under the strong state defines an ideal
style of civic engagement. It is a social engineering tool for determining
identities, to be deployed for an ulterior purpose. Furthermore, in producing and reproducing a certain form of human nature—one directed
by the urge of volunteer subjectivity—the national education system has

impinged upon the population as a whole. The proposal points out how the government and businesses can introduce and support volunteering activities (Central Council for Education 2002). At the practical level, volunteering promotion centers, such as the Tokyo Voluntary Action Center (TVAC), an administrative arm of the Tokyo Metropolitan Government, specializing in promoting volunteerism, encourage people in Tokyo to participate in volunteer work. As I mentioned in chapter 2, social welfare councils, quasi-governmental institutions designed to promote both the growth of volunteerism and the matching of existing community needs with volunteering resources, are nowadays being reorganized as volunteering promotion centers at the prefecture and municipal levels. Volunteer centers such as the TVAC provide information about volunteer opportunities while educating people who are interested in volunteering. What they are advocating, however, is not simply the virtues of volunteerism but the social necessity of surrendering subjectivity to the volunteering impulse. According to a TVAC pamphlet, there are four pillars of volunteerism. They say volunteerism exhibits the following qualities: (1) spontaneity, (2) mutual aid, (3) unpaid service, and (4) problem solving (TVAC 2001, 2).

Japanese society, as a result of such movements, has been experiencing a reformulation of the relations between the state and the individual. In fact, it is being introduced to a new form of rationality of the state aimed at the level of human consciousness. The volunteer subjectivity is becoming "the fictitious atom of an 'ideological' representation of society" defined by the specific technology of power that Foucault has called "discipline" (Foucault 1977, 194). Disciplinary power is insinuated in volunteer activities, penetrating regulation into the details of everyday life through procedures such as examinations and systematic training. These constrain the human consciousness—volunteer subjectivity—into collectively useful aptitudes. In fact, I noticed that the Japanese term *borantia* is never used for "negative" activism under the current system. For example, participating in antigovernment activities, antiglobalization appeals, and the anti-Iraq war movement (to cite a recent case) has never been categorized as part of volunteer activities. The volunteer subjectivity is only praised for maintaining, strengthening, and improving the existing society. In this sense, if we replace the term *New Public* with "the state" in the council proposal, then the meaning of volunteerism in Japan becomes clearer. That is, volunteerism is done for the state. Volunteer work is not to be used against the state, even if the volunteer believes this activity would be for the good of the people. During my fieldwork, I had the impression that volunteers supervised under the NPO system would never become social activists. They are apolitical. In general, those people advocating thoughts different from the dominant political voice are labeled "people in anti-establishment groups," but not as "volunteers." I found this usage to be very conspicuous in media reports, such as in newspapers.

The Colonization of the Volunteering World

As I argued earlier in this chapter, volunteering is generally thought of as informal, unregulated, and spontaneous, as the term *voluntary* brings to mind. Volunteering is an expression of individuals' values and their search for meaning in their lives. It is situated as part of the activities of the *lifeworld*, a term introduced by Edmund Husserl (1970). He describes the lifeworld as the world of immediate experience, the world as already there, predetermined, experienced in the natural, primordial attitude. The lifeworld is the immediate milieu of the individual social actor. The things that make life worthwhile—love, friendship, companionship, good conversations with friends and peer groups in informal discussions, and spending quality time with family—are all part of the lifeworld, through which we are each known and recognized as a person, an individual, and a human being.

On the other hand, throughout my fieldwork, I felt like I observed something different from this. I was witnessing the encroachment of forms of administrative rationality or formal rationality, to use Max Weber's terms, into life spaces (Weber 1978). Volunteerism organized under administrative rationality is not situated in the lifeworld, as Husserl describes it. Instead, to rephrase Jürgen Habermas (1987), this is the "colonization of the volunteering world." By administrative rationality invading volunteerism, volunteerism cannot be synonymous with the lifeworld. As my ethnographic research shows, volunteers were originally seeking their own meaning in their lives. Satisfying their own meaning through volunteering for something was one of the crucial motivations for stepping into volunteering. However, people who were interested in satisfying their own interests through volunteering were strategically mobilized under the NPO Law in Japanese society. They were organized as volunteers under the name of NPOs, in which each had its own special area of social service within seventeen designated areas, including social welfare, community development, and international cooperation. The volunteers are expected to play a significant role in contributing to the existing society through their activities in NPOs. Furthermore, participating in voluntary activities in NPOs, for example, is highly recommended as an ideal civic engagement style for supporting the *New Public*, or the state. Volunteering, supervised under the NPO Law, should be situated in the domain of formal rationality.

The colonization of the volunteering world involves a restatement of the Weberian thesis that the modern world based on formal rationality (determined by expectations of rational action pursuing efficiency and predictability) is triumphing over substantive rationality (determined by conscious, value-oriented action) and coming to dominate areas that were formally defined by substantive rationality. It is a process by which rational actions in social and political life become predominant in the social activity of individuals, and formal rationality becomes predominant in the patterns of action, institutionalized in groups, organizations, and other collective behaviors. Weber characterizes this increasing rationality as an "iron cage" that limits individual freedom and activities:

> No one knows who will live in this cage in the future, or whether at the end of this tremendous development entirely new prophets will arise, or there will be a great rebirth of old ideas and ideals, or, if neither, mechanized petrifaction, embellished with a sort of convulsive self-importance. For of the last stage of this cultural development, it might well be truly said: "Specialist without spirit, sensualists without heart; this nullity imagines that it has obtained a level of civilization never before achieved." (Weber 1992, 182)

In my research context, under the iron cage, people are expected to institutionalize volunteer subjectivity in their bodies and minds as civic engagement for supporting the *New Public*, in other words, the state. In the mobilization of volunteerism in contemporary Japan, all burdens fall on the grassroots volunteers, who are at a loss to suddenly be given such a large assignment. They are at their wit's end trying to determine what they are expected to do. One volunteer, Ms. Takamiya, one of the thirteen *pure* volunteers who spontaneously joined this community-oriented lifelong learning project, told me this:

> I think what I am doing here is work. I know a lot is expected of us from the government. The pressure actually sometimes makes me feel lost—I don't know what I am doing here. I am only a volunteer, looking for my own meaning through volunteering.

Another day, Ms. Tajima, mentioned earlier in this chapter as an *invited* volunteer, told me the following:

> For the past two weeks, I have been sick. I was at home. Dur-
> ing that time, I felt I was very settled. I even felt like that was
> the real me. Volunteering made me very tired. I was always
> thinking about planning new courses. I don't know why I
> was so driven. Nevertheless, it was my daily life.

I will never forget the day that I saw a dispatched government official playing a computer game next to one of the volunteers who was negotiating with an instructor candidate. More able, active, flexible volunteers actually covered his job. Meanwhile, some of the volunteers left the organization as they became annoyed with this reality—the colonization of their volunteer consciousness by administrative rationality. They felt that this was not the volunteer activity they had imagined. These people chose not to be volunteers under the NPO structure.

Before concluding this chapter, I would like to add an ethnographic observation of my old friend, Ms. Suzuki. I met her when I started working as a reporter for a news service in the early 1990s after graduating from college. I used to speak with her because she was (and still is) active in a city northeast of Tokyo, where there were many migrant laborers from Bangladesh, Iran, Pakistan, and Peru working at small- and medium-size factories during the so-called "bubble" economy of the late 1980s and the early 1990s. Many foreign workers, most of whom were illegally staying in Japan, came to this city to perform hard jobs that Japanese people hated to do. When there was an on-the-job accident, the factory owners often refused compensation to these workers, as they were living in the country illegally. As a volunteer, Ms. Suzuki eagerly supported the migrant workers. She created her own network to help them by organizing a group to support migrant workers' rights in Japan. As a reporter, I covered many labor accident cases in which these workers were involved. Ms. Suzuki stood up for anyone she believed was a victim; she also stood up against anyone, whether a government official or a business owner. Ms. Suzuki experienced the students' movements (*gakusei undō*) of the late 1960s when she was a freshman at college in Tokyo. While covering many cases, I saw that Ms. Suzuki's actions originated from her experiences as a student activist.

It was in early January 2003 that I met Ms. Suzuki for the first time in more than five years. We talked about many things during our meeting at a tiny Japanese-style bar; but although I expected her to mention the ongoing NPO phenomenon in Japanese society because she continued to be active in social movements, during our three-hour conversation she never uttered the word NPO once. In the last few minutes of our meeting, I asked her directly what she thought about the current trend of NPOs. All she said was: "Some people might find that easier." That was the only comment she offered. Despite its brevity, her remark was one of the most insightful comments I gathered for my project. She had continued to do what she wanted to do and what she needed to do in Japanese society as an independent, autonomous human being, while remaining deeply rooted in her community. She did not need the state's recognition or control in an NPO to do her "volunteer" activities.

Volunteerism institutionalized under the NPO Law serves the state. This is one reality of "volunteerism" in contemporary Japan. I would say, moreover, that this reality of "volunteerism" is not limited to Japanese society. I believe that it also is true of other countries promoting volunteerism under a conservative neoliberal policy.

Chapter 5

Power and Contested Rationalities

Kyōdō: Policy Collaboration

I have here a 255-page report with an orange cover published by the Mie Prefectural Government NPO team (Mie Prefectural Government 2001). The report specifically deals with 123 successful cases of policy collaboration between municipal governments in Mie Prefecture and local NPOs during the fiscal year 2000, which ran from April 1, 2000, to March 31, 2001. Collaboration, currently called *kyōdō*, between third-sector organizations such as NPOs and the government in policy making has been a fashionable strategy in Japan's public administration since the enactment of the 1998 NPO Law, as it promises to facilitate successful, effective policy implementation while achieving cost cutting for the government. *Kyōdō* is also an active effort of civic engagement in public affairs that aims to build on the resources, skills, and knowledge of community members so that they can, together, improve the quality of life in the community. This is usually realized through the entrusting of projects to NPOs by the government. Third-sector organizations provide specific social services in place of (but promoted by) the government.

Since the late 1990s, Mie Prefecture, located in central Japan, has become established as a role model for the Japanese NPO world for the way in which the prefecture government strongly pushed policy collaboration with local NPOs under the administration of reform-minded Governor Kitagawa Masayasu. Mr. Kitagawa, elected in 1995, aggressively implemented a decentralization policy at the local level of his administration. These represented moves away from the old-fashioned, back-room maneuvering politics of the central government. Mr. Kitagawa's approach to administrative reform inspired an outbreak of reform-minded governors across the nation. Local governments have indeed moved ahead of the central government, usually known for its strong power in Japan, as far as reform is concerned. Acknowledging the significance of this shift, the national daily *Asahi Shimbun* newspaper printed an editorial on July

18, 2002, stating that the central government and bureaucrats could be left behind the times.

Kyōdō was a hot topic at my field site, SLG, a community-oriented lifelong learning NPO in downtown Tokyo. As I mentioned in the previous chapters, SLG is a provider of lifelong learning opportunities to local residents. Volunteers at SLG create various kinds of lifelong learning courses, including classes in literature, foreign languages, sports, and so on. Meanwhile, the municipal government funds its activities. The fiscally constrained municipal government implemented this community-oriented lifelong learning project in four steps. First, in the mid 1990s, the government organized a citizens' group to perform lifelong learning program planning in place of the government. This effort was in direct response to the enactment of the Japanese Law for the Promotion of Lifelong Learning in 1990, which articulates that governments at both the national and municipal levels provide all residents with learning opportunities over their lifetimes. Second, the government led the group to become an NPO in 2000, following the enactment of the NPO Law in 1998. Third, the government entrusted parts of the management of the municipal lifelong learning center—the planetarium and computer facility—to the NPO from April 2002. The final step, which this chapter explores, involved the entrustment of the entire operation of the public facility to the NPO in April 2003. The NPO would take full responsibility for managing a public facility for promoting lifelong learning in the municipality as an entrustment project. That public facility is the place where the NPO is currently housed and where all of the lifelong learning courses SLG offers are held. I was able to document every detail of the series of talks between the NPO and the government geared toward achieving this final step for the six months following July 2002. Despite the attempt, the two sides failed to reach an agreement on the entrustment project.

In this chapter, I first give an overview of the *kyōdō* discourse in Japan and then make an argument regarding the specific entrustment case that failed, identifying two key points—power and rationality—in both the NPO and the government. There was a huge conflict between the two entities in terms of what they sought through policy collaboration. My ethnographic investigation identified a preoccupation with persistent formalism in Japanese administrative politics, the framing of issues, and procedures and practices of the government sector in the dominant discourses of bureaucratic instrumental rationality—in this case, cost cutting. Furthermore, I observed something that the government had not expected: resistance from the volunteer-based NPO to alternative ways of doing things. The government's rationality, which was pushing for the most effective public administration in terms of cost, was never echoed among the volunteers. Local knowledge and practices generated by the NPO were fettered by bureaucratic rationality. In my ethnography, I illuminate how the dynamics of power contributed to determining the dominant rationality over the decision-making process. Rationality is very much power driven. The powerlessness experienced by the NPO participants during the decision-making process led them to feel that they were becoming peripheral in public affairs under the strong state. There was a strong contrast between practices generated by local knowledge and state administrative skills. Pursuing an ideal form of deliberative democracy, Japanese NPOs have shown their fragility and immaturity; meanwhile, the state has, ironically, become more and more dominant.

A New Political Technique

Before moving on to my analysis of the case, I offer a brief review of the discourse of *kyōdō* in contemporary Japanese public administration. *Kyōdō* was introduced as a new political technique between NPOs and governments in policy-making initiatives; it was very much in fashion, as it promised to make possible more successful policies. This was directly in line with a trend seen in the Anglo-American countries; the foundation of the so-called New Public Management (NPM) movement strongly influenced the renewal of public-sector activities in advanced industrial countries (e.g., Pollitt 1990; Osborne and Gaebler 1992; Naschold 1996). Japan is a latecomer to NPM-inspired reform. Only since 1995 have comprehensive reforms—including traditional reform elements, such as cabinet reform, decentralization, and strengthening of local self-government—as well as NPM-specific components, including a spree of agencification, been tackled (Muramatsu and Naschold 1997; see also Masujima 2005 for recent developments).

As Harry Boyte and Nancy Kari (1996) argue, creating collaboration beyond the conventional sector generates new flows of energy in society. Introducing the term *public work* to mean collaborative work that builds basic public goods and resources, they note the following:

> Public work generates new sources of energy. It brings together people, resources, and groups who may never have imagined working together. By creating new working relationships, it also changes the dynamics of power, often in significant ways. (Boyte and Kari 1996, 29)

Further, Boyte continues the argument elsewhere:

> Public work is central to the idea of productive, everyday politics. . . . It leads to people seeing themselves as the co-creators of democracy, not simply as customers or clients, voters, protestors, or volunteers. To highlight the creative, educative, and productive dimensions of politics, public work can be best defined as sustained effort by a mix of people who solve public problems or create goods, material or cultural, of general benefit. Public work is work that is visible, open to inspection, whose significance is widely recognized, and which can be carried out by people whose interests, views, and backgrounds may be quite different. (Boyte 2004, 5)

The political atmosphere in Japan certainly resembles what Boyte and Kari describe. For example, the Tokyo Metropolitan Government, one of the strong public entities promoting collaboration under conservative Governor Ishihara Shintaro, defines the term in a policy proposal for promoting *kyōdō*. It provides an ideal scheme of *kyōdō*:

> *Kyōdō* denotes activities jointly created by the government and NPOs, respecting each other as equal partners and exchanging their respective resources, aimed at achieving some social purpose and offering social services. (Tokyo Metropolitan Government 2000a, 18)

Furthermore, *kyōdō* is meaningful in the Japanese context of deregulation politics and financial economy, which started in the mid 1990s under Prime Minister Hashimoto Ryutaro of the Liberal Democratic Party (LDP). Koizumi Jun'ichiro, prime minister during my fieldwork, was strongly pushing for government services, including postal services, to be privatized. One of his favorite phrases, frequently quoted, was *"Min de yareru koto wa min de [yaru]"* ("If things can be done by the private [third] sector, the private [third] sector should do them.")[1] The government does not need to do them if it does not need to be involved.

This trend has become dominant across the nation as public-private partnership (PPP). In Japan, PPP policy has actually been explained as a panacea for breaking through the deadlocked state of the economy after the collapse of so-called "bubble" economy of the late 1980s through the early 1990s, referring to the British economy, which was galvanized under Margaret Thatcher's strong initiative to implement PPP policies. The idea is associated with using limited taxes more efficiently. It applies not only to government procurement but also to all aspects of the public administration as a whole. According to research done by a think tank in Tokyo, more than 60 percent of local governments are interested in introducing the PPP policies for enhancing the efficiency of public administration.[2]

Aiming to expand the PPP idea, many symposia were held in Japan during the time I was doing my fieldwork. These symposia focused on explaining the ways in which the policy should be introduced, advocating its effectiveness as a cost-cutting measure while at the same time justifying it as a highly recommended platform for increasing citizens' participation in public affairs. Each symposium included invited experts from countries already successful in implementing the PPP policy. One symposium I attended on PPP in Tokyo in May 2002 was sponsored by the Ministry of Economy, Trade, and Industry (METI). The discussants included bureaucrats from the METI, the Ministry of Finance (MOF), and the Tokyo Metropolitan Government; a professor of economics from the University of Tokyo; and a couple of economists and strategists from think tanks in Japan. The PPP expert this time was an Australian businessman. The underlying theme of the symposium was the redefinition of the government's job of providing basic social services. The symposium provided a good forum to consider the true mission of the government. The discussants argued that if the role of the government is to provide the best social services to the public, then the government should consider buying them, or outsourcing them, rather than generating them on its own. The role of the government should be to offer the best-quality service at the cheapest price to its constituents. One METI official said this at the symposium:

> We are now introducing a concept of new public interest in Japanese society. What we are thinking is not social services in a top-down manner but social services jointly produced by both the government and NPOs. I believe the PPP policy aims to utilize the vitality of the private sector to galvanize the current deadlocked society. It is an effective approach to rebuilding the Japanese economy.

The Australian expert said:

> Japan is lucky because it can learn from the UK and Australia, both of which were successful in using a PPP policy for the

past couple of decades. Japan can learn from them in a most effective manner about the cases of successes and failures. We can provide that knowledge.

The symposium specifically discussed what third-sector organizations such as NPOs could do under a PPP policy framework. Examples of collaboration that were mentioned related to child care, the water supply, parking violation ticketing, prison operation, and data input. As an MOF official observed:

> Indeed, those are the main areas the government is considering entrusting to the NPO sector, mainly for cost cutting. Meanwhile, I think the government should take responsibility at the decision-making stage. The government needs to control the decision-making activities, including making budgets and recruiting personnel.

In January 2003, I had another opportunity to participate in a similar gathering: an annual conference on policy analysis hosted by a nationwide consortium of policy analysts, politicians, researchers, and students. While the overall purpose of the conference was to discuss the Japanese policy-making system, the main topic was deregulation. Several participants reported obstacles caused by the Japanese social and political structure—for example, how existing bureaucrats had resisted opening up active policy debates, and how the conventional iron triangle formed by bureaucracy, businesses, and politicians had dominated the decision-making system in politics and the economy. Some participants even argued that Japanese politics is not politics in any real sense; it is just an interest-coordination process. Many people seek to maintain the existing social and political structure, as it promotes their own interests. Against this backdrop, NPOs are being introduced as a way to stimulate such public administration. In other words, supporting a wider role for NPOs is in line with deregulation politics. One of the discussants at this January gathering, a mayor in Gunma Prefecture, northern Tokyo, outlined how he uses NPOs in his municipal administration.

> What I want to do is increase the quality of our public administration for the residents. For example, I want to open our office 24 hours. However, I can't use my staff for that purpose due to labor law regulations. Thus I would use an NPO. If I use NPOs, I can keep the office open 24 hours. The municipal government and NPOs have a good collaborative relationship and are able to make such an entrustment contract.

In order to explain how these macro-policy ideas were introduced to and implemented at the grassroots level in Japanese society, I document later details of a specific case of entrustment planned at my field site. My analysis primarily focuses on local people's responses—their beliefs and practices—toward accepting the entrustment project, which was introduced by the municipal government in a very top-down manner. The case study unveils vulnerability and an unbalanced power relationship between the government and the NPO in a local community.

Talks toward *Kyōdō*: A Japanese Case

I present the development of the entrustment talks between SLG and the municipal government from July 2002 until the end of the year. Formal meetings were held six times and resulted in failure, with six NPO members, including a head, three vice heads, the general secretary and vice general secretary, and four municipal government officials, including the chief of lifelong learning policy, head and vice head of the lifelong learning center, and a lifelong learning specialist from the government. The series of meetings was primarily driven by one word—*benefit*. What are the benefits? The participants from SLG and the municipal government explored their own benefits in achieving the entrustment.

The talks started in early July 2002. Throughout, the tone was oppressive and even unfriendly, due to the dominant presence of the government at SLG. The government held the dominant power as entrustor, while the NPO as entrustee was weak. The government's policy chief for lifelong learning primarily led the discussions. It was the government, not the NPO, which presented the proposal for the entrustment project. At the beginning of the meeting, it was impressive that the policy chief defined the purpose of the meeting and how it would be conducted.

> *Policy Chief:* This meeting aims to create mutual understanding about the entrustment of operations of the public facility to SLG. We need to discuss what this is exactly; what SLG would be expected to do; and what impact this could potentially have on the residents, both positively and negatively. We have not decided exactly when the entrustment would start, although we are targeting April 2003 tentatively. I hope through a series of meetings we can develop some shared vision of the entrustment project.

The head of the lifelong learning center followed the policy chief.

> *Center Head:* Frankly speaking, under the entrustment contract, we would want SLG to do basic facility management; this primarily entails daily maintenance of the lifelong learning center, including both the main hall and the annex.

He was referring to a ten-page handout suddenly presented to the SLG participants. These were filled with details on how to do daily maintenance. The list of things to do was quite overwhelming. It included some sixty items that were too detailed in a sense, including collecting facility rental fees, maintenance of the building, and nighttime patrolling (see Appendix 3).

After the government officials explained the agenda, they started discussions by focusing on the benefits of entrustment for both sides. Why would SLG want to get involved in the entrustment? Why would the government want to entrust management of a public facility to an NPO? The government, while responding to a question from an SLG member, defined the benefit from its point of view. Surprisingly enough, the government also provided rationales to the NPO about why NPOs should accept entrustment contracts from the government, which originally could be presented by NPOs under their own initiatives.

> *SLG Head:* First, may we ask what your intentions are regarding entrusting business to an NPO?
>
> *Policy Chief:* One of the benefits NPOs get from entrustment is stable revenue from earning entrustment fees from the government. This is part of our *support* policy for NPOs. This means we plan to change the current stance on the entrustment contract. We consider that if you can save some part of the entrustment money due to your efficiency efforts, you don't have to give it back to us. You can keep it. Furthermore, from the residents' perspective—and actually this is the strongest reason for entrustment itself—the residents may feel that it is more convenient when citizen-based NPOs operate public facilities than when the government operates them. The crucial aim is to more effectively achieve the purpose that such facilities originally have. In other words, we want

public feasibility to the residents, by the residents, and for the residents. Thus, we are considering entrusting all the current work we do on this to you. The work includes such responsibilities as collecting facility rental fees, maintenance of the building, and nighttime patrolling.

The actual discussion began.

SLG Head: Well, I was thinking that it might be difficult to solidify our financial situation with the entrust-ment money from the government by saving money on our own efforts. . . . The efforts mean that we will do what you were doing with six people, with fewer people, right? If you think it is possible, why don't you do it that way? That's not the issue, though. That is not what we are actually looking for. What we want is when SLG uses the facilities of this center, it doesn't have to pay a fee, or maybe pays a discounted fee. That would benefit us.

Policy Chief: If we specifically do something only for SLG, it would not be fair to all of the residents in this ward. We can't do that. We couldn't intentionally do something like that, not with a public facility.

SLG Vice Head: For instance, could we extend the hours of operation to 9:30 p.m. from 9 p.m. for our course offerings? That would be more con-venient for people working during the day.

Policy Chief: Institutionally, no, to be fair, according to the local ordinance.

SLG Head: Why is this a fairness issue? What is fairness? I think that fairness is not an issue in this case. I believe that the municipal government should seriously think about what it means to entrust something to a citizen-based organization, instead of entrusting to a for-profit company. Otherwise, the entrustment to NPOs will just become another form of subcontracting by

the government. We want to use this public
facility as much as we can. If we can combine entrusted facility management with our
lifelong learning business, that would benefit
us, and we believe that what we want would
also benefit the residents.

Policy Chief: It is impossible. Institutionally, it is impossible.

The discussion clearly revealed a large discrepancy between the two
sides. I felt that the government was trying to manipulate the NPO to
achieve its own policy agenda. The government was taking leadership
in the discussion and justifying the entrustment as an administrative
technique in the new public management framework. It was as though
the government fully knew what the role of the NPOs should be in
this kind of project. The government was teaching the "right" way to
be an NPO. It was the same strategy the government had used when
it introduced a new organizational form—NPO—to the former entity,
as argued in chapter 3. But this time it did not end in success for
the government.

The entrustment project was a package deal that the government
wanted to make. Thus there was no chance for SLG to say anything about
the details of the business contract. SLG was only an entrustee, while
the government was the entrustor. It looked like the government would
reject any proposals from the entrustee about the content of the project.
Further negotiation would be impossible. As far as I know, there was
no *nemawashi* (discussion in advance)—which is part of the traditional
decision-making system in Japanese society—between SLG and the government. The members of SLG appeared extremely annoyed, not only by
the detailed list on the content of entrustment but also by the fact that
there was no *nemawashi* to introduce such an important matter. It might
even have been a shocking experience for the SLG people because they
had believed that the government was an intimate partner. However, there
was no such camaraderie. I observed an oppressiveness the government
had over SLG. Meanwhile, SLG just revealed its fragility. This might be
described as volunteers' amateurism; the government overwhelmed the
SLG side with its professionalism as a business contractor. Clearly, the
NPO and the government entered the discussion with different images,
different meanings, and different purposes for the project.

At the second talk in this process, held at the end of July, the government further explained the details of the facility-management plan.
However, SLG's assertions again sounded powerless; in the end, they
were to have no influence over the direction of the discussion.

Inside Discussion: Challenging the Defined Benefits

By the beginning of August, following the first and second meetings on the entrustment, SLG still could not decide whether to accept the entrustment, due to the wide gap in understanding what the project entailed. It organized an internal strategy meeting focusing on the entrustment project with the municipal government. The following people attended: the SLG head, three vice heads, the general secretary, the vice general secretary, and one government official (the vice head of the lifelong learning center). The meeting also included two directors, one of whom had experience as a business consultant (called *Consul-Director* in the conversation analysis that follows) and another who was a member of the task force on administrative reform for the municipal government (called *Reform-Member*).

For the first internal discussion, I observed that the strategy meeting was interestingly divided into two sides—pro-entrustment and anti-entrustment. The pro-entrustment side included the SLG head (a local lawyer who was directly appointed by the government to be the NPO president) and an SLG director from an administrative reform task force of the municipal government. On the anti-entrustment side were two vice heads—a woman who had been invited by SLG to be a vice head from a local environmental NGO (*Environmentalist*) and a person with a long history as a volunteer firefighter in the community (*Fireman*). One of the vice heads (*Landlord*) missed the first internal meeting, although he played a key role in designating the direction later on.

Reform-Member: It is natural that we have a very different perspective from the government's. We are not a takeover target for the government. We have our own way as an NPO, an organization in the society.

Environmentalist: However, we don't have any vision on the entrustment as an NPO. What makes us an NPO? We were indeed created by the government. . . . Maybe, I think, we are expected to just follow their instructions without saying anything. But it would be ideal if we could operate this lifelong learning center in its entirety, combining the public facilities with our lifelong learning course offerings. How wonderful it would be for the local community! Thinking that way stimulates my imagination. What would we be able to do? What do we want to do? We should have proposed specific plans to the government as an NPO. I believe that's the proper attitude as an NPO. That definitely could lead us to benefit from the situation.

Fireman: Maybe we even lack a shared meaning of what an NPO is. Even if we accept the entrustment project, we need to think more of creating a shared meaning as an NPO. . . . What can we do specifically as an NPO?

Consul-Director: I very much agree with this opinion. We need to present a direction as an NPO. Otherwise, we can't move forward. We need something we all can share.

As the discussion continued, the participants also reflected on the government's attitude and vision on educational policy in the local community.

Environmentalist: I wonder what the role of the government is in community education. It seems like it gave up on its lifelong learning policy. Furthermore, the number of kids in this community is decreasing year by year. Public schools in our community are being closed. Under the circumstances, what action is the government taking? Both school education and lifelong learning are out of their hands. I was wondering why they want to disengage themselves from education issues. Nowadays anything made "hands-off by the government" is justified under the name of structural reform for achieving cost cutting. However, I don't agree with it. I believe that the government needs to take responsibility for it, especially by offering high-quality education as a basic social service for its residents.

Frustration was evident on the discussion floor. It was obvious that the frustration stemmed from the government's inflexible attitude. Also, there was frustration from their own inability as an NPO. They wanted to do something as an NPO. It would be a great chance for the NPO if it could use the public facility according to its will. The members of the NPO fully, albeit silently, acknowledged that they were not empowered at a level necessary to work as equals with the government.

One week later, the internal discussions resumed. How would they move forward? It seemed to me that they were deadlocked. The conversation went around and around. The pro-entrustment people tried to control the meeting, while the anti-entrustment vice heads resisted. At the beginning of the second internal meeting, the SLG head encouraged participants to make some decisions in a hasty manner.

> *Head*:   I need to say yes or no by the next meeting with the government on August 26. This leaves us only three weeks. Otherwise, we can't start full negotiations, including on the budget for the next fiscal year. Should we move forward on it? Should we reject it?

The head tried to assert his power at the meeting. At this stage, I saw different power dynamics starting to dominate the discussion, which provided an opportunity to observe an interesting contrast of micropolitical power. Discussion-leader power, for example, shifted to one vice head (*Landlord*) who had missed the first internal meeting. This person was an influential leader in the local community. He was from a good, established family, one that had been part of the community for more than 300 years. He also had rich experiences in such activities as PTAs and community development. When the head asked him for his opinion about the entrustment project, he responded.

> *Landlord*:   I think we should accept the entrustment business if we can. It would be a good opportunity because we would deal with all of the facets of lifelong learning in this local community. From the government's position, this entrustment project leads to cost cutting. The government thinks that introducing the NPO will stimulate the public administration. However, I believe that the real meaning is more than that. What we need to consider is what we specifically can do for *the residents* when we accept

the entrustment. If we don't make this point clear, we will be a target for criticism from the residents, not the government.

This comment suddenly changed the atmosphere. Nobody, including the anti-entrustment people, rushed to disagree with his comment. There was only silence—positive silence for the pro-entrustment people. I knew that he was a very reliable man among the SLG volunteers. His logic was indeed persuasive, bringing a new key word—*residents*—to the discussion table. However, it seemed to me that the changes to the atmosphere went beyond that. What I observed was power dynamics in territorial politics. Even though my field site is located in a very urbanized part of Tokyo, it still exists. I had the impression that everybody was just following whatever the landlord—a powerful man in the community—said. Meanwhile, it seemed that the SLG head had no place in the politics. He was just a newcomer in the community, having moved to this area a couple of decades ago.

Empowered by this comment, the pro-entrustment side seemed to gain momentum. From this stage, I was actually surprised when I later looked at my field notes, because few negative opinions were written on the entrustment project. The discussion gradually moved toward a shared consensus based on the key term *residents*. In this process, the pro-entrustment people seemed to take tactical advantage of the positive mood generated by this shift of emphasis to the term *residents*.

Environmentalist: We indeed need to think about what we can do specifically for *the residents* when we accept the entrustment project. For example, the center facilities should be more convenient for *the residents* themselves.

Reform-Member: We need to go forward to improve services of lifelong learning for *the residents*. Our counterpart is not the government but *the residents*. We should think about all of *the residents* in this community, regardless of sex and age, since we now take full responsibility for the lifelong learning operation for *the residents*. Maybe we are focusing too much on the relationship between SLG and the government. Instead, we need to look more at *the residents*.

Head: I understand the key purpose of the entrust-
                          ment is to achieve *benefits for the resident*.
                          Both SLG and the government try to realize
                          the same thing, but in extremely different
                          manners. (emphases added)

Distrust Accelerating between the Sides

At the third round of meetings with the government, the SLG people
reported that they wanted to proceed with the discussions on the entrustment project in a positive way. At the discussion table, the SLG head
mentioned the significance of the entrustment project. This was one of
the most impressive moments in the series of talks.

SLG Head: I believe that the entrustment method should not
               be used in the framework of the government's
               logic. NPOs are not subcontractors to the gov-
               ernment. If the government misses this point,
               the meaning of the entrustment to NPOs will
               become unclear. This is a collaborative project
               for both of us—an NPO and the government.

The response from the government was rigid, however. I felt that the
atmosphere was becoming very heavy. The government then stepped up
to clearly mention the purpose of the project from its perspective. That
is, it hoped to realize cost cutting. This had not been clearly expressed
in the first and second series of talks. The policy chief of lifelong learning promptly responded to the head's comment.

Policy Chief: We are promoting cost cutting by the entrust-
                 ment. The entrustment to SLG is a program of
                 rationalization of our public administration. I
                 believe this will lead to the careful use of tax-
                 payers' money. But we are not promoting the
                 entrustment project just because it is economical.
                 What we are interested in is what we can get as
                 a result of the entrustment project. What kinds
                 of services to the residents are newly created by
                 SLG, an NPO organized by local residents? What
                 can you offer to add value?

Landlord: If you say so, I believe that the government needs to revise the local ordinance as soon as possible. Otherwise, we can't do anything. I mean, we can plan new lifelong learning courses by using the planetarium at the center. However, the planetarium is not supposed to be used for such a purpose under the local ordinance. According to the ordinance, the planetarium is a place to see stars, not a place to have lifelong learning courses. The law limits our possibilities and imagination.

Policy Chief: The law guarantees that the public facility—the planetarium in this case—will be equally open to all people in the local community. That is the top priority. We can't treat SLG specially, even though SLG is a partner in the entrustment project.

Fireman: Why don't we discuss the issue more flexibly? Otherwise, we can't achieve the key purpose—enhancing the use of this facility for *the residents*. The planetarium is a facility to see stars. However, for us, the planetarium is a dome-shaped classroom. We plan to have a concert while watching stars. In other words, we can use the facility more creatively. Why don't you think in such a way?

Policy Chief: Institutionally speaking, it is a problem. The law says that the planetarium is not supposed to be used in such a way. (emphasis added)

The government turned a deaf ear to the SLG proposal.

Inside SLG, one issue left unclear was the government's rationale that the entrustment project would create financial stability for SLG as an NPO. This rationale was, as I mentioned in discussing the policy chief's comment earlier, that SLG would save money for the entrustment project due to its efficiency efforts and then use the surplus for its lifelong learning business. The municipal government provided two categories of money to SLG. One was called aid money (*hojo-kin*) and the other was entrustment money (*itaku-kin*). The government had funded SLG's lifelong learning business from the aid-money category. The operation costs for the planetarium and computer facility had been financed from the entrustment-money category, as those facilities are government assets. However, the government had been decreasing the amount of aid money due to its severe financial situation. Every year, the budget was supposed to decrease by 10 percent. According to an SLG vice general secretary, SLG had 66 million yen (approximately $0.6 million) of aid money for the fiscal year 2001. About 35 million yen (approximately $0.3 million) went to personnel costs, and 31 million yen (approximately $0.3 million) went to supporting lifelong learning programs. Meanwhile, SLG received 142 million yen (approximately $1.3 million) as entrustment money.

I had a chance to exchange opinions about this government's logic with the vice general secretary and Mr. Iwata, a volunteer, over coffee. Both of them thought that the logic was wrong. The two kinds of money should not be blurred. They should clearly discern the difference between the funds. If they used the entrustment money to cover the decreased aid money, then what would happen? That was a key concern. The situation would be that there would not be enough money for the entrustment project itself. In that case, just imagine the situation.

Mr. Iwata:	I was actually thinking about what is expected of us by the government. That is, as one of the possibilities, we are required to do the entrustment business by decreasing our staff. There are six full-time staff members currently working for the center management. However, let's say, we try to do it with five people. That move is probably justified as a successful case of structural reform. Using the NPO, the government sector is supposed to be reinvigorated. What is going to happen at the grassroots level, though?
Vice General Secretary:	I think that we can't even hire five staff members. Actually I was told the other day by an accountant that SLG is behind the times since its staff is made up of all regular, full-time workers who are provided with health insurance. This is very rare nowadays. Listening to his opinion, I was thinking we are going to hire part-time staff people and then, finally, our volunteers will

fill the positions on an unpaid basis. In the
near future, our volunteers, instead of a
government official, will sit at the reception
desk of this public lifelong learning center.
That is not an exaggeration.

SLG volunteers were wondering if they saw any serious efforts by the
government in its severe financial situation. Their salaries were double
those of SLG secretariat staff members. The general secretary of SLG told
me one day that personal expenses would be halved when the municipal
government assigned all business related to lifelong learning—course
planning and implementation—to SLG. It seemed to me that for the
government, it would be a successful case of structural reform, because
the residents called volunteers were taking over jobs originally done by
paid government officials. The volunteers did the curriculum planning for
the lifelong learning program. Meanwhile, the SLG staff did the administrative work, but for half the salary of the government officials. As a
result, SLG has been praised, mostly by government officials, as a model
case of residents participating in community-oriented lifelong learning.
However, the reality was that the discrepancy between the perception
and understanding of what citizen participation in local politics should
look like was only becoming wider and wider.

Pushing Cost-Cutting Policy

Around October, discussions about the entrustment project accelerated,
paced by the government. This was because the government had to make
budget decisions for the next fiscal year. Around the same time, there was
a rumor among SLG secretariat staff that the entrustment project might
not happen. According to my investigation, which included informal
conversations with government officials, the government was calculating
the next year's budget. Regarding the total operation cost, for example,
if it entrusted all of the lifelong learning center business to SLG, then it
would cost more than this year's budget, because consumption tax had
to be added to the contract. They came to realize that the government
was not required to pay consumption tax on electricity, gas, and water,
for example, used at the public facilities. But SLG, an NPO—a third-
sector organization outside of the government—has to pay the tax. This
would undermine the original aim of cost cutting. The government was
reconsidering whether entrustment to an NPO was the most effective
measure under the structural-reform movement.

Table 5.1: Government's Calculations (numbers in millions of Japanese yen)

Item	Current	Plan A	Plan B	Plan C
Facility Management	**155.831**	**203.225**	**0.000**	**203.225**
Total Operation Cost	**164.756**	**172.051**	**396.463**	**172.051**
Audio visual library	22.082	16.511	16.511	16.511
Science course for kids	0.971	0.992	0.992	0.992
SLG entrustment fee	141.703	154.548	378.960	154.548
Total Human Resource				
Cost	**54.000**	**54.000**	**27.000**	**37.200**
Regular staff	54.000	54.000	27.000	27.000
Part-time staff				10.200
Education Consulting Fee	**32.205**	**34.853**	**34.853**	**34.853**
TOTAL COST	**406.792**	**464.129**	**458.316**	**447.329**
Difference from Plan A			−5.813	−16.800

A fifth meeting took place in mid-November. As the meeting began, the policy chief of lifelong learning announced what they had been doing over the past month.

> *Policy Chief*: Actually, we estimated the cost of running this lifelong learning center for the next year. We did it in three cases. The first one is Plan A. That is, the government would continue to operate this center; Plan B is that the government would entrust all businesses related to the center to SLG; Plan C entails the government operating the center, while some members of the staff of regular government officials are replaced by part-time staff. Given the calculations, we have realized that Plan C is the most effective in a cost-cutting sense, which means that Plan C is in line with the administrative and structural reform we are now pushing. Plan C is going to save more than 10 million yen (approximately $0.9 million) compared with Plan B. This is just a test calculation, and we have not made any formal decision about this issue. However, I just want to let you know that we are thinking that Plan C is the most realistic.

I was interested in the reaction from the SLG people. I saw that they were more or less relieved. The SLG vice general secretary looked at me and even smiled. I know that she was always discussing SLG's inability to start the entrustment project with the government. According to her, the entrustment would only burden the secretariat. There were no verbal responses to the policy chief's comment. There was silence on the discussion floor. Further talks on specific issues did not develop that day.

At the sixth meeting at the end of December, the government simply announced that there would be no entrustment on facility management of the lifelong learning center in the next year. They had decided to go with Plan C, replacing some of the current regular staff with part timers. The rationale was that this was the cheapest approach and would have no hidden costs, such as the consumption tax. The government finally decided that full entrustment was not the best measure to cut costs, although Plan C was still in line with a process of devolution in public administration. Thus it did not need to discuss the entrustment further. At this stage, SLG did not even have a chance to respond.

I observed the entire series of discussions on the entrustment. I believe that the less-dynamic atmosphere accelerated the failure of the entrustment talks. The government initiated the series of talks, and, throughout the process, was the primary leader for all discussions. SLG was underrepresented throughout the meetings. This further increased SLG's negative feeling toward both the government and its own inability as an NPO. The feeling of being marginalized was increased among SLG people. Furthermore, the meetings were always conducted in a very closed manner. SLG's ordinary volunteers never participated in the discussions with the government. They were never even fully informed. Their frustration drove them to be less interested in the discussions. The meetings were dominated by particular administrative procedures and techniques. People outside the government, myself included, sometimes did not understand the government officials' particular use of words or administrative language. The closed nature of the talks could be justified by the claim that ordinary volunteers would not be able to understand the procedures and language of public administration very well. My interpretation of what was happening in this case was that the government wanted to totally replace its regular staff at the lifelong learning center with unpaid volunteers. The vice head of the lifelong learning center (a government official) often said during the entrustment talks, "Work such as repairs could be done by volunteers." However, SLG rejected the government's intention. Members protected their meaning and value with respect to volunteering for the local community. In this sense, SLG might be said to have won.

Contested Rationalities: A Reality

Since the arguments of both SLG and the government were based on different rationales, the points of discussion never meshed. The government was pushing its argument on rationalizing public administration, demonstrating just the characteristics that Herbert Simon observes in the "administrative man" who recognizes the world as a drastically simplified model of the buzzing, blooming confusion that constitutes the real world (Simon 1997). For the fiscally constrained, conservative government, cost cutting was the highest priority and preference in its rationality. The government is an entrustor. It has money. It has laws that legitimize its actions. It has an administrative logic supported by the PPP policy.

On the other hand, SLG was looking for something different. Since it had its own sense of what the entrustment project should mean, it tried to insert its meaning into the project. Its actions went beyond the rational, purposive function of the work. It was looking for *mētis*, exactly as James Scott (1998, 311) defines it. Scott generates the notion of *mētis* while examining how authoritarian, high-modernist schemes are potentially very destructive. *Mētis*, which is practical knowledge and skills or know-how, was generated from the actual experiences that the NPO had. However, it was denied by the government's rationality, although SLG expected the government to have some understanding of local residents' activities. SLG volunteers thought that the government should have supported the SLG proposal, because their activities greatly contributed to the development of the community-oriented lifelong learning program, in place of the government. SLG and the government were supposed to be good partners to each other. As for the government, as Scott points out, however, its rationality was "not just strategies of production, but also strategies of control and appropriation" (311).

I observed this in rationality for actions throughout my extensive research. One night in December 2002, I went to an interesting symposium, advertised in a newspaper. It was held in Ginza, Tokyo's upscale shopping district, and the symposium was entitled "Moving from Public to Private—We Will Take Leadership for Social Change." The symposium was sponsored and organized by one of the first independent think tanks in Japan. The leader of the think tank explained:

> We are now facing an era in which we are going to offer
> by ourselves such services as social welfare and education,
> which have been provided by the government thus far. Now
> it is time that we take responsibility for our own social lives.

The role of the government is becoming smaller. On the other hand, citizens are becoming a major actor in society. We need to recognize that this is a key social and political trend.

Several NPO practitioners were invited to the meeting. What I saw was a big difference between NPO practitioners and NPO "theorists." Mr. Park is a Korean-Japanese man organizing an NPO in Shinjuku, one of the busiest districts of metropolitan Tokyo, for helping victims of domestic violence. He said:

> I am doing what I feel I need to do. I don't care whether I am doing it as an NPO or not. That doesn't matter. I can't trust the government or the police. Thus I do what I feel I need to do. I am now in my mid-forties. I don't have a wife or kids either. However, I want to leave some verification that I lived.

On the other hand, a bureaucrat, who actually played a significant role under Governor Kitagawa's administration in Mie Prefecture, introduced at the beginning of this chapter, voiced an interesting comment in opposition. He said:

> I was thinking of why various kinds of NPOs don't unite. If they unite for achieving something, they believe they can do something more powerfully. If only one NPO does something, its power is limited. However, if they get together and propose something in the policy-making arena, it would be influential. Why don't they do that more? The move would directly generate social change.

Mr. Park responded:

> I would never do that. I am not interested in it. Why should I get together with other organizations just because we are all labeled as NPOs? Each NPO has a different vision, right? It seems difficult to get together. . . . Before getting together, I want to do something by myself. It's easier. That's why I organized an NPO."

Mr. Machida, another environmental NPO practitioner, concurred.

> I also don't imagine getting together with other NPOs. Each NPO has its own mission. If we strongly felt that we needed

to get together, we would. However, we could get together if somebody (implying not the government) prepares and organizes such an NPO network for policy making. That move would be possible, but it is difficult for me to get involved in such NPO networking (intentionally generated by the government).

I observed this honest thought on policy collaboration between NPOs and the government.

Following this discussion, I became more interested in exploring what both volunteers and government officials thought about building collaborative relationships at my field site. What happened behind the scenes of the formal discussions? I had a chance to speak informally with a vice head of the lifelong learning center, who shared his perspective on the SLG entrustment talk:

I am really worried about SLG. SLG is still dependent on us. They never try to be independent of the municipal government. The government and NPOs are different entities. However, both of us continue to cling to each other, although two years have passed since SLG got NPO status. I thought that the entrustment talks would be a good time to encourage SLG to be independent of the government, but it did not happen.

Another reason the entrustment talks failed was that the government was very doubtful about accountability issues—specifically SLG's business management capabilities as a third-sector organization. It even wondered whether the SLG secretariat could do the office work generated by the entrustment project. One of my key research collaborators, a former SLG volunteer and current member of the board of education in the municipality, observed:

According to one of the government staff members at the center, the concern was amplified when the staff dispatched from the government left SLG at the end of March this year. As you know, the government dispatched them as part of its NPO support policy since its start. He said to me, SLG's ability to do administrative work has surely decreased. I am pretty sure the government staff contributed a lot to SLG.

This interpretation left me with a sense that the government may actually have chosen to distance itself tactically from the entrustment talks with SLG. The government, well informed about the delicate organizational aspects of SLG, may have felt that SLG was too fragile to make the entrustment contract with the government.

On the other side of this story was how NPO people saw the government. An SLG secretariat staff member provided one interesting story. Apparently, for the past year, a dispatched staff member from the municipal government had been giving him a hard time.

> *Staff:* The man wouldn't tell me about the course-making procedures unless I asked. I was never actually trained on my duties by my predecessor. I think he wouldn't be happy if I became successful, since lifelong learning was originally offered by the municipal government and is now being handled by an NPO. The man's job had been snatched by other people.

This story reminded me of an incident wherein the Japanese foreign ministry had rejected a particular NGO's participation in the International Conference on Reconstruction Assistance to Afghanistan in January 2002. Peace Winds Japan, a humanitarian-aid NGO in Afghanistan, was excluded from the conference because a senior lawmaker who had strong influence on foreign affairs was angered by comments made by one of the NGO members in the Japanese daily, *Asahi Shimbun,* on January 18, 2002. What the Peace Winds Japan member said in the interview with an *Asahi* reporter was, "I don't have total faith in the abilities of the government. I don't trust any of them that much." Following this article, the foreign ministry, which was under pressure from the senior lawmaker, said that it was not appropriate for an NGO that had made such comments about the government to participate in a conference organized by the Japanese government. The tone of the media in Tokyo was that the lawmakers were unhappy with NGOs because they were so successful, in contrast to the foreign ministry or the government, which then turned around and put pressure on the NGOs. NGOs were infringing upon several kinds of vested interests of the foreign ministry. The story of the foreign ministry and NGOs sounded familiar to me.

During my time at SLG, I was indeed able to observe a number of incidents of pointless government intervention. Such incidents clearly amounted to the harassment by government officials of SLG people. One instance occurred during an afternoon team meeting discussion on course planning. There were nearly ten housewife volunteers there. They were discussing how to operate a couple of courses that would start in January. A vice general secretary in charge of course planning, a dispatched official, and I attended the meeting from the secretariat. I was struck by the dispatched official's way of talking during the meeting. He often used phrases in speaking to the volunteers such as "do this as soon as possible" and "discuss it and decide promptly." I had never heard anybody use such authoritative language during any meetings held at SLG. The following exchange illustrates this even more clearly:

Vice General
Secretary: In the near future, I would like to propose to discuss the cooling-off period for courses we provide to the residents as other businesses currently do.

Dispatched Man: Don't say such a dream-like thing. We can't do that. Such a thing is never going to be realized. You should be more conscious of your responsibilities as a paid staff member and vice general secretary of the SLG secretariat.

His aggressive attitude left an impression on me. After the meeting, two of the housewife volunteers told me that they had felt very uncomfortable when they saw the dispatched government official yelling at an NPO staff member. This kind of thing happened often, however. This incident aptly speaks to the frailty of the relationship between the NPO and the government.

Kyōdō: A Failed Attempt

In many countries, the role of voluntary third-sector organizations has gained increasing attention in the context of opening up the meaning of democracy. Western intellectual groups, especially communitarian and social capital theorists, rooted in Alexis de Tocqueville's work, have highlighted the function of the third sector in the development of social capital and the formation of civic trust and norms as the basis of effective governance. In *Democracy in America*, Tocqueville (1980) argues that voluntary associations are necessary for providing successful alternatives to problems having to do with the common good and for curbing unbridled governmental power. The growth and development of voluntary associations provide safeguards for checking political despotism, reinforcing the habits of the heart that are essential to stable and effective democratic institutions. Such associations become informal webs of solidarity that unite societies and provide communities with the most basic of social safety nets.

These days, scholars have further promoted the idea of associative democracy to supplement or even supplant representative democracy (e.g., Hirst 1989, 1994, 1997; Cohen and Rogers 1992; Fishkin 1993; Elster 1998; Dryzek 2000; Newman 2001; Gastil and Levine 2005; Ryfe 2005; Urbinati 2006). This idea of associative democracy has been developed around the idea of renovating democracy by extending the scope of associations and remodeling the relation between the state and civil society. The concept emphasizes self-governing voluntary associations as the building blocks of participatory democracy. Advocates of associative democracy assume that this type of democracy will reduce the complexity of the modern state, while drawing citizens close to public life and fostering their civil engagement. Paul Hirst (1994, 19) defines associative democracy as follows:

> Associative democracy is deceptively simple in its most basic political claims. . . . Associationalism makes a central normative claim, that individual liberty and human welfare are both best served when as many of the affairs of society as possible are managed by voluntary and democratically self-governing associations. Associationalism seeks to square the aims of freedom for the individual in pursuing his or her chosen goals with the effective governance of social affairs.

Hirst's conception of associative democracy is in line with the ideological ground of Anthony Giddens' *Third Way* (Giddens 1998), which argues in favor of balancing the energy of capitalism with the need to foster social solidarity and civic values. *Third Way* suggests that it is possible to combine social solidarity with a dynamic economy, and that this is a goal that contemporary social democrats should strive to achieve. Conventional institutions of representative democracy now find it harder to regulate social life and to scrutinize public services. Our activities have become complex, our practices differentiated and flexible, and change both rapid and multidirectional. The result is a complex society that is impossible to control democratically without the decentralization of accountability. Thus associative democracy advocates collective decision making with all stakeholders who will be affected by a decision thorough arguing, bargaining, and voting. To achieve collective decisions, voluntary associations, business corporations, and governments should all come together. Among them, voluntary associations can best provide key sites and processes for effective governance and welfare provision that will foster active citizenship, extend democracy, and even strengthen civil society. It involves shifting control of and responsibility for social development from the administrative institutions of the centralized state to self-governing voluntary associations. In fact, the role of voluntary organizations in promoting democracy has gained increasing attention worldwide, as many countries are experiencing an apparent loss of faith in the formal democratic process, accompanied by decreasing political party membership and voting levels. Under these circumstances, voluntary associations have the potential to become principal organizing forces in society, the key institutions providing public good.

My detailed ethnographic investigation of the aforementioned Japanese case, meanwhile, reveals a number of tensions between the NPO and the government. Because the power of the government is too strong, and because the accountability of the NPO is (still) too weak, the introduction of the third-sector organization into real politics has left many ordinary people confused. The government is now rushing to cut costs under the name of structural reform. Budget cuts target, for example, lifelong learning program planning, where I did fieldwork, nursing and caring for the elderly, museum operations, library operations, and so on. These services are now commonly covered by volunteer-based NPOs under the name of entrustment. The government is outsourcing them more and more. The reality is that NPOs are becoming subcontractors to the government. In fact, of the collaborative cases in Mie Prefecture that I mentioned at the very beginning of this chapter, nearly 80 percent were proposed by the government. Even though Mie Prefecture often has been cited as a successful model in pursuing the collaboration between NPOs and the government in Japanese society, NPOs were mostly receivers of government plans. Throughout my fieldwork on Japanese NPOs, I have wondered what the government is and what local autonomy is. Thinking about the role of Japanese NPOs and the third sector means rethinking what the government should be. NPOs are not "new partnership organizations" primarily intended to form collaborative relationships with the government, although they have the same acronym. Ideally, NPOs will change the rigid characteristics of Japanese politics and even beat the dominant bureaucracy. Only in this context can policy collaboration create a new wave of social resources beyond the conventional sector, human beings, information, and money.

Chapter 6

Shimin in Japanese Society

Shimin—A Genealogy

In this chapter I explore the meaning of civil society, or *shimin shakai,* in contemporary Japan, tracing the history of the grassroots constituents of civil society, known as *shimin* (citizens), in the post-World War II period. Taking a glance at postwar Japanese history, there were people called *shimin* in the citizens' movements (*shimin undō*) in the 1950s and 1960s, for example. They were contentious political activists against the existing authority. You could see them protesting the renewal of the U.S.-Japan Security Treaty, popularly known as *Anpo*, when thousands of Japanese *shimin* marched to the National Diet Hall in 1960. In the late 1990s, meanwhile, *shimin* were seen participating in the NPO phenomenon. The *shimin* could be described as normative subjects having internalized coercive, self-disciplined volunteer subjectivity; they are collaborative partners with the government to jointly produce public good, as I documented in the previous chapters. The subject of *shimin* indeed has been covering those from free spirits to duty-driven people. In fact, the usage of these terms does not reflect any neutral objectivity, and the image conjured up by the term *shimin* has changed through time.

Here I develop an argument that *shimin* are a cultural product reflecting social values in Japanese society on each occasion, comparing and contrasting subjects represented by *shimin* in various historical contexts. In particular, I focus on the coercive *shimin* under the NPO framework; I argue that such *shimin* did not suddenly appear in Japanese society. The subjects should be argued in historical continuity, not in isolated contexts. Linking my ethnographic data to interdisciplinary literature in intellectual history, political science, sociology, and economics in the Japanese studies scholarship, I argue that the contemporary *shimin* internalized volunteer subjectivity under the NPO framework could be originally traced to self-disciplined subjectivity supporting World

War II as total war. It was a standardized subjectivity for all Japanese people contributing to executing war or the state through spontaneous individual actions. My argument in this chapter is based on the more recent reinterpretation made by Nakano Toshio (2001), that Ōtsuka Hisao and Maruyama Masao, two eminent social scientists in Japanese academia, gave rationales through their scholarly works for producing such subjectivity as an effort to rationalize total war mobilization. In the postwar era of the 1950s and 1960s, meanwhile, Japanese society saw the emergence of free, contentious, spontaneous *shimin* in new social movements, popularly called citizens' movements. However, those *shimin* were directed to be normative citizenry by the modernists (*kindai shugi sha*), whose logic was still constrained by such wartime psychology.

Guiding the social movements, the modernist intellectuals aimed, as a foundation of postwar democracy, to internalize the self-disciplined subjectivity—the same subjectivity they advocated during the war—into the contentious *shimin*. They tried to locate such *shimin* within the existing social and political system; their key efforts were toward constructing a more democratic Japanese society through unifying Japanese people as a nation in a modern state. In the following decades, primarily led by Matsushita Keiichi, a student of Maruyama, the normative citizenry was further strengthened; *shimin* in local residents' movements (*jūmin undō*) were expected to become active participants in dialogues with administrative entities and business enterprises. In fact, Matsushita played a significant role in providing a prototype of *shimin*, which led the way to the self-disciplined *shimin* with volunteer subjectivity under the NPO phenomenon. Currently, *shimin* are coerced subjects; they are supposed to be actively involved in promoting public good in a very organized way—the NPO. Furthermore, I locate such Japanese *shimin* as a key actor in neoliberalism—a global phenomenon. The conservative market-oriented ideology seeks the small government, sponsoring the devolution process of social services to civil society. Japanese NPOs are a key form of agency in this politico-economic strategy, and the incorporation of NPOs is part of a calculated, strategic reorganization after the Keynesian welfare state since the 1980s. The contemporary *shimin* play a significant role in the political development. In order to achieve the neoliberal course of action, nowadays the Japanese state is making *shimin* an ideal subject of the state to primarily serve its needs. In fact, *shimin*—a standardized subjectivity like soldiers—have been systematically produced and reproduced by the state-supervised education. *Shimin* are featured as an ideal national subjectivity in contemporary conservative Japan.

Shimin in the Early Postwar Era

Historically, *shimin* were located as a scholarly term in the Japanese academic discourse, which was heavily influenced by Marxism, a fundamental touchstone for Japanese intellectuals. In an influential passage in "On the Jewish Question," Marx wrote, "[T]he so-called *rights of man*, as distinct from the *rights of the citizen*, are simply the rights of a *member of civil society*, that is, of egoistic man, of man separated from other men and from the community" (Marx [1843] 1978b, 42, emphasis in original). Marx continued: "*Practical need, egoism*, is the principle of *civil society*, and is revealed as such in its pure form as soon as civil society has fully engendered the political state. The god of *practical need and self-interest* is *money*" (50, emphasis in original). The egoistic members of society described in the aforementioned passage were recognized as *shimin* by Japanese scholars. Marx further argued in "The German Ideology" that civil society was a society in which the "propertyless" mass of the population was coercively held in subjugation by the owners, or the bourgeois capitalists, of the instruments of production. The relationships of production, and the division of society into the "propertied" classes and the "propertyless" classes, were the defining features of civil society (Marx [1845] 1978a, 155–63; see also Shils 1991, 6). Even today, the term *shimin* still has a negative connotation in Japanese, especially to those whose works are within the Hegelian-Marxist framework. From a Marxist viewpoint, *shimin* were capitalists, members of an exploiting class who pursued their own self-interest without thinking of the public welfare. As political scientist Shinohara Hajime (2004, 93) points out, even though the term *shimin* is recently gaining currency among politicians and journalists, some scholars still hesitate to use the expression. Political scientist Takabatake Michitoshi (2004, 33) further states that for scholars influenced by Marxism, it was difficult to accept the term *shimin shakai* (or civil society), since it overlapped with bourgeois society. The *Kōza-ha*, the Marxism of Lecturers Faction, whose influence over Japanese social science extended into the postwar era, maintained that Japan had no citizens, no autonomous individuals, and thus no civil society—or only the barest beginnings of each—but it had developed a species of capitalism.[1]

Meanwhile, Maruyama Masao, a postwar renowned scholar who was influenced by Max Weber, did not often invest the term *shimin* with positive connotations. In particular, it seems that Maruyama intentionally did not use *shimin* because he thought there was no space in Japanese society for a European-specific civil society to exist, due to the particularities of the Japanese context (Ishida 1997, 11–16; Barshay 2004, 179). Translating the French term *citoyen*, which emerged during the French Revolution, Maruyama used *kōmin* (directly translated as public person) rather than *shimin*, describing the "modern *kōmin* as key leaders of political responsibility" (Maruyama [1951] 1964a, 301).

Oguma Eiji (2002, 242–51) provides detailed accounts of the popular usage of the term *shimin* in the very early postwar period. The term was mostly employed as an administrative term, as in the phrase *Kyoto shimin*, or residents of the city of Kyoto. It was very rare to use the term as a general noun. At the time, the majority of the Japanese population lived in rural or farming areas. Even those who lived in urban settings would never be categorized as *shimin*. Citing Maruyama's writing in 1947 on the Japanese middle class (Maruyama [1947] 1964b, 63–64), Oguma (2002, 243–44) explains that there were two kinds of people in cities in the years following the war. On the one hand, there were owners of small- and medium-size factories, construction workers, mom-and-pop shop owners, carpenters, small landlords, and peasants. On the other hand, there were *salaryman*, journalists, professors, and lawyers. The majority of the members of the urban middle class were in the former group. It was not customary to apply the term *shimin* to carpenters or construction workers. Oguma argues that such explicit social stratification made it difficult to popularize the term *shimin* among the general public. In other words, it is only a scholar's word in the Marxist literature.

I believe that *shimin* first came to have a different tone in the 1950s, when the negative image the term had assumed in dominant Marxist thought was progressively wiped out. During the 1950s, the Liberal Democratic Party (LDP) started the so-called 1955 system, which continued for thirty-eight years, from 1955 through 1993, in Japanese politics. It is a reference to the conservative, one-party-dominated political system based on political tensions stemming from cold war world politics. The feature was illustrated as ideological battles between the conservative forces rallying around the LDP, which had close ties to the United States, and supporters of the left-wing agenda, led by the Japan Socialist Party (JSP). Gerald Curtis (1988, 17–18) points out, "But much of this tension was created by opposition to the LDP's avowed objective of overturning the constitutional order established during the American Occupation. As it turned out, it was the dynamic tension created by the standoff between an 'antisystem' JSP which made up for its weakness in numbers by the intensity of its opposition and by the support it received from mass movements loosely affiliated with it, and an LDP that was in its own way also an antisystem party, that kept that the postwar system on center, so to speak."

It was a crucial moment when Japan experienced citizens' movements, or *shimin undō*.[2] Japanese people could be seen starting to speak freely in public, originally triggered by the emergence of ban the atomic bomb activities in the wake of the Lucky Dragon incident of 1954. It was an incident where the Japanese tuna fishing boat, Lucky Dragon 5 (*Daigo Fukuryū Maru*), was exposed to nuclear fallout by a U.S. hydrogen bomb test on Bikini Atoll in the South Pacific, and one of the crew members died, suffering from acute radiation syndrome. By 1955, John Dower (1993, 19) writes, the Japanese peace movement had come to focus especially keenly on the global abolition of nuclear weapons, supported by a spectacular grassroots petition drive against nuclear testing that collected an astonishing 20 million signatures. In 1956, there were strong grassroots protests against the teacher rating system announced by the government. The citizens' movement was then sparked when Prime Minister Kishi Nobusuke (1957–1960) tried to revise the Police Duties Bill in 1958 to expand police prerogatives to search in anticipation of a crime, as part of efforts to renew the U.S.-Japan Security Treaty (*Anpo*) in 1960. There was nationwide opposition to the revision of the bill, since the political move was intended to broaden police powers; it was intensively opposed, and ultimately blocked, by progressive political forces. The subsequent event was the 1960 struggle against the renewal of *Anpo*, a milestone in postwar Japanese politics. *Shimin* were popularized through the *Anpo* demonstrations of the 1960s, a series of massive protests against the Japanese government's renewal of the treaty and its forcible ratification by the Kishi administration. Amidst growing public furor, Kishi stepped down.

Millions of *shimin* took to the streets for months in protest. Witnessing the ordinary people's commitment to ongoing *Anpo* politics, Kuno Osamu, philosopher and political activist, was one of the first persons to use the term *shimin* in a positive manner. Kuno heralded the rise of citizens' movements capable of mobilizing people whose consciousness was based not on particular, communal interests but rather on their public, occupational lives and ethics, because they cut across organizational loyalties and demanded universal adherence to procedural rules (Kuno 1960; see also Koschmann 1981, 627–28, 1993, 407). Kuno advocated the masses to generate their political subjectivity through their own occupations:

Shimin are based on a strong consciousness as occupational ethics. (Kuno 1960, 10)

Our occupations should be fundamentally separate from national and political authority. How much can we deepen

Picture 6.1 Thousands of Japanese people on their way to the National Diet Hall in Tokyo protesting the renewal of *Anpo*, May 1960 (Reproduced with permission from Mainichi Shimbun)

> awareness that each individual can freely express his opinion for or against the government? How much can we reject any controls and interventions by the state? How much can we build common judgments and senses of values based on occupations beyond national borders, which people in the same occupation would share? (13)

Meanwhile, Wesley Sasaki-Uemura's (2001) vivid description of the *Anpo* demonstration of 1960 illustrates that the *Anpo* movement was composed of diverse groups of politically conscious actors attempting to reshape the public body. *Shimin* indeed attracted many different kinds of people and was used to mobilize people for social movements in Japan. Oda Makoto, a writer and social activist who led *Beheiren* (*Betonamu ni heiwa wo! shimin rengō*, or Peace for Vietnam! Citizens' Committee) in the anti-Vietnam War movement of the 1960s, realized the diversity of the term *shimin* (Oda [1965] 1974, 11–12). Interestingly enough, he described as *shimin* various kinds of people who were uniting for anti-Vietnam War demonstrations, including *salaryman*, housewives, teachers, young people, and the unemployed. The following passage—an excerpt from a pamphlet of a citizens' movement called *Koe Naki Koe no Kai*, or the Voiceless Voices—shows how the term was used during this period.

> Hello. All of you *Shimin*, let's all walk together.
> Even if it is only five minutes or just a hundred meters,
> let's walk together.
> We won't stick to any particular political thoughts
> nor will we loudly stake claims.
> But even the "voiceless voices" can distinguish between what's
>   right and wrong,
> and we really want to protest politics.
> So let's walk together and quietly show our opposition to
>   politics. (*Koe Naki Koe no Kai* 1962, 30–31)

Shimin were realized as independent individuals participating in spontaneous activities. They existed outside of the social class, rejecting any kind of exclusion and respecting diversity. They were very heterogeneous.

Picture 6.2 Rally by *Beheiren* (Peace for Vietnam! Citizens' Committee); demonstrations to protest the Vietnam War were conducted every first Saturday, Tokyo, December 1967 (Reproduced with permission from Mainichi Shimbun)

While creating loose, decentralized networks, *shimin* were representing their own senses of values. Participating in the movements was realized as part of their lives; it reflects their meanings of life. Such a spontaneous, contentious, diversified body against the existing authority became a new key actor called *shimin* in Japanese social and political life.

Observing these social dynamics at that moment, Hirata Kiyoaki, a Marxist economic historian, gave a Habermasian interpretation to *shimin* (Hirata 1969; see also Keane 1998, 12–14; Barshay 2004, 189–91). While rereading Marxist literature, Hirata provided a new image of *shimin*. In particular, he refocused on commerce, or *kōtsū*—a key concept in Marxist literature—"a process in which various sorts of people publicly negotiate each other" (Hirata 1969, 78). He relocated the concept of civil society as a public sphere, focusing on dynamic communication among people. For this new interpretation, Andrew Barshay explains Hirata's difficult text *Shimin shakai to shakai shugi* (Civil Society and Socialism; Hirata 1969). Barshay (2004, 190) introduces one of Hirata's key arguments as follows: The "basic categories" of *Capital* . . . have been "lost." Property, commerce (*Verkehr*; *kōtsū*), and civil society have all fallen victim to the pernicious influence of " 'Marxist-Leninist' cant." Yet, in fact, they constitute a system that must be restored as such. Property has its origins in productive labor (the making of things) and in the acquisition by others of that product. The "intercourse" of ordinary people in civil society as they exchange what they make actualizes both "property as production" and "property as property," introducing the dialectical moment in which the fateful alienation of work from property occurs and is perpetually reproduced. Based on this interpretation, Hirata (1969, 79) argues, "Civil society is, above all, the place where this kind of mutual exchange is taking place by human beings as *shimin*; '*shimin*' could refer to ordinary, concrete human beings in their daily economic lives; they are the real foundation of the free and equal subjects of law." He maintains, "Civil society is a society where concrete human beings independently exchange their products, in other words, their will, with each other" (86).

These movements, as well as the *shimin* subjects, were in line with the new social movements scholarship developed by Alain Touraine (1971), Ernesto Laclau and Chantal Mouffe (1985), and Alberto Melucci (1989), addressing cultural issues as being central to the motivating logic of society. In particular, Melucci's definition of new social movements is relevant, since it focuses increasingly on issues of groups or collective identities, values, culture, lifestyles, and networks. Also, it has a tendency to emerge more from middle- rather than working-class constituencies, major players in the "old" social movements (Melucci 1989; see Edelman 2001; Hourigan 2003; Todd and Taylor 2004; Nash 2005 for the recent development on new social movement theory). As Malcolm Todd and Gary Taylor (2004, 19) plainly argue, the so-called "new" movements tend to be defined by their focus on postmaterial values, their detachment from an identifiable political ideology, and their use of novel and unconventional methods of political action. This is combined with a rejection of hierarchical and bureaucratic organization. It is the march, public demonstration, petition, and the act of civil disobedience in order to exercise their power. Indeed, in the new social movement theory, emphasis usually has been placed on the creation of loose, heterogeneous, decentralized structures (Rucht 1984, cited by Hourigan 2003, 23). In fact, June Nash (2005) argues, new social movements theories opened the stage of history to many new actors by drawing attention to the ethnic, gender, and racial composition of movements that were suppressed by those that gave priority to class position. Nash continues, "The new leaders embodied the muted demands of diverse groups as women, ethnic, and religious groups contested repressive conditions. In the course of their struggles, they expanded the cultural potential for symbolizing their objectives and embodying their concerns" (10, referring Escobar and Alvarez 1992; Alvareze et al. 1998).

Bringing in the Japanese historical, political, and economic contexts to this global social movement scholarship, Kurihara Akira (1999) portrays the dynamism of Japanese social movements. He (8-9) points out that the "old" paradigms for social movements seen until the early 1950s were primarily classified as labor movements (*rōdō undō*) led by political parties, left-wing leaders, and union officials. The identity of the main actor was the worker; the dominant actors were institutionalized interest groups and political parties. The worldview of the movements was broadly based on a class society, and its discourse focused on demands. Kurihara further argues that the old social movement paradigm supported Japan's miraculous economic development in the early postwar period; organized labor worked as a mechanism for distribution and Japanese social stability supplemented capitalism as a growth mechanism. He then illuminates the emergence of "new" social movements in Japanese society:

> [The period of the so-called "1955 system"] gave priority to economic values, avidly pursued so-called development and economic growth according to the principle of productivity-first, and spared no effort to realize the "affluent society" and make Japan a great power economically. This was also the era in which the contradictions and distortions that were caused by those policies erupted in all corners of the society.

> The new social movements appeared when it became clear
> that neither representative politics nor the administration nor
> pressure groups nor the existing social movements could begin
> to resolve those contradictions and distortions. (10)

Shimin played a key role in the emerging social movements. Enjoying
the economic development, they were developing new ways of social
and political life in Japanese society—freely cultivating wide ranges of
identities and building horizontal networks. Compared to the old social
movements, Kurihara (10–11) mentions, the movements measure themselves according to such standards as way of life, identify, self-renewal,
self-determination, symbiosis, and links among different forms of life;
they also are turning in the direction of multifaceted human activity, new
forms of commonality, conviviality, self-government, and self-discipline;
the worldview of the movement amounted to critical acceptance of the
existing system, and the main theme is the public sphere or civil society.
The citizens' movements stemming from the renewal of *Anpo* primarily
influenced the organizational structures and political philosophies of peace
movements (*heiwa undō*), or antiwar movements (*hansen undō*) such as
the anti-Vietnam War efforts, and left-wing students' movements (*gakusei
undō*) in the 1960s and thereafter.[3] Dower (1993, 22) points out that it is
estimated that more than 18 million Japanese took to the streets to protest
the Vietnam War and demand the reversion of Okinawa to Japan. He
continues, "As elsewhere, 'people's power' entered the Japanese lexicon
at this time as a legitimate and essential alternative to bourgeois parlia-
mentary politics; and, as elsewhere, the theory and practice of 'people's
power' ranged from peaceful protest to wanton violence.... [I]t left as
legacies the memory and experience of grass-roots mobilization that could
be evoked in more particularistic causes thereafter" (22).
    As I am finishing this book in early 2007, I observe a social
dynamics—the emergence of the Article 9 Association (*9-jō no Kai*) in
contemporary Japanese society. It is a nationwide network of groups
seeking to defend Article 9 (defining war renunciation and pacifism)
in the Japanese constitution under the ongoing nationalistic politics led
by hawkish Prime Minister Abe Shinzo (Abe's political stance on the
constitutional revision is discussed later in this chapter). The association
was established by nine writers and activists in June 2004, including Oe
Kenzaburo, a Nobel Prize Laureate in Literature, and Oda Makoto. In that
movement, I see an action style—network-based consensus formation,
a strategy used in the new social movements like *beheiren* of the early
postwar period. According to a newsletter of the association (June 13,
2006, issue), 5,174 groups were officially registered across the country.

I will be carefully observing the development of the movement in the upcoming years to see how to locate this associational group within the framework of new social movements' history in Japan (see Junkerman et al. 2004 for further details).

Shimin under the NPO

While pursuing the genealogy of the term *shimin* in early postwar Japan, I often wondered if the connotation of dynamism in the meaning of *shimin* given by Sasaki-Uemura and Oda still held true in people called *shimin* under the emerging NPO sector. At my field site, during a twice-a-month meeting of SLG's volunteer recruiting division that I attended, we discussed a new volunteer recruiting system. SLG often received calls from people responding to the organization's Internet advertisement seeking volunteers. The agenda of the meeting that day focused on the following question: How should SLG respond to such requests for volunteer opportunities? It was discussing specific details about how to welcome newcomers in a series of introductory sessions. As a key principle, it emphasized that cooperation with other volunteers was the highest priority in volunteering. In this context of welcoming newcomers, what does cooperation entail? I sensed that cooperation, in essence, meant "not giving other volunteers trouble." SLG needed people, Ms. Katō, an assistant leader of the division, seemed to be saying, who could follow the rules of the organization without complaining. Volunteers were just expected to come at their appointed times and to devote their time and energy to productive work.

This discussion made me recall a newspaper article that I had read that morning.[4] The article dealt with the recent boom of company mergers in Japan. According to this piece, after such mergers, disparate types of people were forced to work together. Due to the mixture of different corporate cultures, miscommunication frequently occurred. The article went on to say that when people face such situations, they have a good excuse that helps reduce their frustration. They can rationalize, "Now that there are 'various kinds of people' (*tasai na hito tachi*) in our company, it is difficult to communicate with each other very well. It cannot be helped. It is the reality." I believe that the phrase "various kinds of people" originally had a positive nuance in Japanese. Having "various kinds of people" in a company should represent an asset, as the term suggests rich, valuable human resources. In this newspaper article's context, however, the phrase "various kinds of people" sounded quite negative. Various kinds of people colored by different corporate cultures were presented as obstacles to effective management.

I began to wonder whether diversity among SLG volunteers was valued. At my field site, there were more than 100 registered volunteers. The core group, as I noted in chapter 4, consisted of people invited by the government. These people were leaders who contributed to local associational groups, such as neighborhood associations, PTAs, and local amateur sports associations. The rest of the volunteers could be described (using conventional terms of social classification based on occupation) as retirees, housewives, businesspersons, and *salaryman*, as I introduced in the previous chapters. These were, in short, very ordinary members of the Japanese middle class. In Japanese popular terminology, their "ordinariness" is probably described as *futsū*. In fact, I realized the term *futsū* was valued in the process of recruiting new volunteers at SLG. They often told me that they were looking for ordinary people, or *futsū no hito,* as new volunteers.

Again, Oda Makoto also used the term *futsū* when he described the people who participated in the anti-Vietnam War movement. As noted earlier, participants in the movement included *salaryman*, housewives, teachers, young people, and the unemployed. Oda ([1965] 1974, 11) called these people *futsū no shimin,* or "ordinary citizens." In this usage, however, he implied "various kinds of people," as I argued previously, calling them "ordinary citizens." "When he was told, 'I am an ordinary company worker,' Oda responded by saying, 'I am an ordinary writer' " (11). Oda's usage suggests that ordinariness is something that transcends existing social classes and occupations, rejects any kind of exclusion, and respects diversity. Meanwhile, what I noticed in my fieldwork was that SLG volunteers were very much alike. In a sense, they were very homogenous. Although the NPO was located in a blue-collar district of eastern Tokyo, most of the participants were wealthier, college-educated, white-collar workers in the local community. Members of other nationalities, such as Japanese-Koreans and migrant workers from China, the Philippines, and other Asian countries, were not represented, even though these groups were significantly present in the community. The Korean community seems especially big, since there is a Korean elementary and junior high school. Members of the former outcast *burakumin* were not present either, although there was a large district previously called a *buraku* (an outcast community) in Kawazoe. There were no registered volunteers from that community at SLG and no serious efforts to include such people. I even felt that those are "untouchable issues" at SLG.

The homogeneity represented as *futsū* among SLG volunteers was actually reinforced through the recruitment process. Recruiters were looking for persons much like the current volunteers—people who were willing to follow the rules of the organization without complaint—as such, individuals would make it easier to reach consensus on the norms that guide appropriate behaviors within the organization. Further, such volunteers make for a relatively conflict-free environment. From time to time, I observed serious complaints among the volunteers about how to exclude several annoying members of the group, as this was indeed the easier way to achieve consensus in a discussion. In fact, I myself became a target of "exclusion" at one time when I said something against SLG's policy (I explain reflectively the experience in chapter 7). When they often used the term *futsū*, the word suggested a subconscious attempt to exclude otherness. In order to protect their comfort in the small, insular community at SLG, the volunteers tried to reject otherness. Due to a lack of social and political imagination to negotiate diverse views and interests, it seemed that they did not even appreciate otherness.[5] I even wonder whether this kind of voluntary NPO can enhance such values in Japanese society. Belonging to voluntary organizations does not always strengthen the foundation for good citizenship. I believe in a democratic society where freedom of association is important, and the willingness to grant basic civil liberties to people whose views are different is extremely essential.

As I further contemplated the term *futsū*, I had a chance to read a book entitled *Iyashi no nashonarizumu* (roughly translated as *Nationalism as Healing*, Ueno 2003), an ethnography of a group of grassroots conservatives in the late 1990s that supported a neonationalistic history textbook. The textbook was written by nationalistic academics from the Japanese Society for History Textbook Reform (*Atarashii rekishi kyōkasho wo tsukuru kai*), attempting to revise the history texts used in the nation's junior high schools.[6] They advocated an alternative view of history and argued that the root cause of Japan's deadlocked economy and society in the 1990s lay in a masochistic overemphasis on the negative aspects of Japanese history. In fact, according to them, Japanese people had lost confidence due to this historical view. They called for a new type of history education that would help build the identity of the Japanese people. In order to awaken a sense of national pride among Japanese students, the scholars promoted a view of early twentieth-century Japan that refused to acknowledge Japan's invasion and colonization of other Asian countries and that exonerated Japan for its responsibility in World War II. Furthermore, they believed that the acceptance of individualism and the development of democracy—the guiding principles of reform after World War II—neglected the concept of public responsibility, which must counterbalance the recognition of private rights. Thus the deadlock in contemporary Japan can be viewed as the culmination of sixty years of postwar Japanese history.

Ueno Yōko, the author of this ethnography, conducted fieldwork in a grassroots conservative group in Kanagawa Prefecture that supported the neonationalist textbook. In Japan, all textbooks used in public and private schools must be submitted to the Education Ministry for approval. Ueno's ethnography describes how this group of grassroots conservatives supported the history textbook in an attempt to reverse the masochistic view of Japanese history (in particular, Japanese World War II history) and how they justified the textbook's nationalistic discourse. While reading this ethnography, I was especially interested in the following questions: Exactly who supported the textbook? Who were the grassroots conservatives? In the ethnography, Ueno identifies the shared characteristics she observed among the group members. The supporters of the textbook were people who might be labeled "white-collar" workers. They seem quite removed from activists in the social movements of the early postwar era. They emphasized respect for individualism, and they valued their professions and families more than the activities of advocacy groups. Furthermore, they hesitated to take extreme positions. They never even called themselves "right wingers" or "nationalists." When the people in her field site described themselves, they called themselves ordinary citizens—*futsū no shimin*—although they sometimes had difficulties finding the correct words to express themselves accurately.

Throughout the fieldwork, the members of the group often asked Ueno, "Do you think this is a gathering organized by people who are peculiar?" (Ueno 2003, 88). In contexts such as this, the term *futsū* is used to guarantee membership in the majority in Japanese society. In Ueno's ethnography, the movement's supporters are extremely afraid of being excluded from the majority and sense that society may cast a suspicious eye on their activities. Furthermore, Ueno points out that one of the favorite expressions among the group members was "silent majority," or *sairento majoritī* in Japanese (145). In fact, members *were* silent. They avoided conflict. They were passive in a sense, since they attempted never to complain in public. Within the inner circle they created, they had become good spectators in their support of the nationalistic textbook.

In my view, the people supporting the nationalistic textbook movement and the people supporting NPO activities at my field site look very much alike. Both prefer to have people label them as ordinary—*futsū*. They were homogenous—white-collar, educated people. They never tried to instigate conflicts among themselves. They were silent. Indeed, people in the history textbook movements were ideologically right. Meanwhile, the SLG volunteers were far removed from the progressive activism that characterized the new social movements of the 1960s and thereafter. Nevertheless, it did not appear that people at my field site supported the extreme right wing. I believe that they were neither on the Left nor on the Right. Instead, they held the center. If anything, they might have been conservatives who supported the policies implemented by the LDP, the ruling party during most of the postwar era. They probably represented the middle-class people who had been called the "silent majority" throughout postwar Japanese history.

Today's *shimin* under the NPO structure are actually avoiding politics. NPO activities are realized in a very moderate tone, encouraging participation in collaborations, or *kyōdō*, with the government, as I argued in chapter 5. In fact, more precisely, *shimin* are compelled to avoid politics in the NPO setting, as the NPO Law prohibits any political involvement by these organizations. The law explicitly defines NPOs as organizational entities that are not involved in any political activities.

Article 2 (Definition)[7]

"Specified nonprofit activities" under this law shall mean those activities specified in the attached schedule, which are *for the purpose of contributing to advancement of the interests of many and unspecified persons.*

"Specified nonprofit corporation" under this law shall mean an organization that has as its main purpose the implementation of specified nonprofit activities, that conforms with each of the following items, and that is a corporation established under the provisions of this law:

i. An organization that is covered by both of the following items and is not for the purpose of generating profits:

   a. Provisions regarding acquisition and loss of qualifications for membership are not unreasonable;

   b. The number of officers receiving remuneration total no more than one third of the total number of officers;

ii. An organization whose activities conform with each of the following items:

a. The activities are not for the purpose of propagating religious teachings, performing ceremonies, or educating or fostering believers;

b. *The activities are not for the purpose of promoting, supporting, or opposing a political principle;*

c. *The activities are not for the purpose of recommending, sup- porting, or opposing a candidate (including a prospective can- didate) for a public office (meaning a public office as specified in Article 3 of the Public Offices Election Law [Law No. 100 of 1950]; the same shall apply hereafter), a person holding a public office, or a political party.* (emphases added)

The November 1, 2003, edition of the *Asahi Shimbun* newspaper reported an interesting story regarding NPOs' involvement in politics. The Kana- gawa Prefectural Government Community Relations Department (which is in charge of NPO-related issues) sent a letter to all of the NPOs in the prefecture. Anticipating the national election scheduled for the upcoming year, the letter reminded them that NPOs were not to be involved in any political activities related to election campaigns. The letter emphasized the NPO Law's clear prohibition of political involvement and stressed that NPOs were expected to understand this point. The newspaper story introduced voices of annoyance from NPO members responding to the letter. As one NPO person said, "I thought that NPOs were supposed to play significant roles in the process of legislating and objectifying the government. However, this letter put a kind of pressure on us. I am afraid that some NPOs will step back, thinking that it is better to have nothing to do with politics." A newsletter published by an intermediary NPO in the prefecture presented a concern that most of the NPOs in the prefecture kept silent on this issue (Kanagawa Information Center for Citizen's Activities 2003, 21).

As this incident suggests, the contemporary meaning of *shimin* under the NPO Law seems to lack the dynamic connotation; *shimin*, represented as ordinary people, or *futsū no hito*, are a very homogenous population, as I documented. Further, they are expected to become apolitical subjects who simply "contribute to the advancement of the public welfare"—a direct quote from the NPO Law—through NPO activities. Contemporary *shimin* actually conjure up an image of what I have, in chapter 4, called volunteer subjectivity with civic engagement; the predominant language of civic engagement is service, or *hōshi*, not politics. With this term, the NPOs are only presented as vehicles for participation in the problem-solving processes of public affairs for the betterment of society. Such *shimin* are populating "civil society" in contemporary Japanese society.

Volunteer Subjectivity Revisited

> We need to know that the emerging new economic ethics (ethos) is . . . based on individual responsibility for responding to the expansion of productivity demanded by the whole (the state). By discarding private profit-making consciousness, we need to take the responsibility directly and clearly. (Ōtsuka [1944] 1969c, 341)

> In order that the new ethics leads to something really "productive," we need to establish two distinctive characteristics—inner originality and institutional rationality—as the crucial structure of our inner commitment for the whole. . . . The supreme inner originality should be generated through aesthetic training by normative, self-disciplined subjects. (343)

These lines were written in 1944 by Ōtsuka Hisao, an economic historian, while he was witnessing the Japanese army fighting in a national crisis against the United States in Saipan. When I read these lines during my fieldwork, the subjectivity advocated by Ōtsuka for supporting total war sounded familiar to those of us examining Japan in the twenty-first century. It seems to me that Ōtsuka's underlying tone in 1944 is echoed in the discourse of contemporary Japan, which is facing a chronically deadlocked economy and society or another national crisis. In fact, the subjectivity seen today, which I presented in chapter 4 as Foucauldian, coercive, self-disciplined volunteer subjectivity, was originally a political subjectivity supporting total war.

Ōtsuka advocated a type of subjectivity that he believed was necessary if the Japanese were to fight World War II as total war. What he sought was a normative, self-disciplined subjectivity that would support the whole or the state. He understood that the wartime crisis required the Japanese people to establish a new economic ethic. In his 1944 article entitled *Saikōdo 'jihatsusei' no hatsuyō* ("Generating a Supreme 'Inner Originality' "), Ōtsuka argued that people's priorities needed to shift. The Japanese people, according to Ōtsuka, needed to stop working to increase their own wealth; instead, they should direct their efforts toward benefiting the state. In this way, they would accept full responsibility for expanding the productive forces of society.

I also would like to bring into this argument Maruyama Masao, a political scientist and intellectual historian. The most common image of Maruyama, as projected by his pronouncements and writings on post-World War II Japanese politics, is of a man who vehemently opposed the 1960s' version of the Japan-U.S. Security Treaty and the attempts by conservatives to revise Article 9's renouncement of war in the postwar constitution, which was regarded as a symbol of Japan's pacifism (Sasaki 1997, 59). From a broader perspective, Maruyama was a spokesman for democracy and public enlightenment in postwar Japan. As Andrew Barshay (1992, 366) argues, "Maruyama, by publicizing a 'scientifically imagined' notion of democracy in postwar Japan, attempted to create a mass citizenry." Meanwhile, as the current scholarship (Nakano 2001) shows, Maruyama also was committed to Japan's war efforts through his propagation of nationalism; like Ōtsuka, introduced earlier, Maruyama in fact advocated a normative, self-disciplined subjectivity for mobilizing ordinary people for total war. During the war, Maruyama certainly observed the necessity of a political subjectivity that supported and strengthened the nationalistic atmosphere of total war. The following is a well-known quote from Maruyama's "Becoming a Nation":

> It is said that a nation means subjects who try to form a nation. In a modern sense, a nation does not mean an objective fact that people simply belong to a national community or share in a common political institution. That just means people, not a nation. In order for people to become a nation, it is inevitable that people positively evaluate their own commonalities, or at least have a strong consciousness about them as desirable. (Maruyama 1944, 93)

On the relationship between the state and individuals, Maruyama presented a model in which he often cited the work of Meiji-period enlightenment thinker Fukuzawa Yukichi. Referring to Fukuzawa, Maruyama wrote, nationalism and his individualism were not, as had often been assumed, contradictory but were rather complementary aspects of a coherent political approach (Maruyama [1943] 1976a). In fact, as Barshay (1992, 384–85) argues, Maruyama's strong affirmation of the universality within European culture being relevant to Japan came at a time when a defensive exceptionalism had developed into one of the most brutal forms of nationalism in Japanese history. One cannot read Maruyama in context without sensing a powerful intellect marked by a national concern. Maruyama's work, like that of the modernists as a whole, was actually nationalistic in its intent. For Maruyama, nationalism was "an instrument of universalization" (Maruyama 1969, 95, quoted by Barshay 1992, 385).

By the postwar era, the 1940s' subjectivity—a normative, self-disciplined subjectivity originally advocated in the context of supporting total war by Ōtsuka and Maruyama—permeated Japanese society and would even become a solid foundation in postwar social and political life. In fact, scholars, such as Ōtsuka and Maruyama and their students, played significant roles in leading the widespread social movements in the early postwar era, rationalizing them as legitimate expressions of the ideals of modern democracy. In his early postwar writings, for example, Ōtsuka's essentially Christian zeal to foster a new "human type" (*ningen ruikei*)—the modern personality—indeed came to form a leitmotiv in his professional work (Koschmann 1998). Citing Daniel Defoe's Robinson Crusoe as a prototype of the modern human being, Ōtsuka sought economic subjects who could supervise and motivate themselves through self-discipline. He encouraged the Japanese people to adopt a rational, autonomous way of life. Of Robinson Crusoe, Ōtsuka wrote:

> He generated his life in an extremely rational and planned way. What impressed us was he was organizing the reality he was facing by creating a rational system of production (albeit it is reproduction, more precisely speaking) on such an isolated island. (Ōtsuka [1947] 1969b, 215)

Ōtsuka continued to explain the modern human type he advocated:

> Like our country, where modern human types are rarely established, it is particularly important to build an interior ethos (human type) among ordinary people for the right development of the economy (productivity). It is achieved by industriousness, frugality, making careful preparations, and organizing autonomous and rational life which makes it possible to get the internal ethos, and "strong" and courageous power of construction. Building such internal ethos among ordinary people should be specifically emphasized. (221)

Further, he explicitly posited the generation of such a human type as a prerequisite of democracy and economic reconstruction in postwar Japan.

Japanese people must learn to appreciate their individuality
and their worth as human beings. They must become free
individuals capable of creating a new social order and promoting public welfare on their own initiative. An internally
fired, living democracy can emerge only out of a society
of free individuals. They are also the root force behind the
power of production—the material foundation of our economic development. A free citizenry is not only the decisive
source of productive power, it is that power itself. (Ōtsuka
[1946] 1969a, 172)[8]

That is, Ōtsuka's theory of normative, self-disciplined subjectivity working for the benefit of the whole (i.e., the state) remained consistent during total war and throughout the postwar democratic revolution. He
intentionally tried to insert the subjectivity into the postwar social order.
On this point, Nakano Toshio (2001, 78–79) argues that Ōtsuka created
a macro discourse on postwar enlightenment, mobilizing people under
a slogan of postwar reconstruction by instilling his sense of modernity
arising from economic subjects supporting total war.

For Maruyama, the generation of such self-motivated subjectivity
also was a key agenda item in his postwar writing. He saw postwar
democracy as entailing the awakening among the masses of modern
political subjectivity. On this point, Hiraishi Nao'aki (2004, 12, 2003) argues
that Maruyama emphasizes the necessity of the intellectual revolution
of each citizen, enabling the people to participate in democratic political reform to create a new nation from below, in place of the "national
polity" from above. Imagining the intentional construction of a political
subjectivity, Maruyama referred to John Locke, who advocated positive,
rational, self-disciplined subjects.

Locke was one of the first thinkers to "systematically" establish
the principles of political liberalism by generating the notion
of liberty based on self-legislating—a subjective liberty that
human beings assign normativity by themselves. What he
was doing was enhancing the notion of liberty from a passive
definition of the lack of regulating to a positive, constructive
notion. (Maruyama [1949] 1976b, 404)

Maruyama continued this argument by citing phrases from Locke's
Second Treaties of Government:

[F]or in all the states of created beings capable of laws, *where
there is no law, there is no freedom*: for *liberty* is, to be free from

restraint and violence from others; which cannot be, where there is no law" (§57). Thus "[t]he *liberty of man*, in society, is to be under no other legislative power, but that established, by consent, in the common-wealth; nor under the dominion of any will, or restraint of any law, but what that legislative shall enact, according to the trust put in it" (§22). In other words, political liberty means people's political autonomy, which is only established by the popular representative politics. (404, emphases in original)

What they expressed through the prism of Robinson Crusoe and John Locke was a single logic—seeking the normative citizenry, or self-disciplined subjectivity, that could serve as the agent of postwar democracy and construction, and leading Japanese people to a nation as a certain ideal subjectivity in a modern Japanese state. Indeed, the self-disciplined subjectivity would be later overlapped with the one I argued thus far as volunteer subjectivity—a key subjectivity in the contemporary NPO phenomenon.

All of the modernist intellectuals, including Ōtsuka and Maruyama, followed by the intellectuals of the next generation—the civil society youth (*shiminshakai-seinen*) who were influenced by modernists—have been referred to generically in Japanese academia as the civil society school (*shiminshakai-ha*).[9] They were leading Japanese social sciences in the post World War II era, and their intellectual concern had a great deal to do with the discourse of civil society (Carver et al. 2000, 546). What the civil society school scholars sought was to speak to mass meetings about the ideal of democratic revolution. Victor Koschmann (1993, 407) describes the role of those intellectuals in the emerging social movements: "Their objective was not socialist revolution but rather an extension of the early postwar ideal of democratic revolution, which would catalyze the formation of a civil society composed of modern citizens. . . . [S]ome citizen-society theories attempted to radicalize the Anpo movement by providing it with a more principled political commitment. That is, they held up certain ideals, or fictions, which they hoped would guide the movement toward construction of a more democratic society." Yamanouchi Yasushi (1993, 1996, 1998) further develops the argument on the role of intellectuals in the early postwar social movements. Yamanouchi pointedly argues that the civil-society school scholars who contributed to develop postwar democracy could not, however, escape wartime psychology (1996, 41). In fact, he continues, postwar democracy guided by them has been largely constrained by a theory of "system society that is organized on the basis of functional principles" (1998, 4), the course for which was set by total war mobilization in World War II.[10] The civil society school

scholars in postwar social movements made serious efforts to locate the
contentious grassroots *shimin* within a system society where each individual is principally expected to play some normative role and make a
positive contribution in maintaining, strengthening, and improving the
existing social, political, and economic life as a self-disciplined subject.
This has a different tone from the original characteristic of new social
movements aiming to bring together independent individuals in spontaneous free activities outside of the existing system, which I presented
in a brief review of the social movement literature earlier in this chapter.
Instead, the Japanese social movements guided by those intellectuals
obviously were aimed at integrating people into the existing system. On
this point, as Kurihara (1999, 11) maintains, this tendency of Japanese
social movements to define issues to invite administrative solutions was
still mired in the "old paradigm" of postwar progressive movements.
The Japanese movements, in principle, attempted to gain access to the
state and willingly participate in an administrative public realm.

In this context, I focus on Matsushita Keiichi, a political scientist
among the postwar intellectuals. He was one of the students working
with Maruyama at the University of Tokyo. As Carver et al. (2000, 549)
point out, the politicization of the civil society discourse was mainly
an achievement of younger political scientists under Maruyama's influence, and Matsushita was a key theorist who gave rationales to the new
social movements of the 1970s and thereafter. In fact, Matsushita was a
key figure who formally institutionalized social movements in Japanese
representative politics. He explored the possibilities for democratizing
local politics through citizen participation under the liberal Tokyo Metropolitan Governor Minobe Ryōkichi. Governor Minobe, who was first
elected in April 1967 and served until his third term ended in 1979,
was well known for being a progressive (*kakushin*) politician. It was an
era in which progressive mayors were elected across the country, such
as in Sendai, Yokohama, Kawasaki, Nagoya, and Kyoto. This was a
by-product of people wanting change from the high economic growth
policy implemented by Prime Minister Ikeda Hayato (1960–1964), which
had allegedly resulted in nationwide industrial pollution (see Rix 1975
for further background). Minobe was a front-runner on this political
trend, and his political stance was that local politics should have greater
involvement of residents in the form of citizens' movements (Minobe
1979; see also Snow 1973; Hein 2004, 187–211). During his administration, Minobe repeatedly stressed words such as *sanka* (participation) as
ways of enhancing the local autonomy guaranteed by the constitution.
He also stressed *taiwa* (dialogue), and he himself was engaged in active
dialogues in the form of *taiwa shūkai* (dialogue assemblies) as a way of
exchanging ideas and opinions.

Political scientist Matsushita supported Governor Minobe's administration theoretically. Matsushita's rationales featured a central concept: "civil minimums" (1971a)—an idea that all citizens have the right to a specified set of healthy, comfortable conditions to ensure minimum standards of life. Further, local citizens should work with politicians and government officials to develop policies for improving the quality of their lives. Matsushita wrote:

> Citizens' movements must become involved in the entire scope of progressive self-government in order to establish "civil minimums." They must take part in the planning and construction of government, and then guard its operations vigilantly and critically. It is essential that the citizens' movement remain aloof from internecine party politics, regardless of local conditions, for their unique function and contribution lies in their ability to influence political developments from outside the immediate, formal political process. For this reason, citizens' movements will differ structurally from professional political groups, such as the parties and the clubs that support parties. The preservation of an amateur quality will assure the citizens' movements of greater freshness and vitality than would otherwise be possible; it will allow them to continue focusing on problems more basic than structure and traditional politics. (Matsushita 1971b, 224–25)[11]

Here I argue that, in fact, Matsushita explicitly provided a prototype of the contemporary *shimin* as internalized self-disciplined volunteer subjectivity supporting NPO activities, which I have argued for thus far: *shimin* became a certain kind of normative subject, expected to bear the responsibility for defining the public interest. As such, they were to take part in the planning and construction of the state. Matsushita wrote:

> The word "citizen" (*shimin*) is not meant to refer merely to the residents or a particular administrative area. Neither is it used to refer to the petite-bourgeoisie or any other particular strata or society. "Citizen" describes the autonomous human being who, ideally, embodies the republican spirit of freedom and equality. He is not a godlike being with powers beyond that of the average man. He is an ordinary individual like ourselves, filled with ordinary hopes and fears, joys and sorrows. He is likely to be a member of the working class, as are most of his countrymen. Yet he does not fit the classical working class stereotype; his character is new and different.

This citizen is free, a self-respecting human being, capable of effectively organizing and initiating political policy. He is active in politics because he is concerned with the problems of daily life rather than with an abstract sense of duty to the nation; as a result, he does not regard his own opinion as infallible, but remains open-minded and flexible. (Matsushita 1971b, 198–99)[12]

What Matsushita advocated was political participation, in other words, civic engagement by ordinary people in ordinary places, a form of integration that would make self-government the nation's highest priority. The movements were repudiating the irresponsibility of the traditional political system, in which policy decisions were initiated at the national level and then trickled down to the prefectural and local levels. At this moment, people labeled *shimin* were not expected to be contentious against authorities. Removing such characteristics, instead,

Picture 6.3 Governor Minobe (left, standing) having a dialogue with local residents (right) who were against the construction of a waste-management facility in Suginami, Tokyo. He asked them to provide the land for the facility site, November 1973. (Reproduced with permission from Mainichi Shimbun)

they became collaborative partners with the authorities. They would sit and have dialogues with government officials. In Matsushita's words, "The citizens' movements seek a one-hundred-eighty degree reversal in the flow of authority to create a 'citizen participation model,' where decisions originate with the citizen and flow out to the national level" (Matsushita 1971b, 197). They were primarily expected to participate in the policy-making process beyond the conventional framework of party politics (Matsushita 1991). Indeed, I have an impression that this era was the tipping point for normative citizenry advocated by modernists in the early postwar era. This was gradually but solidly superseded by *shimin* supporting neoliberal politics, which I argue later in this chapter, without their realizing it.

This prototype of *shimin* was solidly absorbed by grassroots Japanese people, and it guided their way of social and political life thereafter—in local residents' movements (*jūmin undō*) such as environmental movements (*kankyō undō*) and consumer movements (*shōhisha undō*) in the following decades of the 1970s and 1980s.[13] The characteristics of the movements were shifting from appealing strong criticism toward existing authorities, which was apparently seen in the 1960s' citizens' movements, to generating concrete proposals and collaborative partnership with them. On this point, Kurihara (1999, 11) maintains, the interpretive scheme encompasses affirmation of the system as long as it allows piecemeal modification and reform, and the main themes include preservation of life and community formation. One of the environment movements focused on widespread industrial pollution under the economic development, such as the mercury poisoning that became known as Minamata disease in Kumamoto (see George 2001 for comprehensive social research on Minamata disease in English) and Niigata Prefectures, and severe lung disease in such industrial cities of Kawasaki in Kanagawa Prefecture and Yokkaichi in Mie Prefecture. Meanwhile, some of the consumer movements' activists formally developed their activities as a political party, which became known as *Seikatsusha Network* (see LeBlanc 1999 on *Seikatsusha Network*; see also Maki 1976 for the earlier movement; see also Ueno 1988 on the rise of the Japanese women's movement). The party focuses on social welfare, the environment, gender equality, food safety, and peace from the perspective of women and children. Their representatives are regularly elected to local assemblies, as I introduced in chapter 2.

Such normative citizenry has appeared in Japanese society in various guises. In the 1980s, the self-disciplined subjectivity was confirmed by some voluntary social activities. For example, during the era of the "bubble economy," this subjectivity emerged in the form of corporate philanthropy (London 1992). One of the most common terms in the business sector during this period was "contribution to making society better" (*shakai kōken*; Deguchi 1993). Japanese businesses preached the importance of corporate citizens, or *kigyō shimin*, and they began to learn the way of corporate philanthropy from American enterprises. Philanthropic activities were actually energized largely from the "supply side" by corporate philanthropy. After the Plaza Accord of 1985 triggered a dramatic appreciation of the yen, the Japanese economy, viewed in U.S. dollar terms, loomed as a huge international presence. The combination of a weak U.S. dollar and a strong yen encouraged direct Japanese investment in countries around the world, particularly the United States, and opened the way for American-style nonprofit activity. However, it seems that philanthropic activities gradually faded away in Japanese popular discourse when the "bubble economy" burst in the early 1990s.

In the 1990s, when Japanese society faced another national crisis, the self-disciplined subjectivity reappeared in a more explicit and strategic way. Japan suffered its longest recession since World War II, and this plunge into recession is known as the bursting of the "bubble" economy. As a slump in domestic demand pushed the economic slowdown, a real GDP growth rate presented –2.82 percent for 1998, the first negative growth since 1974, after the 1973 oil crisis, according to the World Economic Outlook (International Monetary Fund 1999). Under the circumstances, the normative self-disciplined subjectivity—what I have called volunteer subjectivity—was reexamined. At this time, the government at various levels stepped in to play a significant role in generating that subjectivity, in place of the intellectuals in the early postwar era. Further, buoyed by the surge of volunteerism after the Great Hanshin-Awaji Earthquake, the subjectivity has been formally institutionalized as *shimin* through activities within the framework of the NPO, a new third sector in Japanese society. The nationwide campaign of volunteerism, introducing the phrase—*You can volunteer with a single finger!* (presented in chapter 4)—was a part of its serious efforts. NPO activities supported by volunteer subjectivity are expected to provide alternatives to existing social, political, and economic institutions, all of which worked well in the Keynesian welfare and development state over the past couple of decades. Many sources, including the government, foundations, and businesses, are eagerly funding NPOs as if they see their activities as a panacea for galvanizing the deadlocked society and economy.

NPO as an Agency in Neoliberalism

The last questions I have to explore here are the following: Why does Japanese society have NPOs now? Why are they in vogue? One of the popular arguments has been made largely by NPO practitioners (e.g., Yamamoto 1996, 1998, 1999; Wanner 1998; Yamaoka 1999; Yamauchi 1999a, 1999b, 2000, 2001; Yamauchi and Shimizu 1999; Yamauchi and Deguchi 2000; Anheier and Kendall 2001; Deguchi 2001; Nakamura and Japan NPO Center 2001). Following the impressive disaster-relief activities of 1.3 million volunteers after the Great Hanshin-Awaji Earthquake in January 1995 (Economic Planning Agency 2000), they argued that there was a consensus among Japanese people that the society needed to support volunteer-based social movements. A new formal and institutional framework to support these social movements—one that would be controlled neither by the government nor by for-profit businesses—was necessary. After the earthquake, there was not much of a system in place to provide long-term, efficient support to the disaster-stricken area. That experience led Diet members to bring forward new legislation to encourage the establishment of more volunteer-based NPOs by granting them corporate status, which would enable their members to share their assets and make contracts in the name of the organization. Without this status, members had to open bank accounts as individuals, as I mentioned in chapter 1. To form an NPO, one does not have to prepare capital; thus it is much easier for an NPO to achieve corporate status than it is for other types of corporate bodies. The NPO Law was based on the vision that people could freely become organized in newly conceptualized entities called NPOs. Many hoped that NPOs would present effective alternatives to the government (and also to for-profit business entities) and would break the social, political, and economic gridlock that Japanese society faced after the burst of the so-called "bubble" economy of the late 1980s and early 1990s.

The 1990s, popularly called the "Lost Decade," witnessed a paradigm shift in Japanese social and political life. Jeff Kingston, a Tokyo-based American historian, describes the era as follows in a book documenting postwar Japanese history:

> Mired in recession during the 1990s, Japan is facing the consequences of prolonged economic malaise. It enters the twenty-first century as the world's leading debtor nation, with total public debt amounting to 123 percent of GDP, a result of massive counter-cyclical government-spending packages aimed at stimulating recovery and rescuing the financial sector from insolvency. From a nation that enjoyed double-digit growth and minimal unemployment throughout the miracle years . . . , growth has become anaemic and unemployment has sky-rocketed. The twin pressures of recession and economic deregulation have generated a powerful riptide with

considerable consequences for the employment system. This system seems to be unraveling as companies discover that measures which saw them through past slumps are exhausted. Corporate Japan can no longer afford the rigidities and high costs of lifetime employment and seniority-based wage scales (*nenko*). The social contact between employers and employees based on security and loyalty is a likely casualty as firms gradually pursue more aggressive restructuring. What went wrong? (Kingston 2001, 90)

This situation was exacerbated by the fact that the bureaucrats have lost much of their prestige and trustworthiness due to a nationwide flurry of bribery scandals, such as *kankan settai,* which involved lower bureaucrats who entertained higher bureaucrats at the taxpayers' expense. Some Finance Ministry officials even accepted entertainment from businesses at a *no-pan* restaurant, where the waitresses wore short skirts and no underwear. Curtis (1999, 56) points out that these incidents "symbolized how far bureaucratic behavior had strayed from the lofty ideal of the selfless professional who dedicated his life to serve the interests of the nations." This fall from grace was finally and decisively highlighted by the bureaucrats' woeful performance in disaster-relief activities following the great earthquake. "The governments cannot respond to our needs promptly and flexibly." I think this was the shared impression among us Japanese, which I reported as a journalist in the mid 1990s from Tokyo. Japanese people were becoming distrustful of the government—in particular, of the bureaucrats, the people who had once been labeled as the cleverest in the society and had led the miraculous postwar reconstruction. The bureaucrats no longer seemed to have the answers, and they no longer seemed able to cope with new challenges. As we came to learn of their incompetence and malfeasance, we felt a solid need for increased scrutiny and monitoring of their activities. Under this social and political circumstance, the concept of the NPO was strategically introduced to the society in a very timely—and, in a sense, tactical—manner. The NPO, or the third sector, was officially instituted in Japanese society, gaining popular support. NPO generation has been recommended amid a rosy discourse in line with the associational revolution that I cited in chapter 1, as illustrated in this passage:

NPOs have been particularly effective in areas where government bureaucracy does not have sufficient flexibility or resources to respond effectively. As social needs and values became more diverse and the government budget became more constrained, the space for NPOs widened. (Yamamoto 1999, 101)

The NPO was justified by this rationale and was described as a citizen-based organization, a term that connoted something correct, ideal, and desirable in contrast to the scandal-tainted bureaucracy. In fact, no political parties were against the generation of the NPO Law (see Pekkanen 2000), and Japanese political parties—both the ruling LDP and the opposing Democratic Party of Japan (DPJ), regardless of their political creeds, supported the NPO.[14]

I contend that Japanese society would have NPOs even if the great earthquake had never occurred. Arguably, the current NPO phenomenon derived from the context of the social movements. By the early 1990s, the development of the Japanese nonprofit sector had already been discussed in an American think-tank journal as a new dynamism stemming from a convergence of domestic and global developments that were "awakening Japanese citizens to the possibility of new ways of relating to their government and the private sector—and eventually to the outside world" (Frost 1993, 28). In fact, official activities supporting the institutionalization of a nonprofit sector began in November 1994, about two months before the earthquake, when a citizens' group, known as the C's (formerly the Coalition for Legislation to Support Citizens' Organizations), was organized by twenty-four citizens' groups to facilitate citizen-based activities. The C's was widely known as the group that played a significant role in lobbying for the legislative process of the NPO Law in 1998.[15]

I see the NPO, or "civil society," as a key form of agency in neoliberalism. I argue that the Japanese NPO is a representation of the way in which a global trend—neoliberalism—is placed, shaped, understood, and operated in a society. Neoliberalism is a politico-economic ideology centered around the values of a global economy—a free market, free trade, and the unrestricted flow of capital—which became widespread during the last quarter of the twentieth century (Drucker 1986; Harvey 2003, 2005; see Ferguson and Gupta 2002; Hoffman et al. 2006 for anthropological accounts on neoliberalism). Neoliberalism originates from the 1980s assault on the Keynesian welfare-state model pioneered by conservative politicians, most notably Margaret Thatcher in the United Kingdom and Ronald Reagan in the United States, and the gurus of monetarist economists in the Chicago School of American Neoliberalism, promoted most noticeably by Milton Friedman (1962). These conservatives sought to withdraw the government from society to some extent while giving greater rein to the free market and to individuals. In Japan, Nakasone Yasuhiro, a political leader of the conservative LDP and Japanese prime minister from 1982 to 1987, promoted neoliberal ideology under his administration. He privatized three state-owned businesses: the national railways, telephones and telegraphs, and tobacco and salt. Those businesses are currently known as the Japan Railway (JR), Nippon Telegraph and Telephone (NTT), and Japan Tobacco (JT), respectively. The government thus downsized, transferring its businesses to the private sector.

The Japanese NPO phenomenon should be situated in line with the neoliberal policy implementations of the 1980s and early 1990s. It is an inevitable extension of the neoliberal politics we have experienced over the past two decades. As I argued, the NPO gained strong attention in the context of devolution from the state to the third sector. Volunteers invited by the local government were key actors in the devolution process. That was a part of structural reform, or *kōzō kaikaku*, a key term in neoliberal politics since the late 1990s under the Hashimoto Ryutaro administration of the LDP. Hashimoto is a key political figure in the context of my argument, since he strongly pushed deregulation (*kisei kanwa*) politics. Hashimoto sponsored the financial Big Bang program in the Tokyo market under the name of structural reform. Further, he was the prime minister when the legislation of the NPO Law was primarily discussed. In the argument vis-à-vis structural reform, the NPOs were definitely expected to play a powerful role in setting the terms of the debates by mobilizing key constituencies and coordinating grassroots companies to effect change. They are expected to be a device that will drastically alter the conventional social, political, and economic customs in Japanese society by tapping volunteers to create a better society and revitalize the economy. In fact, in 1999, the Economic Strategy Council (*Keizai senryaku kaigi*), an advisory body to the prime minister, officially proposed introducing NPOs into the existing system to enhance dynamism in society. In the proposal, the role of NPOs is mentioned—for example, as partners in private finance initiatives (Economic Strategy Council 1999, 59–71). In this context, the Ministry of Economy, Trade, and Industry (METI), the Japanese business daily, *Nihon Keizai Shimbun,* and the conservative Japan Business Federation (*Nippon keidanren*) have been ardent supporters of NPO activities.

The institutionalization of NPOs is a calculated reorganization of the Japanese public sphere designed to establish a small government in the postwelfare state through the transfer of social services originally delivered by the state to volunteer-driven NPOs. Further, the process of restructuring conventional administrative techniques using the NPO redefines the relationship between the state and the individual, while articulating an ideal subject—*shimin*. That process has been justified by the logic of associational revolution, which, I would argue, can be located in the reverse discourse of neoliberal ideology of outsourcing state responsibilities to civil society.

Shimin as Cultural Product in Neoliberalism

Using Foucault's concept of governmentality (Foucault 1991), we can develop a more theoretically specific analysis of the relation between *shimin* and neoliberalism. Thomas Lemke (2001, 203) plainly characterizes as follows:

> Neo-liberalism is a political rationality that tries to render the social domain economic and to link a reduction in (welfare) state services and security systems to the increasing call for "personal responsibility" and "self-care."

One of the key features of neoliberal governmentality is the withdrawal of the state from social services. This policy, characterized by "a 'folding back' of the objectives of government upon its means" (Dean 1999, 174), entails breaching the conventional divisions between the state and the individual. Another significant attribute of neoliberal governmentality, as Lemke points out, is the development of particular techniques for leading and controlling individuals at the grassroots level. In an article contributed to *Audit Culture*, a collection of anthropological studies on accountability, Cris Shore and Susan Wright (2000, 61) claim that neoliberal governmentality as a whole shifts the role of government, using the norms of the free market as the organizing principles not only of economic life but also of the activities of the state itself, and, even more profoundly, of the conduct of individuals.

The term *jiko-sekinin* (self-responsibility) reminds me of the relevance of the code of individuals. I often read and heard this term while I was doing fieldwork on the Japanese NPO. It contains a metaphor suggesting that the seed sown for oneself is reaped for oneself. During my series of conversations with NPO practitioners, I discovered that most NPOs did not offer health insurance to employees, whereas most Japanese companies did. Thus, many NPO workers were forced to purchase state-sponsored health insurance by themselves. Citing this as an example, one NPO practitioner told me that all people who want to work for NPOs should embrace the principle of self-responsibility, or *jiko-sekinin*. The reality that this term actually implies is not so rosy.

At my field site, the SLG secretariat staff's salaries were half of those of the government officials who previously performed the same administrative work, as I mentioned in chapter 5. SLG staff members could fortunately subscribe to health insurance sponsored by the municipal government, mainly because the former entity of SLG was established by the municipal government, but they had no other employee benefits, not even bonuses, which are granted by most Japanese companies. During my fieldwork, all of the male staff members, one after another, left SLG because they could not support their families on their low incomes. One young staff member in his mid-twenties told me that he was fully aware that his salary at the NPO would be low. He did not expect much in terms of benefits. However, when he actually faced this reality, he said, "I can't even support myself, much less expect to marry and start a family." Over time, the staff became composed entirely of women, mostly housewives who could work for SLG because they had the spare time and did not need to make much money. According to the national survey of the Research Institute of Economy, Trade, and Industry (RIETI 2003, 15), for example, the average annual salary in early 2003 for a full-time paid staff member of an NPO was 1,184,000 yen (approximately $11,000). This is far below the national average. The average salary in the calendar year 2003 was 4,439,000 yen (approximately $40,000) a year for both men and women (with an average age of 43.5 years); 5,442,000 yen (approximately $49,000) for men (43.6 years); and 2,748,000 yen (approximately $25,000) for women (43.4 years), according to annual statistics from the National Tax Agency (2003).[16] The reality of Japanese NPOs as a workplace is often harsher than idealism would suggest. This even shows that people's goodness actually destroys the wage system in this society, which was won by laborers in the development of capitalism.

The low wages paid in the sector were justified by the term *paid volunteers* at my field site. There seemed to be a consensus among SLG volunteers that the secretariat staff should not expect to earn a significant amount of money. Frankly speaking, NPOs are not places to pursue money making. Unpaid work, beautifully labeled as "volunteerism," was a key concept at SLG. SLG volunteers worked for their local community. They worked to promote lifelong learning through *voluntary* activities. These NPO activities were primarily operated by unpaid volunteers, who paid a membership fee to participate in activities on behalf of the community. As these volunteers needed personnel to coordinate their activities, secretariat staff members were hired to arrange and organize pleasant environments for volunteering while working with the volunteers. In essence, these staff members were part of the volunteer force.

According to the organizational philosophy, their spirit should be identical to that of the volunteers. They are paid for the privilege of organizing the volunteers' activities, thus a little money should be enough. I once heard an SLG volunteer say, "We are working on an unpaid basis. But we are doing more than the secretariat staff. Why are they paid?"

I often read the term *jiko-sekinin* in news reports on Japanese hostages in Iraq when I was completing my dissertation on Japanese NPOs in the spring of 2004 in Tokyo. Three Japanese youth—an independent aid worker, a peace activist, and a freelance photojournalist—had been kidnapped. In return for their freedom, their captors demanded the withdrawal of Japan's Self-Defense Forces (SDF) from Iraq. At the time, Japan had deployed about 500 ground SDF troops in southern Iraq for rehabilitation operations. The three hostages, who spent nine days in captivity, received a chilly response from some politicians and members of the general public, who claimed that they had acted irresponsibly by going to Iraq in defiance of government travel warnings. According to a news report (*Kyodo News*, April 16, 2004), one senior politician of the ruling LDP stated at a press conference, "I want people to be aware of the concept of self-responsibility." Following the comment, another politician mentioned the possibility of urging the three hostages or their families to shoulder the costs the government paid for their rescue. He argued, "We have spent a large sum of money, funded by taxes. It is necessary to make them aware of their self-responsibility by asking them to pay for what we spent on them." Similarly, Prime Minister Koizumi Jun'ichiro severely criticized the situation. "Think about how many people handled the hostage crisis by working around the clock," he remarked. Such comments by politicians were supported by the public. In one survey, 68.4 percent of respondents positively evaluated the government's handling of the hostage crisis, and 61.3 percent said the government had made the right decision not to yield to the captors' demand for the withdrawal of Japan's SDF troops from Iraq (*Kyodo News*, April 17, 2004).

These episodes seem to reflect a discourse of the neoliberal governmentality that dominates Japanese society and politics in the early twenty-first century. Lemke (2001, 201) explains the critical features of neoliberalism's discourse:

> The key feature of neo-liberal rationality is the congruence it endeavours to achieve between a responsible and moral individual and an economic-rational actor. It aspires to construct prudent subjects whose moral quality is based on the fact that they rationally assess the costs and benefits of a certain act as opposed to other alternative acts. As the choice of options

for action is, or so the neo-liberal notion of rationality would have it, the expression of free will on the basis of a self-determined decision, the consequences of the action are borne by the subject alone, who is also solely responsible for them.

Today, Japanese individuals are indeed expected to become such responsible, moral, and economically rational actors. They are encouraged to voluntarily give their lives a specific type of entrepreneurial form—embodied in the NPO, for instance. The individuals who are organized into the NPO are expected to voluntarily respond to demands placed upon them by society and to supply services in areas once considered the domain of the state—which indeed resonates in Lemke's explanation, cited earlier.

Such individuals are *shimin*. *Shimin* are a cultural product of discursive norms; they are one of the "categories of individuals to be governed" (Wedel et al. 2005, 30) in contemporary Japan. Policy increasingly shapes the way in which individuals construct themselves as subjects, as Shore and Wright (1997, 4; see also Moore 1987; Rose 1999; Ren 2005; Wright 2006) argue, and through policy, the individual is categorized and given such statuses and roles as *shimin*. Recently, the Japanese state, at various levels—national, prefectural, and municipal—has indeed tried to produce this particular type of individual with an internalized volunteer subjectivity.

One of the major differences that I observed between the initial and final stages of my fieldwork at SLG from 2001 through 2003 was that the number of students who participated in NPO activities as volunteers was increasing. Student participation occurred through a volunteer "experience" (*taiken*) program developed by Japan's Ministry of Education, Science, Sports, Culture, and Technology (MEXT),[17] which aims to generate a nationwide structure to promote volunteer involvement among students at the elementary, secondary, and college levels through actual volunteer experiences with local nonprofit social service providers. The program has established support centers at both the national and prefectural levels for promoting such activities and maintaining related information. Program implementation has been supported by a report released in July 2002 from the Central Council for Education recommending volunteer activities—*hōshi* (literally, services), in the report's language—in the regular school curriculum. Under this MEXT-sponsored program, SLG regularly accepted students from local junior high schools and colleges as interns. These students worked with paid staff members of the secretariat for a week or so, thereby earning credits they needed for graduation. SLG assigned some projects to the students. The projects included data entry using computers with secretariat staff members, helping in course administration with instructors and volunteers, and delivering newsletters on lifelong learning opportunities published by SLG to local facilities such as city halls, public libraries, senior citizens centers, banks, metro stations, and neighborhood associations. Through the projects, students are expected to learn how volunteer activities actually work in real settings, and how NPOs work with entities in other sectors in their community. One local junior high school student who completed an internship at SLG commented that he was impressed with the fact that the organization's activities were primarily organized by volunteers. He said, "I helped with administrative work at the secretariat. Before doing this internship, I was thinking that this kind of experience would not mean so much to me. But, having actually done it, my impression has totally changed. I learned a lot through this real experience."

This education is a strategy of governance, a technology for the production of *shimin*.[18] This MEXT policy seeks to produce *shimin*, an

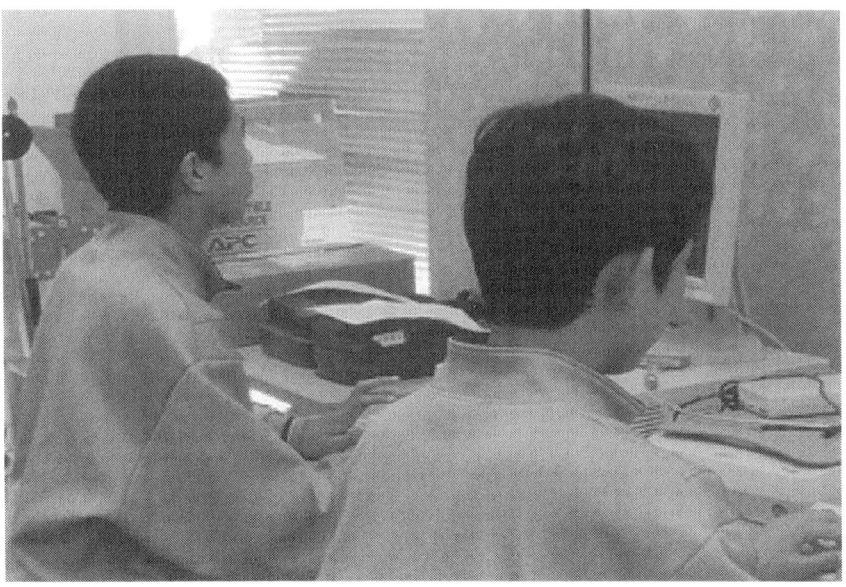

Picture 6.4 Student volunteers, interning for credit under the regular school curriculum, enter data at the SLG secretariat

ideal subject, while the government is redefining its role, instead of providing social services for their citizens, toward the aim of empowering the population to generate social services for themselves based on their needs. Furthermore, this policy has significant meaning in a society facing a huge demographic change—an aging populace. In December 2005, the Japanese government announced that Japan's population started shrinking in 2005 for the first time on record (MHLW 2005).[19] With society aging and women giving birth to fewer children, social security costs are likely to increase for future generations. The policy generates a particular type of population to support the social welfare system originally operated by the government. Policy makers hope that these new "volunteer" subjects, working within the NPO framework, will be able to take care of the expanding aging population, thus solving a major problem for government. As I observed in the previous chapters, the neoliberal government first tactically mobilized active associational leaders and housewives as resources, labeling them volunteers, in the process of devolution from the state to the NPO. Now the government strategically targets students as volunteers or unpaid workers amid the rapid demographic changes.

The Japanese NPO has been believed to provide greater accommodation and space for diversity in contemporary Japan while breaking a rigid bureaucratic rationality. Japanese people, myself included, are expected to play significant roles in this newly created social space. However, the NPO has been strategically co-opted by the state, like many other Japanese third-sector organizations such as incorporated foundations and incorporated associations, into the social and political structure. The standardized volunteer subjectivity embodied in *shimin* is creating docile subjects who fit the ideology of the current neoliberal system. These individuals are to be collaborative partners participating in public affairs for the betterment of society. To me, this move looks ironically as though it is intensifying bureaucratic rationality at the grassroots level. The process of dispersal of social services from the state to the third sector or the NPO has actually strengthened government control through performance targets or cost cutting in public administration and the growth of managerialism by the government as a mode of collaboration with the NPO. The Japanese state continues to be strong, and NPOs—products of the state's deliberate institutionalization of "civil society"—have become nearly synonymous with the state. The state, an unusually strong actor in Japanese social and political life, retards the development of a dynamic civil society. One might say that the state is using underhanded tactics to institutionalize a "civil society" that will exclusively meet its neoliberal goals.

However, at the grassroots level, I observed strong internal tensions or disagreements, coupled with frustrations and resistance, to such artificially created state discourse on civil society. People were becoming alienated from the strategies of the neoliberal state. In fact, in an article in the *Asahi Shimbun* (September 29, 2002), a handicapped person expressed this sense of mounting frustration:

> I, a handicapped person, am always supposed to be "given to" (*hodokoshi wo ukeru*). I am always supposed to be helped. If those activities are standardized, becoming something normative under the name of volunteerism, I will be really uncomfortable living in this society. For me, it is really difficult to survive. I feel I must be small and weak. . . . I wonder what this society is trying to achieve. Even I can push a button on the elevator.

I have introduced a story of the state attempting to depoliticize people at the grassroots level, which suggests that this was not being meekly accepted. I hope, optimistically, that most Japanese people will become aware of this ongoing, calculated reality, even if only vaguely. As I mentioned in chapter 2, it is a fact that more than 60,000 citizens' groups (*shimin dantai*) have existed in Japanese society (Cabinet Office 2001). Only a small percentage of them, however, have sought recognition under the NPO Law. In fact, most of the NPOs currently incorporated exist because there is the NPO Law (RIETI 2003, 4–6).[20] There may be a self-selection bias among those who are less inclined to challenge the government. As I confirmed in chapter 4, some people—in particular, social activists who participated in the new social movements in the early postwar era—have been very cautious about participating in this NPO phenomenon. In a survey conducted by the Cabinet Office, released in 2005, only 7.2 percent of the surveyed population had participated in NPO activities over the past five years, just 39.7 percent knew the meaning of the term *NPO*, and only 30.6 percent thought of NPOs as trustworthy organizations (Cabinet Office 2005b). There also is criticism that the NPO is a new way of interest distribution. The *Yomiuri Shimbun* (October 6, 2006) reports that Fukushima Prefectural Government established an NPO for generating jobs for its retired officials. The NPO, which was nominally registered in the area of disaster relief, primarily received more than 300 million yen orders from the prefecture office to inspect bridges and tunnels between November 2002 and August 2006. The NPO is actually used as another way of producing *amakudari*, a Japanese traditional practice where retired bureaucrats land cushy jobs in the private sector that they supervised in their previous jobs.

Finally, I put forth a concern that I had throughout my fieldwork. I realized that the huge upsurge in NPO incorporation, now more than 30,000 groups over the past eight years, proceeded simultaneously with a series of nationalistic policy moves by the Japanese government starting in the late 1990s. Certainly, neoliberalism and nationalism, although each has a different worldview, might be highly compatible in crushing diversities and challenges. The nationalistic policy moves include the passage, in August 1999, of the Communication Monitoring Law and an amendment to the Citizens' Residence Registration Law, which allowed the government to monitor all citizens by assigning each a number. At almost the same time, the Diet formally adopted the *Hinomaru* (the Rising Sun flag), a symbol of the Japanese military invasion of Asia in World War II, as Japan's national flag, and *Kimigayo* ("His Majesty's Reign") as the national anthem, imposing a legal duty on all schools to adopt both. In 2000, Prime Minister Mori Yoshiro stunned the nation with his statement that Japan was a divine country with the emperor at its center. During his tenure, from 2001 to 2006, Prime Minister Koizumi regularly visited Yasukuni Shrine, which honors—among others—Class A war criminals. In 2002, a right-wing group, the Japanese Society for History Textbook Reform, successfully campaigned for the elimination of "masochistic" war clauses in a history textbook that I spoke of earlier in this chapter.[21] This was among the textbooks under the state-supervised education system that China and Korea, which both suffered under Japan's wartime aggression, strongly criticized the Japanese government for approving. According to a news report, the textbook will be used in a limited number of schools; it will be used by 0.4 percent of all junior high school students nationwide beginning in April 2006 (*Kyodo News*, September 1, 2005).[22] The issue is that such a contentious textbook was formally approved by the Japanese government, and that some schools are actually using it. The campaign to select the textbook is becoming more powerful at the municipal government level. One of my key research collaborators in this project, a board member at the committee of education in the municipality in which SLG was located, candidly told me that she faced incredible, intermittent pressure from municipal assembly members in the conservative camp to adopt the textbook when she was involved in the text-selection process. In January 2004, the Japanese government dispatched its SDF to Iraq. This was a historic moment, because it marked the first time that the Japanese military had been sent to a war zone since World War II.

Today, it seems to me that all of these moves converge on a political course—the revision of the Japanese constitution, in tandem with the revision of the Fundamental Law of Education, stressing the need for a compassionate, patriotic sprit in which volunteerism, called *hōshi,* is central. In particular, they converge on the revision of Article 9, which distinctively articulates Japanese pacifism and the renunciation of war in the post-World War II political discourse. The ongoing discussion also has included calls for amendments to Article 24—the clause protecting gender equality in postwar Japan—in a bid to lock conservative family values into the legal and social framework at the expense of individual freedom. In September 2006, Abe Shinzo, an ardent nationalist, was appointed by the parliament as prime minister, proposing the revision of the Japanese constitution. Abe said to a reporter of Britain's *Financial Times* (October 31, 2006):

> There are three reasons by which I judge we need to revise the Japanese constitution. The first is that the current constitution was written before Japan became independent after the war. The second point is that with sixty years past, there are provisions within the constitution that no longer befit the reality of the day. Third, new values have emerged since, and I believe that by taking up those values and to encourage the spirit of writing our own constitution, we shall be able to open up a new era for Japan. . . . Now speaking of provisions that no longer fit the times, one typical example would be Article 9. . . . I believe this article needs to be revised from the viewpoint of defending Japan, and also in order to comply with the international expectation that Japan make international contributions. My term of office is three years and the president of the LDP can sit for up to two terms. Within that term of office, I shall strive [to] achieve the revision.

In December 2006, the Fundamental Law of Education was revised with patriotic emphasis on nationalistic identity formation. In early January 2007, the Defense Agency, an affiliate of the Cabinet Office, was upgraded to a full ministry with budgetary and policy-making functions. In May 2007, Japan's parliament passed a bill to set referendum procedures for constitutional amendments, preparing its first legal framework for rewriting the pacifist constitution. The bill's passage initiates a step to boost national debates, although the law will not come into force for another three years, under Prime Minister Shinzo Abe's plan to revise the constitution in a move to depart from what he calls Japan's "postwar regime."

Admittedly, my ethnography does not offer an all-inclusive account of the Japanese NPO phenomenon, which has only a short history. Indeed, what I documented in this book is one actor among a vast array of Japanese civil society organizations, most of which might remain invisible in the society. But some observations can be made about this newly institutionalized civil society organization—*NPO*. Here I put again my original research questions: Can civil society successfully be constructed by a state? What are the ways in which states seek to shape their relations with their populations, and how effective are those policies likely to be? From the policy makers' perspective, the institutionalization of the NPO, or "civil society," could be deemed a success, since NPOs have been more formally and successfully institutionalized as effective social services delivery entities, acting like other existing third-sector organizations in this society. My impression after conducting this research project is that Japan's conservative government is successfully taking advantage of this type of civil society organization. The government is using the enthusiasm for volunteering to streamline the social system generated in the current framework of public administration under the neoliberal state. At the same time, the government does not reciprocate the goodwill, such as by giving active tax incentives to NPOs. In other words, Japanese NPOs do not benefit under the NPO Law by earning any active tax-exempt status.[23] Meanwhile, from a grassroots point of view, it is likely believed to be a failure of civil society, as people were just conveniently mobilized under the name of civil society for the neoliberal state. Labeled *shimin*, they were forced to become apolitical under the NPO Law, and they were expected to be collaborative partners with the conservative state and co-opted as subcontractors to the government. In so doing, the Japanese NPO sector, or "civil society," limits dynamic social and political participation—a key component in democracy. It serves the state at different levels in maintaining, strengthening, and improving the existing social, political, and economic system, and it does not directly serve people at the grassroots level. Meanwhile, this ethnography illuminates challenges, represented as difficulties and conflicts from the grassroots level, to maintain this civil society for the state. Japanese civil society pays a high price for becoming involved with the state.[24]

In this book, I believe I have identified an important reality in examining the relationship between the state and individuals under the name of civil society in contemporary Japan. My current concern centers on what will happen when the concept of society is extended to include the state. A parallel can be seen in the 1920s and the 1930s, when the political discourse emphasized loyalty to the state, which was symbolized by slogans such as "sacrifice personal interests for the good of the state" (*messhi hōkō*).[25] Sentiments along the same lines were articulated when a nationalistic Japan advanced into World War II as total war. *Shimin* survive as a new ideal type of national figure under this political landscape in Japan at the twenty-first century's beginning.

Chapter 7

Epilogue:
Initiating Change

A gardener said one day,
"We are going to plant a flower garden."
However, the flowers of the garden never fully bloomed.
The trimming is only an appearance.
The arrogant gardener prunes according to his taste.
He never considers each individual flower.
The gardener gives water and fertilizer haphazardly.
The flowers can't get their necessary nutrition.
The roots have begun to rot.
The garden has beautiful stone walls.
However, the stone walls hurt the flowers' roots.
To make matters worse, the walls disturb the draining.
The gardener wondered why the flowers were withering.
Without serious consideration, he pulled out the flowers,
although some of the flowers had buds.
He bought new flowers and planted them.
But the newly planted flowers again started withering.
The day after a heavy rain fell,
the garden lost all of the flowers,
leaving only the beautiful, but cold, empty stone walls.
—Ms. Andō, SLG volunteer

I received this poem from a female volunteer during the initial stage of my fieldwork at SLG. This poem confirmed to me what I needed to do as an action-minded anthropologist: to become deeply involved in helping SLG get out of a deadlocked situation and to facilitate change so the organization could operate more effectively for its members. Suspending my objectivity as a researcher, I set off on a mission of action.

Research for Social Change

The research strategy I chose is called Action Research (AR), a social research strategy that combines collaborative research and an impulse toward social change with a strong democratic emphasis (Greenwood and Levin 1998). I am not a silent, passive observer, a note taker, or even just a participant. I am actively involved with my research subjects. I do socially relevant research, that is, research for social change.

I came to know AR when I was frustrated with a type of social science research—the number-oriented, rational-choice-based knowledge production, a dominant trend in social science in the U.S. academia. When I did assigned readings in the political science program, honestly speaking, I felt like they were something far from the real world. I even felt like it was knowledge for the sake of knowledge, looking for a linear causal relationship as a form of theory. While thinking about my real-world experience as a journalist before going back to graduate school, it seemed to me that such kind of research would not well reflect complicated daily lives at the grassroots level. Further, I believe that everyday life is a dynamic texture of social meaning. Where is the meaning as human beings in such theory making? I definitely needed another research paradigm.

On snowy winter days one December, I spent a lot of time at the methodology section of the Olin Library at Cornell. At that time, I happened to encounter a book titled *Introduction to Action Research: Social Research for Social Change* (Greenwood and Levin 1998). I had never heard the term "Action Research," but the word "action" definitely sounded attractive to me. While reading chapter by chapter, I felt very comfortable with the content, thinking this might be what I had been looking for. The book was on a style of cogenerative knowledge production, whereby researchers and members of a community jointly identify a problem, gather information, analyze the collected data, plan for transformation, take action, interpret the results, and have reflection. The research aims at achieving positive results through broad participation of the stakeholders in the research process.

One of the authors of the book was a Cornell professor of anthropology, and luckily enough, he offered a course on AR in the upcoming spring semester. Without hesitation, I attended his course. The course was fascinating, something I had never previously experienced. The course had no preset syllabus. Instead, the students wrote a syllabus based on what they wanted and what they could offer. We formed several groups based on our interests. Each group chose readings, presented materials to the class, facilitated the discussion, and led the reflection.

The professor also joined the group based on his interest. I felt that AR democratized, even destabilized, conventional classroom learning. This AR strategy came naturally to me: it reflected my dual role as involved participant and friendly outsider; it was well suited to my being a native anthropologist interested in democratizing my own society through social reform, and it defined my research style as a scholar from that point. My encounter with this research strategy motivated me to transfer to the anthropology program.

I decided to do research on Japanese civil society, or the voluntary third sector, which is associated with neither government nor businesses and is called NPO. The NPO was formally institutionalized in the Japanese civil society following the surge of disaster volunteerism after the Great Hanshin-Awaji Earthquake in 1995 and was incorporated under the NPO Law in 1998. Civil society has been a popular topic among postwar Japanese political scientists. But I, as an anthropologist, argue that most of the work in the field contains normative theoretical formulations or analyses of high-level political institutions and a small number of political elites. The research agenda that runs through my project is that the civil society argument needs a grounded analysis of grassroots values and practices expressed by local actors struggling to frame common definitions of what Japanese "civil society" is. We need to analyze the dynamic micro-politics of everyday interactions between the state and ordinary people. In order to explore the meaning of "civil society" in contemporary Japan, I thus chose the NPO as a research topic. What do Japanese grassroots people experience under the new civil society making? This was my immediate research question.

In this chapter, I offer a reflexive account of my struggle with a research strategy framed by the interconnection of my three identities: a Western-trained or an American university graduate student, an action-minded researcher, and a native (Japanese) anthropologist. One of the products I sought from my research effort was an ethnography of the new Japanese NPO movement. At the same time I hoped my ethnography might transcend being merely descriptive and serve the larger agenda of generating movement toward the democratization of the institutional environment of civil society in Japan.

Establishing the Field Site

During the summer after finishing my course work, I returned to my native country, Japan, to conduct fieldwork on the Japanese NPO movement. At that point, I had targeted no specific organization as a pertinent example of the emergent third sector. I wanted to set my field site in Tokyo, or the greater Tokyo metropolitan area, where my wife had begun her job. Initially, I attended gatherings for people who were interested in the NPO movement. The 1998 NPO Law had encouraged a number of salon-style gatherings across the country for people who wanted to learn more about NPOs. The gatherings were advertised on the Internet and in newspapers and were open to the public. At the beginning stage of my fieldwork, I attended many of these events, exchanging my business cards with as many NPO practitioners as I could. I asked them what they were doing at the grassroots level so I could get a real sense of these types of activities. If a particular NPO sounded interesting to me, then I visited its offices.

At the first salon-style gathering I attended, I happened to sit next to Mr. Hasegawa, general secretary of SLG. We exchanged business cards, along with a brief self-introduction. In early August, I e-mailed him, requesting a meeting, since I was still in the process of data collection on several types of the NPOs. In his response, he asked for information on my research. I simply told him that I wanted to conduct research on the voluntary citizens-based NPO. (I did not use the term *ethnography*. I did not think that Mr. Hasegawa, as a member of the general public, would be familiar with this research method and writing style.) I told him I was looking for an NPO to use as a basis of my research, which was to analyze the dynamic development of third-sector organizations. Further, I wanted to be involved in the NPO as much as I could, if possible, as an unpaid staff member. I wanted to establish some collaborative relationship with NPO participants. I did not want to be treated like a visitor or an outsider. In his response, however, Mr. Hasegawa rejected my request on the grounds that his NPO was not in line with my research purpose. According to him, SLG was a "quasi-governmental organization" and was not part of the dynamic movement of the third sector in Japanese society. Although I did not exactly understand his use of the term *quasi-governmental* at that time, the term itself intrigued me. I sent him an e-mail, saying, "I want to see various kinds of NPOs in the initial stage of my research. Even quasi-governmental organizations, as you said, are a reality of the Japanese NPO sector. If they are less dynamic, I would like to think about why these types of NPOs are less dynamic. Anyway, I would like to see you and know your NPO."

In mid-August, I took a train to a tiny station on a minor metro line, two stops from Asakusa. The district is a major industrial area in Tokyo, for medium- and small-size manufacturers of products such as toys, soap, erasers, and shoes, while one- and two-story houses also populate the landscape. As I was approaching the neighborhood, I suddenly saw a modern building rising above the landscape. As I got closer, I could see that all of its walls were made of glass, and every door was automatic. At the entrance was an artificial river. The contrast of this contemporary compound against the traditional flavor of the neighborhood was striking. The building was SLG. Mr. Hasegawa's office was on the second floor.

Mr. Hasegawa soon appeared, and we spoke briefly about the typhoon that had hit the Tokyo metropolitan area the previous day. He then gave me some information about SLG. According to him, this organization provides lifelong learning courses in the local community. More specifically, local residents are organized as volunteers under the NPO, and the volunteers plan such courses as foreign language, literature, *haiku* (Japanese-style poetry), sculpture, pottery, social dance, and so on for all of the residents. The volunteers are expected to decide the content of the courses, look for instructors through their networks, organize the courses with the instructors, and help in the routine course-related activities, including taking attendance. This sounded to me like an independent, community-oriented, lifelong learning project. "But," Mr. Hasegawa told me, "the municipal government fully funds all of the business operations of SLG. What we are doing in the name of the NPO are social services formerly provided by the municipal government." I was aware that the Japanese Law for the Promotion of Lifelong Learning, enacted in 1990, articulates that both national and municipal governments must support the promotion of lifelong learning. Mr. Hasegawa said that in 1994, the municipal government in downtown Tokyo opened a public facility for promoting lifelong learning in the ward where SLG is currently located. In order to operate the center, the fiscally constrained government, which did not want to spend more money for the social services, decided to ask that course content creation be done by local residents as volunteers. The government initially organized the local volunteers as a citizens' group, and it functioned as a part of the government. Following the enactment of the 1998 NPO Law, the government decided that this citizens' group should apply for NPO status. Lastly, Mr. Hasegawa honestly told me that he was frustrated with the way the government implemented cost-cutting measures in public administration by employing voluntary NPO activities. He wondered if the government had made any serious efforts in reducing the administrative costs, before transferring the business operations to this third-sector organization.

One of the most important revelations in my conversation with Mr. Hasegawa was that SLG had been established by the municipal government, not by a voluntary third sector of the community. "What was the government doing creating a third-sector organization?" I thought to myself when I went back home by train. In my graduate course work, I read a lot of literature on Japanese civil society. Much of the reading focused on the rosy discourse of the emerging Japanese NPO movement. The literature often argued that Japanese society had finally matured through the institutionalization of the NPO since 1998. It stated that Japan has formal, functionally differentiated, and professional nonprofit or third-sector organizations that actively interact with the state and private businesses. (While reading, I was wondering if Japanese society, usually known as having a strong state, could easily have experienced such changes in such a short time.) On the other hand, what I heard today sounded very different from the rosy discourse described in the formal writings. While thinking about my conversation with Mr. Hasegawa, I thought that SLG was indeed a case of the state-led institutionalization of civil society, which was primarily argued in the Japanese civil society literature. The phenomenon itself might be nothing new, but I wanted to know what opinions the grassroots people had to offer about the operation of SLG. I confirmed that my key interest was to go beyond the formal discourse and to study the values and practices expressed and conducted by grassroots people. I thought that SLG would be a great case study for my research.

Later in the day, I sent an e-mail to Mr. Hasegawa saying that I was strongly interested in his organization. I would like to study his organization, since I could share in his frustration, in particular. I wrote to him that I wanted to be involved with his NPO and help initiate some change, if at all possible, through my research involvement. Further, I asked him to accept me as a staff researcher. Of course, I would not expect to be paid.

One week later, I received an offer to act as an unpaid staff researcher at the SLG secretariat. Mr. Hasegawa had negotiated with several directors at SLG and created the position especially for me; I accepted it. I was told that I would be in charge of course planning at SLG and had to be at the office from 9 a.m. to 5:45 p.m. from Monday through Friday and every other Saturday, like other regular staff. I was told that in exchange I would be free to conduct research there. The next day, I visited SLG to submit my curriculum vitae and proof of enrollment at Cornell, upon his request. Thus SLG became the focus of my research.

Knowing My Field Site

I joined SLG in early autumn, one year after its official incorporation as an NPO, and continued my fieldwork from September 2001 to April

2003. I started my research by attending meetings held at SLG and had as many conversations as possible with participants. I also planned lifelong learning courses with the SLG volunteers. As an organizational ethnographer, I understood that the meetings I observed and the stories I heard at SLG would yield significant information about the organizational culture. At the meetings, I observed and collected evidence of basic organizational values, such as dominant rationality, and power relations. Further, I collected stories through open-ended interviews. I usually spoke with people at SLG in informal settings over coffee or drinks. The interviews might be better called informal chats, as we relaxed and enjoyed conversations.

My primary interest at this stage was: Why did these people participate in SLG? How did they feel about their activities? Did they see any difference between the previous citizens' group affiliated with the government and the current NPO style? While continuing to make observations and collect stories, I realized that the volunteers were very frustrated, or even extremely weary, with their environment. Ms. Imai, one of the oldest volunteers in the organization, voiced her concern.

> This organization has become more bureaucratic ever since it got the NPO status. I imagined we would act more actively and freely. However, we cannot. In particular, I even feel that the relationship between volunteers and the secretariat has become rigid. We were more flexible before.

When I spoke to Ms. Tajima, a housewife volunteer, about the difference between the former entity and the current NPO style, she told me this:

> After becoming an NPO . . . everything is driven by a theory of organization. SLG as an organization is the top priority. Many people say, "We have to do this since we are now an NPO." Instead of what we are doing, the organizational form—NPO—seems important. Before becoming an NPO, we really enjoyed discussions. All kinds of decisions were made in free, open forums. Anybody could join the discussions. Now we volunteers are divided, based on our interests, into four divisions, like the course planning division. I am sure it is an easier way to control us in the name of organization. All we often hear now are orders from the SLG president. He said you should do this, and you should do that. . . . We are not his subordinates.[1]

What SLG volunteers complained about most was the inflexible, bureaucratic decision-making style inside the organization, led by the government-appointed president, all of which materialized after SLG changed its organizational style to NPO. The poem, which I introduced in the beginning of this chapter, was part of this story collection. In particular, the volunteers faced certain difficulties due to their confusion under the president, described in the poem as a gardener whose methods led to the garden's ruin.

Even though the SLG volunteers were organized under the NPO rubric, I realized that they did not understand why they were organized this way. Some volunteers even thought that the arrangement of SLG was improper for a third-sector organization. SLG was not a proper NPO because it was organized by the government, not by the spontaneous will of citizens. Further, many volunteers had strongly expected that the transition to the NPO would bring about an organizational structure different from the exiting government and businesses; they felt that the operations of the NPO should be in their hands. Instead, it seemed the organization was becoming increasingly inflexible, isolating its members. In fact, the NPO was ironically run in a more bureaucratic way. They even were annoyed with the term *NPO* and the concept behind it. Many people asked me, "What is an NPO?" Since I was introduced to SLG's volunteers as a researcher in the area of the NPO, I was supposed to know a great deal about NPOs and how they work. Furthermore, there was one point that the volunteers never said but I realized: SLG was even losing sight of *manabi*, or learning—SLG's primary agenda as a provider of lifelong learning opportunities in the local community. I wonder if it is the NPO, or "civil society," that could directly provide "potential spaces both for learning free from domination and also engagement with social change" (Murphy 2001, 347; see also Jarvis 1993 for comprehensive accounts on lifelong learning and civil society). But I did not hear any active discussions on its philosophy of learning from the members. Under such circumstances, several volunteers left SLG due to disillusionment. The remaining volunteers struggled to understand their position in the hasty "NPO-ization" of Japanese society, led by the government.

As a scholar, I believe that Foucault's concept of the technologies of the self—a series of techniques allowing individuals to work on themselves by regulating their bodies, their thoughts, and their conduct—would afford useful insight into how to survive this predicament (Foucault 1988). Technologies of the self are ways of attempting to live the truth, to tell the truth, and to be changed by the truth. One of the important technologies of the self is self-knowledge, or "knowing the self." This concept, which involves self-examination, provides a great hint regarding the enhancement of our social and political life. Foucault emphasizes the need to verbalize one's thoughts as a way of examining and knowing oneself. What we can do, I believe, is generate self-reflective accounts of our actual activities under the framework of the NPO and discuss our future activities among ourselves, while repeating these questions: Why do we participate in these activities? Why do we collaborate with the municipal government? What is our ultimate goal? My hope is that we come to the following realization: we will make an effort to democratize our own NPOs from the inside so that we initiate change by empowering ourselves in opposition to the state's top-down discourse on civil society.

Initiating Collaborative Inquiry

Confronted with this context, I decided to actively employ an AR strategy to address this issue. AR was already embedded as my meta strategy. But from this stage I believe I implemented the strategy in a more direct and specific way. I thought that the current organizational deadlock at SLG stemmed from a lack of self-reflexive evaluation of the organization's activities. I hoped that the AR approach could be useful in resolving this central issue; hopefully, a self-evaluation system would be a good starting point for initiating changes. I thought that creating such a system would require generating a reflexive space in the organization to think about itself and its activities. I was wondering if I could start the evaluation process in the area of course planning instead of broadening the issue within the whole organization. SLG volunteers and I would collaboratively begin to accumulate concrete knowledge and explore solutions on our own. As a researcher, I could provide feedback from the ethnographic data I collected on the organization to help them understand the reality they faced. Although most of the people at SLG had never encountered an anthropologist, I believe they found the evidence I collected on the organization and its needs extremely helpful.

An immediate goal was to establish a collaborative inquiry group made up of SLG members who shared a desire to change this situation while pursuing new possibilities for the organization. For the past three months, I had been establishing solid networks among the volunteers through my involvement. The first person I had in my mind was Mr. Harada, one of the directors in charge of course planning. Mr. Harada, in his fifties, was a professional architect. He was one of the most influential directors at SLG and had a rich background in community development. He also seemed to have a strong sense of SLG's purpose. He had said many times that SLG should offer high-quality, interesting courses to its customers—that is, local residents—and monitor their satisfaction through evaluations. Otherwise, SLG as a business would not meet the need for which it was established.

At the end of November, I went to Mr. Harada's office and honestly and directly expressed my concerns. I told him, "I have observed that many people are frustrated. I was wondering if we could make a more open, diversified discussion space in the organization through the evaluation process. I remember that you mentioned several times the necessity of creating an evaluation system within SLG. I think that would be the first step. That is why I came here today. I would like to participate in evaluation activities as a part of my research activities here at SLG. How about if we create a path to make a breakthrough?" I explained this, drawing a flow of actions of the linear relationship—clarification of problems, the problem-solving process, and then reflective evaluation. While listening to my proposal, Mr. Harada agreed that a bottom-up style of discussion would be interesting. Further, he drew up a more developed cyclic and dynamic diagram to represent his way of thinking. I thought that his diagram was more evolved than mine. It showed a dynamic learning process that was circular, moving through recursive processes of planning, action, and reflection. While drawing the diagram, Mr. Harada said to me, "What we need is more active and positive interactions and reflections among us—volunteers. I want to generate such flows within the organization too."

Mr. Harada and I then started to recruit group members for this evaluation project. We thought that the most crucial point was to diversify the group. Up until this point, I had had many chances to talk to the SLG volunteers about our shared concerns. Among the SLG volunteers, in particular I wanted to invite Mr. Iwata into the group. Over the past months, I had built a strong relationship with him. He was an engineer from western Japan and was around my age. He joined SLG primarily because he wanted to meet people in the community where he now lived. He positively participated in SLG activities; he attended the meetings, planned a couple of courses, and organized an event for children. Through the SLG activities, he got to know local people; he became a member in the local community.

It looked like Mr. Iwata enjoyed the activities, but, on the other hand, I knew he was frustrated with SLG because of its organizational culture—its top-down decision-making style and government-dependent stance. He and I spent a good deal of time exchanging ideas about what we could do to make changes at SLG. In late November, I asked him to come to the secretariat office after he finished his work, and I explained to him what I wanted to do. I mentioned that he often said, "We, as an NPO, could do things in a different way." That night, I said to him, "If you feel frustrated, why don't you initiate change? Let's start something together, instead of just being frustrated." I was sure he could be a key person in the evaluation group, but I observed that he hesitated.

Mr. Iwata said to me, "I am not sure this project will go well; recently, we volunteers have become very tired and have lost motivation and autonomous attitudes, as you know." But, I pushed him to make a positive decision, asking, "Why don't you work with me? I want to offer everything I can. Otherwise, nothing will be changed." He finally said, "Okay, I can work with you. Nothing will be changed without action."

Mr. Harada and I then invited five other volunteers to be the core members of the evaluation group, taking into consideration the balance of gender and age. At the December directors' meeting, Mr. Harada asked the board for approval to set up an evaluation group under his direct supervision. He obtained the board's consent.

Taking Action

Shortly after the evaluation group received the directors' approval, as a facilitator of the group, I started building relationships with its core members through e-mail discussions. I realized it was extremely difficult to get all of the members together in one place at one time, since they were volunteers who were participating in SLG activities during their free time. Thus e-mail was a convenient device to enhance our discussions, and through e-mail discussions, we gradually reconfigured the purpose of the group. We formulated the premise that self-evaluation would improve the planning and offering of the lifelong learning courses, the main business of SLG. By strengthening the foundation, the organization would improve. Thus we started the evaluation process by focusing on the course planning with other volunteers from the course planning division. We also agreed on our strategy: first we would know our current situation—identify problems; second, we would prioritize objectives—which problem should be solved first. We emphasized that we would solve the problems by ourselves, which we believed would lead to empowering ourselves to function better in the current oppressive atmosphere.

It was time to move ahead. A regular meeting of the course-planning division in February was scheduled for that night. As I distributed note-paper and colored markers to the twelve people present, including the core members of the evaluation group and some other volunteers, I said to them, "Write down anything you want to change. Bring to the table the causes of your frustrations. Otherwise, we can't solve anything." At the beginning, it seemed that the volunteers hesitated a little bit. However, after Ms. Kunimatsu, one of the core members of the evaluation group, said, "This is interesting. Hmmm, I can write whatever I want to change," other volunteers gradually participated in this process. The participants appeared to enjoy the process, changing the color of the markers they used every so often. Surprisingly, in fifteen minutes, we had collected more than fifty pieces of notepaper from the attendants. We divided them into various topics, such as items related to course planning, volunteers themselves, directors, the secretariat, and so on.

In the next meeting, ten days later, we classified all of the problems that the volunteers wanted to solve. Based on their interests and their areas of expertise, they formed smalls groups. For example, volunteers interested in setting a mission for course planning next year comprised one group; those who had accounting backgrounds formed a group to work on the budget for the next year. We agreed that each group was expected to analyze the problem, identify the cause, and write a proposal on how to improve the situation.

From March to July, I facilitated monthly meetings to address the problem-solving process. I also attended the subgroup meetings as much

Picture 7.1 A discussion scene in the collaborative inquiry

as possible and helped the subgroup write a proposal and present the material. This collaboration was a highlight of my fieldwork experience. I felt that it was a joint learning exercise among us—not just a problem-solving process but a meaning-making process, one in which we discovered ourselves. These activities reflected our sincere wishes for SLG; they were not just a process to resolve frustration. We confirmed to each other why we were here and why we participated in SLG, although our reasons varied. Mr. Iwata was looking for friends in the local community; Ms. Tajima wanted to use her free time for the good of the community; Ms. Andō wanted to learn about her own community through planning literature and history courses related to the community; and I was doing research on the Japanese NPO but wanted to improve the organizational situation by my research involvement. Despite the different motivations, each person shared a common interest in doing something positive for the local community. The SLG activities were not only for the local residents but also for us. The activities would enhance our own quality of life, and we wanted to enjoy the activities.

After five months, we had a reflection session. We confirmed what we tried and achieved. I asked the participants of the evaluation process whether they wanted to continue this problem-solving process. Ms. Andō said, "I want to repeat this process. If we stop at this level, we will have frustration again. I am sure that we are moving ahead through this process." "I don't want to postpone dealing with problems either. We need to do it again," Ms. Murase added. We thus started another cycle of the problem-solving process. Meanwhile, the government-appointed president of SLG was aware of this activity. Although he did not express any interest in participating in this process, he watched from a distance and seemed bothered by it. As the process went on, he would not even make eye contact with Mr. Iwata or me. He finally directly intervened in my research.

My Positionality

Being an action-oriented researcher is overtly political, and surviving organizational politics is a key issue in this approach. Apparently some people had difficulty understanding my active stance as a researcher. They expected me to be a conventional researcher who collected data but did not participate in the activities of the subject being researched. I was just expected to be a silent observer. One experience I had in my field site drove this point home. That was a conflict with Mr. Nakamoto, the president of SLG. Here is an excerpt from my field notes.

Field Notes 90
Name: Am I being blackballed?
File Number: 060302

This afternoon I was told by Mr. Kuroda, general secretary of
SLG, that Mr. Nakamoto said that I am no longer allowed to
attend a monthly strategic meeting, which I had been attending from last October to June. Some board members, including
the president, vice presidents, the director in charge of course
planning, and the director of recruiting and training, had been
attending the meetings. I had been allowed to attend as a staff
researcher of the secretariat. I deemed the meetings to be a
crucial part of my fieldwork because I could observe active
interaction among the members who take initiatives in SLG
management. As the board of directors was not functioning
well at SLG due partly to its big size, the strategic meetings
had become a significant place for making decisions.

As a reason for my "exclusion" (I was surprised that
some people used this term to describe my situation) from
the meetings, Mr. Kuroda said that the next meeting was going to deal with an entrustment contract with the municipal
government. Mr. Kuroda said, according to Mr. Nakamoto,
"It should be a secret meeting because it deals with how SLG
talks to the government. The content of the meeting must not
be leaked. Thus Mr. Tanase from the government would not
be allowed to attend the meeting either."

I was very upset by this decision. I had never disrupted
the meetings. I was only an active listener. Sometimes, some
members asked me to make comments. Only in those cases
did I say something. I have no idea what I should do as a
researcher. Later that afternoon, I had a chance to talk to Mr.
Aota, vice president of SLG. He already knew that I would
be "excluded" from the meeting. He was also upset. I asked
him, "Was there any discussion about my position in the
meeting among the members?" He said, "No. We didn't have
any discussion about this decision. Mr. Nakamoto made the
decision by himself. I don't understand why you are not allowed to attend the meeting. A possible reason I can guess
is that you presented some questions at the annual general
meeting in mid-May. One question was exactly a point that
Mr. Nakamoto did not want to touch upon. He is scared
of you."

Showing me the agenda for the next strategic meeting, which Mr. Nakamoto had faxed to him, Mr. Aota continued, "Now nobody controls him, even the municipal government that assigned him as president of SLG. See this agenda. It portrays a one-man style of management just as medium/small-sized companies have. All decision making is concentrated around Mr. Nakamoto.

The agenda even mentions expanding the SLG president's term of office. He seems to have misunderstood his position. He is parading around like the emperor with his new clothes."

I was thinking that this kind of situation might happen some day. However, I never expected somebody to be offended by my research activities in such an unconcealed way. Facing this situation, I was mainly concerned about keeping my position at SLG, primarily because of my commitment to the volunteers' cause, and also because of continuing my dissertation fieldwork. My collaborative involvement in the evaluation group had just begun. My mission of action was not completed yet. Also, I could not leave SLG at this stage, since I wanted to know more about this NPO as a research subject.

I asked the general secretary if I could attend the meeting, while reiterating my research purpose. He gave me permission to attend and said that I was under his direct control as a secretariat staff member. On the next Monday night, the strategic meeting was held. Mr. Tanase, an official from the municipal government, did not appear at the meeting. The discussion was primarily about how to deal with the negotiation of an entrustment contract between the municipal government and SLG. During the meeting, Mr. Nakamoto proposed creating another committee to prepare the negotiations. The committee was to be organized by the SLG president, three vice presidents, the general secretary, the vice general secretary, and two more directors; he excluded me from this group. At that time, I asked Mr. Nakamoto, "I would like to attend the meetings as an observer. May I?" He promptly said, "Of course not." There was no explanation.

I was doubly shocked. First, I was surprised at the fact that the new meeting would be organized by just excluding me from the list of current members. Second, I was dumbfounded by the fact that my request was turned down so quickly, with a sharp "no" in a public discussion. I had never experienced this kind of reproach. Furthermore, I was not given a chance to reply to him. Others in attendance also said nothing. The way I had understood it was that all meetings at SLG should be open, as it was an organization operated by volunteers, and most of its funding came from taxpayers via the municipal government.

The next morning I faxed Mr. Nakamoto in order to clarify my purpose of research at SLG. I wrote to him, "I am doing research on the Japanese NPO. SLG is a case. But I do not intend to just observe as a researcher. Since I am here, I want to be involved with activities as much as possible. You might not accept a researcher like me. No, I am not a conventional researcher. In a sense, I test a research style. Through my research involvement, I want to improve the situation I observe and experience. I test my own possibilities about whether I can do something to improve the situation for the people with whom I work. This is an action I am taking not only as a scholar but also as a citizen. I am testing what it means to be here." With some help from the general secretary in negotiating with Mr. Nakamoto about my further involvement, I was in the end allowed to attend the meetings. After this experience, I tried to speak up clearly about my research stance whenever I had the chance. In so doing, SLG volunteers and I also confirmed the meaning of my involvement with SLG activities. Meanwhile, Mr. Nakamoto never spoke to me again.

During my fieldwork I was always thinking about my positionality in this field site. "Who am I in this organization? What kind of role am I expected to play? How do I define myself? I am a doctoral researcher from an American university," I told myself, "but I am also a secretariat staff member at my field site." Even though I was from an American university, I was not just a "visiting" researcher. I was not a journalist—as I had been in my previous job—just reporting on incidents happening in front of me, nor did I write newspaper articles only based on interviews. I was a Japanese anthropologist doing research on his own society. I always confirmed myself like this: "Thanks to this AR strategy, I believe I can be involved with making positive changes happen at my field site instead of just formulating arguments from afar (like an armchair theorist). By actively participating, I can generate small but solid moves with people at the grassroots level to affect positive outcomes with regard to the state's effort to institutionalize civil society." I also strongly believe that there was a crucial responsibility I had to take in doing this type of research as a native anthropologist. I must write this ethnography in Japanese if I am to label myself as a native anthropologist doing research on his own society, and I have gradually started publishing my narratives in Japanese (Ogawa 2005, 2006b, 2007a, 2007b). Without assigning myself this project, I cannot share the knowledge represented in my ethnography with my grassroots research collaborators.[2]

Now, as I finish my fieldwork, I believe my research results will, more or less, meet my expectations. It became possible to build collaborative research relationships with people at the grassroots level. In fact, what I actually did in this research was to help empower ordinary people and to forward the democratization of my field site NPO by practicing action-oriented social research. In one sense, achieving these results, or at least discovering whether I could, was my research. I tried to facilitate moves that the grassroots volunteers in my field site could use by themselves and for their activities, as a gardener waters flowers for them to freely grow. I wanted people in my field site to have a chance to speak up and empower themselves. Further, I believe that the knowledge I generated on the Japanese NPO under the AR strategy will definitely contribute to the overall academic scholarship on Japanese civil society. I believe research should explore the meaning of civil society not by examining the stated ideas by a small number of elites and leaders but by participating with ordinary, grassroots members of it in the construction of their social and political life.

My hope is that when I am able to return in the near future, the evaluation process we started collaboratively will have taken root, giving the people at SLG more colorful flowers within their beautiful stone walls. I was there to act with them. We initiated a spark of change.

Appendix 1

Courses Offered at SLG from Fall 2001 to Summer 2003

Kawazoe Studies	Shrines in Kawazoe	Fall 2001
	Traditional Crafts: Making Eraser Seals	Fall 2001
	Traditional Crafts: Aizome	Fall 2001
	Traditional Crafts: Wood Sculptures	Fall 2001
	Traditional Crafts: Leather Goods	Spring 2002
	History of Bridges over River Sumida	Spring 2002
	Experiencing Ryōtei	Fall 2002 & Spring 2002
	Tourist Guides in Kawazoe	Fall 2002
	Traditional Crafts: Edo Komon	Fall 2002
	Traditional Crafts: New Year Decorations	Fall 2002
	Exploring Kawazoe, My Own Town	Fall 2002 & Spring 2003
	History of Tokyo Bay	Spring 2003
	Traditional Crafts: Byōbu	Spring 2003
Career Development	Introduction to PC (for Northern area residents)	Every Semester
	Introduction to PC (for Southern area residents)	Every Semester
	Introductory Word and Excel	Every Semester
	Consumer Law	Fall 2001
	Advanced Excel	Spring 2002
	Studying for Kanji Certificate Level 2-4	Spring 2002
	Bookkeeping Certificate 3rd Level	Fall 2002 & Spring 2003
	Self-Expression Seminar	Fall 2002
	Color Coordination Seminar	Fall 2002
	TOEIC 470	Fall 2002

	Second-Life Seminar	Fall 2002
	Applying Makeup (for New Graduates)	Winter 2003
	Bookkeeping Certificate 2nd Level	Spring 2003
Languages	English Conversation (Elementary)	Every Semester
	English Conversation (Intermediate)	Every Semester
	Japanese for Foreigners	Every Semester
	Chinese Conversation (Elementary)	Fall 2001 & Spring 2002
	Business English	Fall 2001
	French for Travelers	Fall 2002
	Elementary Korean	Fall 2002
	Chinese Conversation (Intermediate)	Fall 2002
	Advanced Japanese for Foreigners	Fall 2002, Winter 2003, & Summer 2003
	English Conversation (Advanced)	Fall 2002 & Spring 2003
	Chinese (College Level)	2003
	Reading Harry Potter	Spring 2003
	TOEIC Bridge Test	Spring 2003
Kids	English for Kids	Every Semester
	Rhythmics (~ 2 years old)	Every Semester
	Rhythmics (2 years old ~)	Every Semester
	Cake Making	Fall 2001
	Storytelling for Children	Fall 2001
	Enjoy Drawing	Spring 2002
	Ceramic Art for Kids	Summer 2002
	Japanese Art for Kids	Summer 2002
	Making Animals with Origami	Summer 2002
	Making Illustrated Books	Summer 2002 & Spring 2003
	Terra Cotta	Fall 2002
	Making Kaleidoscopes	Summer 2003
	Making Clocks	Summer 2003
	Making Windmills with Pet Bottles	Summer 2003
Liberal Arts	Europe: Travelers' Experiences	Fall 2001
	China: Introduction	Fall 2001
	Autobiographies	Fall 2001

	Japanese Literature: Heike Monogatari	Fall 2001
	Italy: Travelers' Experiences	Winter 2002
	Japanese Cultural History	Spring 2002
	Eki: Traditional Oriental Fortune-Telling	Spring 2002
	Japanese Literature: Mori Ogai	Spring 2002
	Psychology of Juvenile Delinquency	Spring 2002
	Music: Introduction to Orchestra	Spring 2002 & Spring 2003
	History & People in the Middle East	Spring 2002
	Music: Introduction to Orchestra II	Summer 2002
	Japanese Literature: Ise Monogatari	Fall 2002
	Ethics: Introduction	Fall 2002
	History: Japanese Ancient History	Fall 2002
	History: Japanese Fortune-Telling	Fall 2002
	Japanese Literature: Higuchi Ichiyou	Fall 2002
	Japanese Poem: Tanka	Fall 2002
	History: Japanese Ancient History II	Winter 2003
	China: Travelers' Experiences	Spring 2003
	Japanese Culture: Takehisa Yumeji	Spring 2003
	Japanese Poem: Senryū	Spring 2003
	Art History: Olser Museum	Spring 2003
Hobbies	Ceramic Arts (Elementary)	Every Semester
	Ceramic Arts (Intermediate)	Every Semester
	Ceramic Arts (Advanced)	Every Spring
	Drawing: Spring Flowers	Fall 2001, Spring 2002, & Spring 2003
	Drawing: Japanese Art	Fall 2001
	Musical Instrument: Okarina	Fall 2001
	Musical Instrument: Harmonica	Fall 2001
	Music: Tango	Fall 2001
	Magic	Fall 2001
	Japanese Paper Crafts	Fall 2001
	Wood Seal Making	Fall 2001
	Reading-Aloud Drama	Fall 2001
	Food: Japanese Tea	Fall 2001
	Food: Wine	Fall 2001
	Food: Herb	Fall 2001
	Food: Making Miso	Winter 2002
	Traditional Folk Instrument: Nankin-tamasudare	Winter 2002

Music: Japanese Songs	Winter 2002
Silver Clay	Winter 2002, Fall 2002, & Winter 2003
Drawing: Pastel	Spring 2002
Drawing: Faces of Buddha	Spring 2002 & Fall 2002
Let's Enjoy Gospel	Spring 2002
Singing Chanson	Spring 2002
Kimono Making	Spring 2002
Musical Instrument: Taiko (Zenidaiko)	Spring 2002 & Spring 2003
Kimono: How to Wear Kimono	Spring 2002
Flower Arrangement	Spring 2002
Pantomime	Spring 2002
Let's Play Igo	Spring 2002
Photography Techniques I	Spring 2002
Tarot	Spring 2002
Drawing: Introduction	Summer 2002
Drawing: Contemporary Art	Fall 2002
Calligraphy	Fall 2002
Japanese Folk Songs: Minyō	Fall 2002 & Spring 2003
Musical Instrument: Taiko (Wadaiko)	Fall 2002
Musical Instrument: Ukelele	Fall 2002
Food: English Tea	Fall 2002
Making Accessories with Old Clothes	Fall 2002
Chinese Embroidery	Fall 2002
Oshibana (Flower Pressing)	Fall 2002
Food: Cooking for Men	Winter 2002
Food: Cheese and Wine	Winter 2003
Ceramic Arts: Coffee Cups	Winter 2003
Origami: Sakuradama	Winter 2003
Drawing: Still Life	Spring 2003
Let's Sing Pops	Spring 2003
Making Kaleidoscopes	Spring 2003
Japanese Patchwork	Spring 2003
Food: Chinese Tea	Spring 2003
Food: Herb Spice	Spring 2003
Food: Soba	Spring 2003
Making Accessories by Beads	Spring 2003
Photography Techniques II	Spring 2003
Japanese Traditional Music: Dodoitsu	Spring 2003

Sports & Refreshment	Kikø (Chinese Deep Breathing Technique)	Fall 2001
	Tap Dance	Fall 2001 & Fall 2002
	Shigin (Recitation of a Chinese Poem)	Fall 2001
	Walking	Fall 2001
	Taikyokuken (Chinese Shadow Boxing)	Fall 2001
	Fitness	Fall 2001
	Goshin-bics (Self-Defense Techniques)	Winter 2002
	Jogging	Winter 2002
	Aqua Walking (daytime)	Spring 2002
	Aqua Walking (nighttime)	Spring 2002
	Stretching	Spring 2002
	Easy Exercise	Fall 2002
	Massage	Spring 2003
Special Events/ Lectures	Learning and Community	Fall 2001
	Life in Shitamachi	Fall 2001
	Noguchi Ken: Alpinist's Dream	Winter 2002
	Culture and Traditional Crafts	Spring 2002
	Storytelling by Shimoda Kageki	Fall 2002
	What Is Volunteering?: Supporting Each Other	Spring 2003
	Learning and Traditional Crafts	Spring 2003
	Summer Festival for Kids	Every Summer

Appendix 2

Government Proposal toward "NPO-ization"

1. From Volunteers' Groups to NPOs

(1) The Importance of NPOs

Recently, various kinds of citizens' activities at NPOs have been promoted in this country. The activities include social welfare, lifelong learning, culture, arts, sports, environment protection, international exchange, and community development. After the Great Hanshin-Awaji Earthquake in January 1995, we Japanese were impressed with the fact that more than 1 million volunteers across the country participated in relief efforts after the disaster. One of the reasons why the activities were successful was that citizens' groups in that region organized the volunteers, establishing a system to work effectively.

(2) The Government and NPOs

In this country, we believe that solving social problems is a mission of the government. We believe that social services should be provided by the government. Social services have been based on key political principles of equality and fairness, however, it is doubtful nowadays that social services are responding to complicated new social problems and the diversified values of citizens. The government was expected to respond to such problems and values in a prompt manner and on an individual basis, however, if the government does this, its costs will increase.

On the other hand, NPOs make it possible to respond to such problems promptly and individually, taking advantage of volunteers and their contributions, meanwhile achieving cost cutting to the government by providing the services. Social activities generated by NPOs, whatever they are, will make people realize the importance of independent, spontaneous activities for human beings and society. The expected role of NPOs will further increase in the twenty-first century, when the government tightens its budget.

The practical social function of the organization is to provide social services by citizens. However, NPOs are not meant to be subcontractors of the government, nor cheap service providers. We realize that NPOs organized by citizens are in charge of producing highly valuable social services by themselves. NPOs are expected to play key roles in changing the social structure of Japanese society from being government centered to citizen centered.

The relationship between the government and NPOs is complementary. Both the government and NPOs are expected to respond to various social needs while making use of their characteristics. NPOs have strong images of providing nonprofit, volunteer-based social activities. At the same time, NPOs have an economic function. They are expected to generate employment in local communities.

2. The Meaning of Incorporation as an NPO

(1) The Institutionalization of the NPO Law

Citizens' groups without incorporation often have faced some difficulties in their activities due to a lack of legal status. In order to improve this situation, the Law to Promote Specified Nonprofit Activities (the so-called NPO Law) was established in March 1998. (The actual enforcement date was December 1998.) The law aims to facilitate activities that positively contribute to public welfare in society and give status as an NPO to informal, not-for-profit citizens' groups.

The First Article of the NPO Law clearly states:

> The purpose of this law is to promote the sound development of specified nonprofit activities in the form of volunteer and other activities freely performed by citizens to benefit society, through such measures as the provision of corporate status to organizations that undertake specified nonprofit activities, and thereby to contribute to advancement of the public welfare.[1]

When a citizen's group receives NPO status, the group is recognized as a legal entity. It can enter into contracts with others, open bank accounts, and register real estate under the name of the NPO. Moreover, the group can enhance social trust because it is required to disclose information based on the NPO Law.

(2) Lifelong learning activities must be in line with the NPO Law.

In the NPO Law, twelve areas, including social welfare, social education, and community development, are mentioned. Promoting lifelong learning can surely be categorized as social education. Lifelong learning activities promoted by local residents provide learning opportunities as one of the basic social services and contribute to the development of lifelong learning in the local community. They offer independent, spontaneous learning activities that contribute to the betterment of society, deserving of NPO status. By achieving NPO status, the group can expand its activities. This also will make it possible to form collaborative relationships with the government and other private sector companies as an equal partner.

3. The Agenda for Incorporation
(1) The need to strengthen organizational power as a business entity
The current citizens' group heavily depends on the government, for example, it lacks management skills. For this group to become a continuous and professional lifelong learning service provider in the local community, it is necessary to make solid articles of association as an independent organization. NPO status will show that the organization is dedicated to operating lifelong learning services as a business. The ultimate purpose as a lifelong learning NPO is to plan and offer lifelong learning courses, tailored to the residents' needs. To achieve this purpose, the group needs to secure human and financial resources, supported by public relations activities. As an incorporated entity, management's ability to pursue efficiency is strongly enhanced.

(2) The need to secure human resources for NPO operation
The group needs to secure persons who have strong abilities in strategic management and financial affairs. We believe that qualifications for personnel under an NPO are similar to those in for-profit businesses. People are expected to work effectively based on a business plan. Teamwork also is highly valued. People should be self-starters.

In the main business of lifelong learning course offerings, the current group is too dependent on individual voluntary minds. To operate the business as an NPO, the group is expected to create a shared vision among volunteers. At the same time, volunteers are expected to be trained in how to design organizations and how to operate organizations effectively. The group needs to think about hiring paid staff to operate the group as an NPO from a professional business perspective, while keeping the resident-volunteers strong promoters of lifelong learning activities in the community.

(3) The need to secure stable financial resources
Even though NPOs are not-for-profit organizations, they can make money, although profits are not to be distributed among NPO members. Even though they are not-for-profit, operating costs such as personnel

expenses are incurred. Currently, the government provides money to a group as aid. When a group receives NPO status, it needs to solidify its financial backing in multiple ways. One way would be to enter into a contract with the government. Another way would be to collect donations from for-profit businesses. It also is reasonable to step into new businesses to secure stable financial resources.

We strongly expect that the current group will receive NPO status in the near future and will further contribute to developing lifelong learning activities in Kawazoe as a professional service provider.

Appendix 3

Content of Entrustment

1. Collecting the rental fee for the Lifelong Learning Center facilities
2. Maintaining the LifeLong Learning Center facilities
3. Maintaining the grounds around the LifeLong Learning Center
4. Collecting the rental fee for the public facilities below
   - municipal sanatorium
   - municipal parks
   - municipal gymnasiums
   - municipal athletic field
   - municipal theater hall
   - municipal social welfare facilities
   - municipal women's participation promotion center
   - municipal industrial center
   - municipal medium-size company support center
   - municipal indoor pool
   - municipal sports center
   - municipal home economics center
   - municipal community center
5. Administrative works of the facilities mentioned above, which the mayor designates
6. Supplying the collected fee to the government by the fifth day of every month

Specific Items of Facility Management of the Lifelong Learning Center Main Hall
1. Entrance Hall (every day 9:00–21:00)
   - reception to visitors
   - provide information on the center
   - telephone handling
   - making daily reports to the government

2. Renting the facilities (every day 9:00–21:00)
   - accepting reservation for the facilities
   - manipulating the facility terminal
   - collecting the rental fee
   - delivering the facility keys
3. Music Studio, Audiovisual Studio, Recording Room
   (Monday through Friday 17:00–21:00; Saturday, Sunday, and
   holidays 9:00–21:00)
   - helping to find audiovisual materials
   - renting out the audiovisual equipment
   - instructing on the use of the facilities
   - maintaining the facilities
4. Security
   - leading evacuations in the case of an emergency
   - guiding to a parking lot at night
   - restraining prohibited activities
   - checking on security of rooms, plaza, and terrace
   - notifying the government of broken or damaged parts of the center
   - controlling Lost and Found
   - finding and doing appropriate response to suspicious persons
     and goods
   - preventing dangerous activities which would damage the center
     facilities
   - locking and unlocking all of the room doors and emergency
     doors
   - locking and unlocking the main entrance
   - safekeeping and delivering the keys
   - setting the automatic security system
   - securing security for visitors and all facility users
   - presenting when renting out and returning the center equipment
   - preventing demonstrations or appeal activities in/around the
     center
   - maintaining an area for parking bicycles
5. Fire prevention
   - checking fire prevention equipment—monthly and annually—
     asking specialists
   - checking the smoke extraction apparatuses and the fire doors
   - preventing fire in the smoking corner
6. Utilities (Electricity, Gas, and Water)
   - doing daily maintenance, including turning off the lights
   - testing the electricity breakers regularly

- checking the electricity equipment—monthly and annually—asking specialists
- maintaining the electricity equipment through the remote watching system
- responding appropriately to emergencies
- maintaining the elevators
- maintaining the parking meter equipment in the parking lot
- maintaining the air conditioning system—three times a year
- checking the water system—asking specialists

7. Cleaning
   - cleaning daily
   - having professionals clean monthly

Annex
Same Requirements as the Main Hall

Notes

Chapter 1

1. NPOs are scattered across Japan (Cabinet Office 2007b, 2007d), however, they are most heavily concentrated in three areas with great population density: the Tokyo metropolitan area (Tokyo, Kanagawa, Chiba, and Saitama), the Kansai area (Osaka, Kyoto, and Hyogo), and the Chukyō area (Aichi, Gifu, and Mie). Among the 31,115 NPOs in existence as of March 31, 2007, 15,588, or 50.1 percent of the total, are located in Japanese metropolises (2007d).

2. I use the term *third sector*, which is typically referred to as the nonprofit sector in the United States (see DiMaggio and Anheier 1990; Himmelstein 1993; Anheier 1995). Third sector designates "all organizations which are neither profit-oriented businesses nor governmental agencies or bureaucracies" (Seibel and Anheier 1990, 7). Further, according to Gidron et al. (1992, 3–4), what distinguishes these organizations is that they are constitutionally separate from government, are not primarily commercial or profit seeking in purpose (even though they may earn profits that are plowed back into the primary mission of the agency), have their own procedures for self-government, and serve some public purpose. The organizations include services such as health, education, arts, and culture, but others have an essentially representational role, such as advocacy. In Japanese, there is a direct translation for "third sector": *daisan sekutā*. However, this term refers to corporations established through joint investments of the government and for-profit businesses. In the present context, I am referring to the common Western usage, not to the Japanese term.

3. Permission (*kyoka*) entails significant bureaucratic discretion. This is used for public interest corporations created by special laws. Meanwhile, approval (*ninka*) is used for incorporated associations and foundations. In practice, it can approximate *kyoka*, but there is, technically, less bureaucratic discretion involved in the former term. Recognition (*ninshō*) is a term for which there is no discretion. This last administrative technique is used for NPO.

4. Nowadays, however, a reform of public interest corporations is taking place in Japanese society. As of December 2008, people can set up a general incorporated association (*ippan shadan hōjin*) or a general incorporated foundation *(ippan zaidan hōjin)* simply through registration (*tōki*) at the Legal Affairs Bureau (*hōmukyoku*). No approval or permission by central or local government

217

is necessary. Further, a general incorporated association or foundation can apply for charitable status. For more details, see Japan Association of Charitable Organizations (2006).

5. Permissible NPO activities include the following: (1) promotion of health, medical treatment, or welfare; (2) promotion of social education; (3) promotion of community development; (4) promotion of science, culture, the arts, or sports; (5) conservation of the environment; (6) disaster relief; (7) promotion of community safety; (8) protection of human rights or promotion of peace; (9) international cooperation; (10) promotion of a society with equal gender participation; (11) sound nurturing of children; (12) development of information technology; (13) promotion of science and technology; (14) promotion of economic activities; (15) development of vocational expertise or expansion of employment opportunities; (16) protection of consumers; and (17) administration of organizations that engage in the aforementioned activities or provide liaison, advice, or assistance in connection to these activities.

6. As of March 31, 2007, 32,552 groups had applied for NPO status. Among these applications, only 379 were rejected. At this point, 31,115 NPOs have been incorporated, 1,202 NPOs have been dissolved, and 129 NPOs have been forced to dissolve by the government (Cabinet Office 2007d).

7. I referred to "Concept and History of Civil Society" by H. Islamoglu in the *International Encyclopedia of the Social and Behavioral Sciences*, pp. 1,891–97.

8. Hemment (2000, 2004), who studied postsocialist civil society in Russia, and LeBlanc (1999), who analyzed women's roles in the Japanese political arena, pointed out the same advantage of analysis in ethnography.

Chapter 2

1. The *Nihon Keizai Shimbun* (September 16, 1985) reported that the term was intentionally designed by local government officials to enhance the image of this district.

2. According to the 2005 issue of the *Annual Report on the Aging Society* (Cabinet Office 2005a), among the total population of 127.69 million, the number of elderly persons age sixty-five and older had reached a new high of 24.88 million. The percentage of the elderly to the total population increased to 19.5 percent.

3. *Chōkai* has been a popular research topic for scholars for decades. For example, urban sociologists such as Okui (1940), who was influenced by the Chicago school of sociology, conducted research on *chōkai* and concluded that these networks are typical of feudalistic Japan. Bestor (1989) analyzed *chōkai* as a key social institution that produces and reproduces traditionalism as an important process sustaining contemporary Japanese patterns of social organization. The role of *chōkai* was reexamined after Japan achieved high economic growth during the late 1970s. Iwasaki et al. (1989) focused on the positive role that *chōkai* networks played as the center of residents' movements against environmental pollution. On the description in this ethnography, I also referred to the section on associational activities in the local history book (SWG 1978a, 351–80), as well

as data generated from informal conversations with *chōkai* members. Among others, Kurasawa and Akimoto (1990) and Pekkanen (2004b) provide comprehensive accounts of *chōkai*.

4. Amano (2005) provides a rich introduction to a variety of citizens' groups in Japan, locating their activities in the historical development of the post-World War II era.

5. Most of the Japanese shrines are members of the association, but there are some exceptions; major shrines, such as Yasukuni Shrine and Meiji Shrine in Tokyo, were not members as of October 2006.

6. My argument on social capital was especially inspired by Greenwood (2002) and papers presented at the workshop on social capital, held at Cornell University in collaboration with the University of Turin, September 12–14, 2002. Some of the presented papers were compiled in *Social Epistemology* 17:4 (2003).

Chapter 3

1. Many terms have been used to refer to lifelong learning, such as *social education, continuing education, adult education, recurrent education, lifelong education,* and *community education*. Social education (*shakai kyōiku*) encompasses organized educational activities (including those for physical education and recreation) for adults and young people other than those provided in the curriculum of elementary and secondary schools or at institutions of higher education, according to Article II of the 1949 Social Education Law. This term was used from the late 1940s to the mid-1980s to describe adult education activities. During this period, the Faure Commission Report, *Learning to Be,* led by Edger Faure (Faure et al. 1972) of the International Commission on the Development of Education of UNESCO, was influential. The term *lifelong education (shōgai kyōiku)* was then introduced in the 1981 report submitted by the Central Council for Education, which expressed that learning was to be based on individual voluntary will, with individuals allowed to choose measures and ways to learn when they felt it necessary to do so (Central Council for Education 1981). Meanwhile, the term *lifelong learning (shōgai gakushū)* was gaining in popularity due to its broadness of meaning. Lifelong learning encompasses learning that takes place at all stages of life. It includes both formal learning at school and other places and nonformal learning; consequently, it includes all types of social education activities. These activities may be carried out at companies, formal schools, community centers, libraries, museums, or other facilities. In 1989, the Social Education Division of the Ministry of Education changed its name to the Lifelong Learning Division, thus in this book I primarily use the term *lifelong learning*.

2. Donations are not popular practice in Japanese society. According to a household economies survey made by the Ministry of Internal Affairs and Communications (MIAC 2004), the average annual donation per household was 3,224 yen (approximately $28) in 2004. This amount was up by 430 yen ($4) compared to the previous year and returned to the 3, 000 yen ($26) level for the first time

in four years. The highest amount was 5,834 yen ($54) in 1995, when the Great Hanshin-Awaji Earthquake occurred. The rise in the average donation could be attributed to the donations to those who suffered from a series of typhoons and earthquakes in the fall of that year, since the giving was concentrated in October, November, and December, according to the survey.

3. I referred to "Forty-seven Ronin" in the *Columbia Encyclopedia,* 6th ed.

4. When it was first put into effect on December 1, 1998, the law defined only twelve areas. On May 1, 2003, five newly defined areas were added, including the development of information technology, the promotion of science and technology, the promotion of economic activities, the development of vocational expertise or the expansion of employment opportunities, and the protection of consumers.

5. The names of volunteers and committee members are not available in the meeting records, thus I have simply identified speakers by their titles.

Chapter 4

1. I use the term *subject* in a Foucauldian sense, where human beings are transformed into subjects by different modes of objectification. See Foucault 2003.

2. I use this term *individualization* in line with Ulrich Beck's definition (1994, 13). He writes, " 'Individuation' means, first, the disembedding and, second, the re-embedding of industrial society ways of life by new ones, in which . . . individuals must produce, stage and cobble together their biographies themselves. Thus, the name 'individualization.' "

3. The Fundamental Law of Education was created in 1947. There were four attempts to revise the law prior to November 2001. The first one was in February 1956 by Education Minister Kiyose Ichiro. The second one was in August 1960 by Education Minister Araki Masuo. In 1984, the Ad Hoc Council on Education was organized under Prime Minister Nakasone Yasuhiro. It was this council that actually formed the foundation of the current education reform policy. Under the administration of Prime Minister Obuchi Keizo and Mori Yoshiro in the late 1990s, the National Commission on Educational Reform, a private advisory body for the prime minister, urged the government to review the basic education law and adapt Japan's educational agenda to better meet international needs. The council recommended that Japanese schools reiterate traditional values, reaffirming Japanese culture and community. One of the key points in the recommendation was that all schoolchildren perform community service, which was deemed coercive and compulsory. Education Minister Tōyama then ordered the Central Council for Education to take into account the recommendations made by the National Commission on Education Reform. In fact, a current review of the law gained momentum after being recommended by the final report of the National Commission on Educational Reform in 2000.

4. Although at this point, July 2002, when this proposal was presented, the term *New Public* was not officially introduced, the concept can be seen in

the content of the report. The term first officially appeared in the 2003 report by the Central Council for Education.

Chapter 5

1. I believe in this context Koizumi intends to mean, by the term *min*, an arena that is not associated with the government. Koizumi's usage of *min* broadly includes both for-profit and non-profit businesses, attempting to flexibly and dynamically transfer government's businesses to other sectors. In addition to the direct translation of the word—private—I thus also use the term *third sector*. My usage of this term is in line with a definition made by Seibel and Anheier (1990, 7), that "[t]hird sector" was intended to express an alternative to the disadvantages associated with both profit maximization and bureaucracy by combining the flexibility and efficiency of markets with the equity and predictability of public bureaucracy. Koizumi reiterated this political stance in the policy speech at the regular Diet sessions during his tenure (see, for example, *Nihon Keizai Shimbun*, January 31, 2003).

2. *Nikkei sangyō shōhi kenkyūjo*, a think tank affiliated with the *Nihon Keizai Shimbun* newspaper, conducted a survey on Private Finance Initiatives (PFI) in local governments, including forty-seven prefectures and 700 municipal governments, from March to May 2003. According to the survey, 9.5 percent of the governments, including eighteen prefectural and fifty-three municipal governments, had already introduced the policy. Just over 50 percent, including twenty-six prefectural and 361 municipal governments, were considering implementing the policy. Their primary interests included the areas of garbage recycling, lifelong learning, and social work. Some forty-four prefectures said that the policy was effective in cutting the budget and enhancing the efficiency of public administration (*Nihon Keizai Shimbun*, June 16, 2003).

Chapter 6

1. In the debates over Japanese capitalism, this group of Marxist social scientists argued that the Meiji Restoration of 1868 ushered in an "absolutist" imperial regime whose social foundation was a "semi-feudal" peasantry. In dissent, the so-called Worker-Farmer Faction, or *Rōnō-ha*, contended that, while pusillanimous, Japan's bourgeoisie had in fact triumphed in 1868, and the Meiji regime rested on a properly capitalist, albeit backward, foundation. From this perspective, it might be said that for the *Kōza-ha*, Japan was a nation of subjects, while for the *Rōnō-ha*, it was already, incipiently, a society of citizens.

2. See Irokawa (1988) for an overview of Japanese social movements. The article provides a comprehensive account of the development of social movements in Japan since the Meiji era. In addition, Ishida (1984) argues the emergence of *shimin* in the citizens' movements during the early postwar period.

3. Studies in English on the new social movements in Japan include Packard (1966), McCormack (1971), Krauss (1974), Koschmann (1978), Krauss et al. (1984), Steinhoff (1989), and Kersten and Williams (2006).

4. The article, *"Tasai na hito ga irukara"* [Because There Are Various Kinds of People . . .], appeared in the *Asahi Shimbun* on November 12, 2002.

5. The similar phenomenon is reported by Theiss and Hibbing (2005) in the U.S. context.

6. The major figures of the scholars' groups are Fujioka Nobukatsu, a professor at Takushoku University, Nishio Kanji, a professor emeritus at the University of Electro-Communication, and Yagi Hidetsugu, a professor of Takasaki City University of Economics. Among articles available in English, for extensive analysis of neo-nationalism, see Gayle (2001), Kersten (1999), Layland (2001), Oshiba (2002), and *Social Science Japan Newsletter* (2004). Among them, Layland (2001, 7) nicely cites a comment made by Tessa Morris-Suzuki on the ongoing situation. She says, "[S]ome texts had begun to acknowledge uncomfortable subjects—like the existence of 'comfort women.' Now, a backlash is in progress, tied inextricably to Japan's economic woes, rising unemployment and concern about the future. Such conditions have fostered a climate where simplistic neo-nationalism can flourish."

7. This is from an unofficial translation of the NPO Law, which is available on the Web site of the Japan Center for International Exchange: http://www.jcie.or.jp/civilnet/monitor/npo_law.pdf.

8. This is an excerpt from a translation of the original article, which appeared in *Japan Interpreter* 6(1): 1–5. The citation is from page 3.

9. This theoretical school included Ōtsuka Hisao and Maruyama Masao, as well as Kawashima Takeyoshi, Takashima Zenya, Uchida Yoshihiko, and Ōkochi Kazuo.

10. Importantly enough, Yamanouchi (1998) argues that the reorganization from a class society to a system society was achieved through the total-war experience in Japan. Japanese traditional class-based society was transformed through the wartime mobilization to fight World War II. Yamanouchi (1998, 3–4) says:

> [T]he total-war system attempted to unite all the people under the slogan of a common destiny as citizens of a single national community and to intervene against the momentum toward social exclusion and conflict that had been inherent in modern societies since their inception. . . . The prerequisites of the total-war system are a keen awareness of the potential for intrasocietal conflict and turmoil, the active incorporation of these impulses within the system, and their redirection through reform to enable them to contribute to social integration. Thus conceived, the total-war system undoubtedly played an important transitional role on the way to the establishment of a system society that is organized on the basis of functionalist principles. Although each nation returned to a peaceful and routine social order at the close of the Second World War, such a return did not signify a restoration of prewar conditions. Even

after the Second World War, nations continued to opt for the type of social reorganization based on functionalist principles that had been accelerated by the total-war system; and they restored their way of life in that manner.

11. This is an excerpt from a translation of the original article, which appeared in *Japan Interpreter* 9(4): 451–65. The citation is from page 463.

12. This is an excerpt from a translation of the original article, which appeared in *Japan Interpreter* 9(4): 451–65. The citation is from page 453.

13. Studies in English on the Japanese new social movements in this era include Steiner et al. (1980), McKean (1981), and Apter and Sawa (1984).

14. For example, the *Asahi Shimbun* (January 9, 2004) reports that the LDP is trying to generate a collaborative relationship with NPOs and NGOs prior to the national election in the upcoming summer. Meanwhile, the DPJ clearly promoted NPOs' participation in the policy-making process in its *Manifesto*, which was released in October 2003 (Democratic Party of Japan 2003).

15. When the C's was established, it sought three objectives: a system for citizens' groups to easily receive corporate status, a tax exemption system for citizens' activities, and information disclosure relating to citizens' activities, according to the group's Web site (http://www.npoweb.jp/cs/cs_home_info. php?article_id=1963), accessed February 8, 2006. Meanwhile, C's itself is not an NPO under the 1998 NPO Law. C's started in 1994 as a limited-time project—for promoting the institutionalization of nonprofit groups in Japanese society. Initially it worked for the achievement of the NPO Law in 1998. Since then, the group has always worked on time-specific projects. According to Matsubara Akira, secretary general of the group, in the group's Mail Magazine (C's 2007, NPOWEB Mail Magazine No. 095, May 11, 2007), C's does not expect its activities to be "continuous," which is a primary reason groups receive the NPO status, as I argue in chapter 3. Thus, C's has not sought NPO status. However, on April 28, 2008, C's gained NPO status. According to the articles of association, the group's activities will focus on supporting NPOs, exclusively aiming to continue improving the situation for current civic activities in Japanese society. The articles are available at http://www.npoweb.jp/modules/introduction/index. php?content_id=7, accessed July 1, 2008.

16. Further, the Research Institute of Economy, Trade, and Industry (RIETI 2003, 14) reported that part timers at NPOs are paid only 440 yen (approximately $4) per hour. This is far below the minimum labor wages that prefecture-level governments mandate. In Tokyo, for example, on October 1, 2003, the minimum labor wage was 708 yen (approximately $6.50), according to the Tokyo Labor Bureau (telephone inquiry on June 1, 2006). At a pay rate that is typically quite low, paid staff members work 7.18 hours per day or 32.24 hours a week, while unpaid staff members work 4.47 hours per day or 12.30 hours a week (Japan NPO Research Association 2001, 4). See Japan NPO Research Association (2001) for further examination of Japanese NPOs as workplaces.

17. The program was formally titled *Chiiki to gakkō ga renkei shita hōshi katsudō, taiken katsudō suishin jigyō* (Program on Social Service Experiences through

the Linkage of Communities and Schools). MEXT has funded the program since 2002 (see MEXT 2003).

18. I believe this educational development echoed "service learning" in the United States, although the term has not (yet) become popular in Japan. Hyatt (2001) points out, in the U.S. context, that the political shift from the Keynesian welfare state to new forms of neoliberal governance has resulted in a new emphasis on the teaching of service learning courses, which means that students spend some period of time engaged in volunteer work in community-based organizations, agencies, or programs. Regarding the recent development of service learning in Japanese schools, see Ogawa (2008).

19. The Ministry of Health, Labor, and Welfare's annual survey (MHLW 2005) shows that the balance of domestic births of Japanese minus deaths in that year was estimated to be minus 10,000, marking the first "natural decline" since the data were first compiled in 1899.

20. According to a report produced by the Research Institute of Economy, Trade, and Industry, most incorporated NPOs are relatively new. Of the 1,910 NPOs that responded to a 2003 survey by the Research Institute of Economy, Trade, and Industry (RIETI 2003), 82.5 percent were formed after the Great Hanshin-Awaji Earthquake in January 1995, and 67.5 percent were formed after the enactment of the NPO Law in December 1998; only 17.5 percent of respondents reported that their organizations had been operating prior to official incorporation and before the earthquake. It seems reasonable to assume that the groups that operated before the enactment of the NPO Law were functioning as informal citizens' groups or *shimin dantai*. Sixty-four percent of the NPOs surveyed had no record of activities prior to incorporation under the NPO Law. This statistic indicates that the NPO Law itself accelerated the incorporation of NPOs in Japanese society.

21. Saaler (2005) provides detailed accounts on this textbook examination (*kentei*) process and the reactions it prompted in Japan and beyond.

22. The Kyodo report (*Kyodo News*, September 1, 2005) further says that the education boards of Ōtawara, Tochigi Prefecture, and Tokyo's Suginami Ward adopted the history textbook for use in municipally run schools. In addition, the book will be used in middle schools, which offer six-year programs integrating junior and senior high schools, and schools for handicapped children run by the Tokyo Metropolitan Government and the Ehime and Shiga prefectural governments. Further, nine private schools chose the textbook. A total of seventy-seven schools used the history textbook in April 2006; the total number of students using the textbook was estimated at 16,300, constituting 0.44 percent of all junior high school students.

23. A new tax legislation was enforced in October 2001 as the first legislation to address the eligibility of NPOs under the NPO Law to receive tax-deductible donations. Under the 1998 NPO Law, NPOs do not have any tax-exempt status. Under the new law, NPOs will receive tax-exempt status as approved specified nonprofit corporations (*nintei NPO hōjin*) if they pass the public support test, which includes requirements that their total amount of donations and grants must comprise more than one third of the total amount of income (this has

been eased to one fifth only between April 1, 2003, and March 31, 2008), and others. Meanwhile, donors may claim tax write-offs for contributions made to these organizations. Unfortunately, however, the conditions that NPOs must satisfy according to this law are very strict. Only sixty incorporated NPOs among more than 30,000 NPOs were approved as of May 1, 2007 (National Tax Agency 2007).

24. Interestingly, Hodgson (2004) points out a similar phenomenon in a UK context. She argues that British civil society has become increasingly utilized in policy initiatives, especially in regard to regenerating communities, and finds itself engaged in various types of partnerships with both the state and businesses. She maintains that this has had the effect of redrawing the boundaries between civil society and the state and calls it "manufactured" civil society, that is, groups that look like civil society but are in fact a mixture of state and voluntary sector organizations.

25. This point was inspired by accounts produced by Sato (2003).

Chapter 7

1. When I spoke with her in the fall of 2001, there were only four departments at SLG. The planetarium operation was newly established in April 2003.

2. This point was particularly inspired by accounts produced by Kuwayama (2004).

Appendix 2

1. This is from an unofficial translation of the NPO Law, which is available on the Web site of the Japan Center for International Exchange: http://www.jcie.or.jp/civilnet/monitor/npo_law.pdf.

References

Ad Hoc Council on Education (Rinji kyōiku shingikai). 1987. *Kyōiku kaikaku ni kansuru tōshin (Report on Educational Reform)*. Tokyo: Ad Hoc Council on Education.

Alagappa, Muthiah, ed. 2004. *Civil Society and Political Change in Asia: Expanding and Contracting Democratic Space*. Stanford, CA: Stanford University Press.

Alexander, Jeffrey C., ed. 1998. *Real Civil Societies: Dilemmas of Institutionalization*. London; Thousand Oaks, CA: Sage Publications.

———, with Philip Smith. 2003. "The Discourse of American Civil Society." In *The Meanings of Social Life: A Cultural Sociology*, 121–54. Oxford: Oxford University Press.

Allison, Anne. 1994. *Nightwork: Sexuality, Pleasure, and Corporate Masculinity in a Tokyo Hostess Club*. Chicago, IL: University of Chicago Press.

Alvarez, Sonia E., Evelina Dagnino, and Arturo Escobar. 1998. *Cultures of Politics, Politics of Cultures: Re-Visioning Latin American Social Movements*. Boulder, CO: Westview Press.

Amano, Masako. 2005. *Sākuru, nettowāku no hiraku chihei: "Tsukiai" no sengoshi* (Expanding Horizons of Circles and Networks, Postwar History of Relationships). Tokyo: Yoshikawa kōbunkan.

Amenomori, Takayoshi. 1993. *Defining the Nonprofit Sector: Japan (Working Papers in Comparative Nonprofit Sector)*. Baltimore, MD: Johns Hopkins University Institute for Policy.

Anheier, Helmut K. 1995. "Theories of the Nonprofit Sector: Three Issues." *Nonprofit and Voluntary Sector Quarterly* 24(1): 15–23.

Anheier, Helmut K., and Jeremy Kendall, eds. 2001. *Third Sector Policy at the Crossroads: An International Nonprofit Analysis*. London; New York: Routledge.

Apter, David, and Nagayo Sawa. 1984. *Against the State: Politics and Social Protest in Japan*. Cambridge, MA: Harvard University Press.

Arato, Andrew. 1981. "Civil Society against the State: Poland 1980–81." *Telos* 47: 23–47.

———. 2000. *Civil society, Constitution, and Legitimacy*. Lanham, MD: Rowman & Littlefield.

Aristotle. 1981. *The Politics*. Translated by Trevor J. Saunders and T. A. Sinclair. New York: Penguin Classics.

Asahi Shimbun.

2001. (November 27). "Kyōiku kihon hō minaoshi shimon" (Fundamental Law of Education Revision Requested).

2002. (January 18). "Afugan zantei seiken tomo watariau NGO daihyō" (NGO Leader Negotiates Evenly with Leaders of the Afghanistan Interim Government).

2002. (April 9). "Shin ni 'atarashii kōkyō' wo" (On Creating a True *New Public*).

2002. (July 18). "Kaikaku ni sakinjiru chihō" (Locals Are Ahead of Reform).

2002. (September 29). Shōgaisha wa 'hodokoshi' no taishō?" (Handicapped People Should Always Be Helped?).

2002. (November 12). "Tasai na hito ga iru kara" (Because There Are Various Kinds of People).

2002. (December 19). "NPO wo tachiageyō, mijikana mondai nakama to kaiketsu" (Let's Make an NPO. Solving Ordinary Problems with Friends).

2003. (June 7). "Naniyue NPO" (Why NPOs?).

2003. (November 1). "Senkyo katsudō dame? Tomadou NPO" (Not Allowed To Be Involved with Election Campaigns? NPO Members Are Annoyed).

2004. (January 9). "Jimin, NPO to renkei mosaku" (LDP Explores Collaboration with NPOs).

2004. (February 5a). "Aki kyōshitsu geijutsu no kyoten ni" (Using Abandoned School Classrooms for Art Education).

2004. (February 5b). "For Kids in Danger, Help Is a Mere 10 Seconds Away." English ed.

Avenell, Simon. 2006. "Regional Egoism as the Public Good: Residents' Movements in Japan during the 1960s and 1970s." *Japan Forum* 18(1): 89–113.

Baker, Gideon, and David Chandler, eds. 2005. *Global Civil Society: Contested Futures*. London; New York: Routledge.

Barshay, Andrew E. 1992. "Imagining Democracy in Postwar Japan: Reflections on Maruyama Masao and Modernism." *Journal of Japanese Studies* 18(2): 365–406.

———. 2003. "Capitalism and Civil Society in Postwar Japan: Perspectives from Intellectual History." In *The State of Civil Society in Japan*, ed. Frank J. Schwartz and Susan J. Pharr, 63–82. Cambridge: Cambridge University Press.

———. 2004. *The Social Sciences in Modern Japan: The Marxian and Modernist Traditions*. Berkeley: University of California Press.

Batliwala, Srilatha, and L. David Brown, eds. 2006. *Transnational Civil Society: An Introduction*. Bloomfield, CT: Kumarian Press.

Beck, Ulrich. 1994. "The Reinvention of Politics: Towards a Theory of Reflexive Modernization." In *Reflexive Modernization: Politics, Tradition, and Aesthetics in the Modern Social Order*, ed. Ulrich Beck, Anthony Giddens, and Scott Lash, 1–55. Cambridge, UK: Polity Press.

Befu, Harumi. 1963. "Network and Corporate Structure: A Structural Approach to Community Interrelations in Japan." In *Studies in Asia*, vol. 4, ed. Robert K. Sakai, 27–41. Lincoln: University of Nebraska Press.

Ben-Ari, Eyal. 1991. *Changing Japanese Suburbia: A Study of Two Present-Day Localities*. London; New York: Kegan Paul International.

Benthall, Jonathan. 2000. "Civil Society's Need for De-Construction." *Anthropology Today* 16(2): 1–3.

Berman, Sheri. 1997. "Civil Society and the Collapse of the Weimar Republic." *World Politics* 49(3): 401–29.

Bestor, Theodore C. 1989. *Neighborhood Tokyo*. Stanford, CA: Stanford University Press.

———. 1990. "Tokyo Mom-and-Pop." *The Wilson Quarterly* 14(4): 27–33.

———. 2004. *Tsukiji: The Fish Market at the Center of the World*. Berkeley: University of California Press.

Bestor, Victoria Lyon. 2002. "Toward a Cultural Biography of Civil Society in Japan." In *Family and Social Policy in Japan: Anthropological Approaches*, ed. Roger Goodman, 29–53. Cambridge: Cambridge University Press.

Bourdieu, Pierre. 1977. *Outline of a Theory of Practice*. Cambridge: Cambridge University Press.

Boyte, Harry C. 2004. *Everyday Politics: Reconnecting Citizens and Public Life*. Philadelphia: University of Pennsylvania Press.

Boyte, Harry C., and Nancy N. Kari. 1996. *Building America: The Democratic Promise of Public Work*. Philadelphia, PA: Temple University Press.

Broadbent, Jeffrey. 1998. *Environmental Politics in Japan: Networks of Power and Protest*. Cambridge: Cambridge University Press.

Cabinet Office (Naikakufu). 2001. *Shimin katsudō dantai nado kihon chōsa (Basic Survey on Citizens' Groups)*. Tokyo: Cabinet Office Quality-of-Life Policy Bureau.

———. 2003. *Sōsharu kyapitaru: Yutakana ningen kankei to shimin katsudō no kōjunkan wo motomete (Social Capital: Pursuing Positive Synergy between Rich Human Relations and Citizens' Activities)*. Tokyo: Cabinet Office Quality-of-Life Policy Bureau.

———. 2005a. *Kōreika shakai hakusho (White Paper on the Aging Society)*. Tokyo: National Printing Bureau.

———. 2005b. *NPO (minkan hieiri soshiki) ni kansuru yoron chōsa (Public Opinion Survey on the NPO)*. Tokyo: Cabinet Office.

———. 2007a. *Hōjin ga teikan ni kisai shiteiru bunya no kazu (The Number of Activity Areas NPOs Stated in Their Articles of Association)*. http://www.npo-homepage.go.jp/data/bunnya.html. Accessed May 25, 2007.

———. 2007b. *NPO kako no ninshōsū (The Number of Recognized NPOs)*. http://www.npo-homepage.go.jp/data/pref_history.txt. Accessed May 25, 2007.

———. 2007c. *Teikan ni kisai sareta tokutei hieiri katsudō no shurui (Areas of Activities Stated in Their Articles of Association)*. http://www.npo-homepage.go.jp/data/bunnya.html. Accessed May 25, 2007.

———. 2007d. *Tokutei hieiri katsudō sokushinhō ni motozuku shinsei jurisū oyobi ninshō sū, funinshōsū nado (The Number of Applications for Seeking the NPO Status, Number of NPOs Recognized, and Number of NPOs Not Recognized)*. http://www.npo-homepage.go.jp/data/pref.html. Accessed May 25, 2007.

Calhoun, Craig, ed. 1992. *Habermas and the Public Sphere*. Cambridge, MA: MIT Press.

———. 2001. "Civil Society/Public Sphere: History of the Concept." In *International Encyclopedia of the Social and Behavioral Sciences*, ed. Neil J. Smelser and Paul B. Baltes, 1,897–1,903. Amsterdam: Elsevier.

Carver, Terrell, with Shin Chiba, Reiji Matsumoto, James Martin, Bob Jessop, Fumio Iida, and Atushi Sugita. 2000. " 'Civil Society' in Japanese Politics: Implications for Contemporary Political Research." *European Journal of Political Research* 37: 541–55.

Central Council for Education (Chuō kyōiku shingikai). 1981. *Shōgai kyōiku (Life-long Education)*. Tokyo: Central Council for Education.

———. 2002. *Seishōnen no hōshi katsudō, taiken katsudō no suishin hōsaku nado ni tsuite (On Promoting Youth Social Service Experience Activities)*. Tokyo: Central Council for Education.

———. 2003. *Atarashii jidai ni fusawashii kyōiku kihonhō to kyōiku shinkō kihon keikaku no arikata ni tsuite (On the Fundamental Law of Education and Basic Plan for Education Promotion for the New Era)*. Tokyo: Central Council for Education.

Chan-Tiberghien, Jennifer. 2004. *Gender and Human Rights Politics in Japan: Global Norms and Domestic Networks*. Stanford, CA: Stanford University Press.

Cicero. 1998. *The Republic and the Laws*. Translated by Niall Rudd. Oxford: Oxford University Press.

Cohen, Jean L., and Andrew Arato. 1992. *Civil Society and Political Theory*. Cambridge, MA: MIT Press.

Cohen, Joshua, and Joel Rogers. 1992. "Secondary Associations and Democratic Governance." *Politics and Society* 20(4): 393–472.

Columbia Encyclopedia. 2001–2005. 6th ed. New York: Columbia University Press., s.v. "Forty-seven Ronin." http://www.bartleby.com/65/fo/Fortyseve.html. Accessed May 24, 2007.

C's (Coalition for Legislation to Support Citizens' Organizations). 2007. NPOWEB Mail Magazine No. 095. May 11.

Curtis, Gerald L. 1988. *The Japanese Way of Politics*. New York: Columbia University Press.

———. 1997. "A Recipe for Democratic Development." *Journal of Democracy* 8(3): 139–45.

———. 1999. *The Logic of Japanese Politics: Leaders, Institutions, and the Limits of Change*. New York: Columbia University Press.

Curtis, James E., Edward G. Grabb, and Douglas E. Baer. 1992. "Voluntary Association Membership in Fifteen Countries: A Comparative Analysis." *American Sociological Review* 57(2): 139–52.

Dean, Mitchell. 1999. *Governmentality: Power and Rule in Modern Society*. London; Thousand Oaks, CA: Sage Publications.

Deguchi, Masayuki. 1993. *Firansoropī: Kigyō to hito no shakai kōken (Philanthropy: Social Contribution by Business Corporations and People)*. Tokyo: Maruzen.

————. 2001. "The Distinction between Institutionalized and Noninstitutional-ized NPOs: New Policy Initiatives and Nonprofit Organizations in Japan." In *Third Sector Policy at the Crossroads: An International Nonprofit Analysis,* ed. Helmut K. Anheier and Jeremy Kendall, 153–67. London; New York: Routledge.

Democratic Party of Japan (Minshutō). 2003. *Manifesto.* Tokyo: Democratic Party of Japan.

Diamond, Larry. 1994. "Rethinking Civil Society: Toward Democratic Consolida-tion." *Journal of Democracy* 5(3): 4–17.

Diamond, Larry, Marc F. Plattner, Yun-Han Chu, and Hung-Mao Tien, eds. 1997. *Consolidating the Third Wave Democracies: Themes and Perspectives.* Baltimore, MD: Johns Hopkins University Press.

DiMaggio, Paul J., and Helmut K. Anheier. 1990. "The Sociology of Nonprofit Organizations and Sectors." *Annual Review of Sociology* 16: 137–59.

Doi, Takeo. 1971. *Amae no kōzō (Anatomy of Dependence).* Tokyo: Kōbundō.

Dore, Ronald Philip. 1958. *City Life in Japan: A Study of a Tokyo Ward.* Berkeley: University of California Press.

————. 1973. *British Factory-Japanese Factory: The Origins of National Diversity in Industrial Relations.* Berkeley: University of California Press.

————. 1978. *Shinohata, a Portrait of a Japanese Village.* Berkeley: University of California Press.

Dower, John W. 1993. "Peace and Democracy in Two Systems: External Policy and Internal Conflict." In *Postwar Japan as History,* ed. Andrew Gordon, 3–33. Berkeley: University of California Press.

Drucker, Peter F. 1986. "The Changed World Economy." *Foreign Affairs* 64(4): 768–91.

Dryzek, John S. 2000. *Deliberative Democracy and Beyond: Liberals, Critics, Contesta-tions.* Oxford: Oxford University Press.

Ducke, Isa. 2007. *Civil Society and the Internet in Japan.* London; New York: Routledge.

Eberly, Don E., ed. 1994. *Building a Community of Citizens: Civil Society in the 21st Century.* Lanham, MD: University Press of America: Commonwealth Foundation.

Economic Planning Agency (Keizai kikaku chō). 2000. *Kokumin seikatsu hakusho: Borantia ga fukameru kōen (White Paper on the National Lifestyle: Good Net-working Deepened by Volunteering).* Tokyo: Ministry of Finance Printing Bureau.

Economic Strategy Council (Keizai senryaku kaigi). 1999. *Nihon keizai saisei ye no senryaku (Strategy for the Revitalization of the Japanese Economy).* February 26. Tokyo: Economic Strategy Council.

Edelman, Marc. 2001. "Social Movements: Changing Paradigms and Forms of Politics." *Annual Review of Anthropology* 30: 285–317.

Edwards, Bob, Michael W. Foley, and Mario Diani, eds. 2001. *Beyond Tocqueville: Civil Society and the Social Capital Debate in Comparative Perspective.* Hanover, NH: University Press of New England [for] Tufts University.

Edwards, Michael. 2004. *Civil Society*. Cambridge, UK: Polity Press.

Ehrenberg, John. 1999. *Civil Society: The Critical History of an Idea*. New York: New York University Press.

Elster, Jon, ed. 1998. *Deliberative Democracy*. Cambridge: Cambridge University.

Embree, John F. 1939. *Suye Mura, a Japanese Village*. Chicago, IL: University of Chicago Press.

Engels, Frederick. [1852] 1975. "Engels to Marx in London, Manchester, 23 September 1852." Translated by Richard Dixon and others. In *Karl Marx and Frederick Engels: Collected Works. Vol. 39, 1852–55, Letters*, 188–92. New York: International Publishers.

Escobar, Arturo, and Sonia Alvarez. 1992. *The Making of Social Movements in Latin America: Identity, Strategy, and Democracy*. Boulder, CO: Westview Press.

Evans, Sara M., and Harry C. Boyte. 1992. *Free Spaces: The Sources of Democratic Change in America*. Chicago, IL: University of Chicago Press.

Faure, Edger, Felipe Herrera, Abdul-Razzak Kaddoura, Henri Lopes, Arthur V. Petrovsky, Majid Rahnema, and Frederick Champion Ward. 1972. *Learning to Be: The World of Education Today and Tomorrow*. Paris: UNESCO.

Ferguson, Adam. [1767] 1995. *An Essay on the History of Civil Society*, ed. Fania Oz-Salzberger. Cambridge: Cambridge University Press.

Ferguson, James, and Akhil Gupta. 2002. "Spatializing States: Toward an Ethnography of Neoliberal Governmentality." *American Ethnologist* 29(4): 981–1,002.

Financial Times. 2006. "Exclusive Interview: Shinzo Abe." (October 31). http://www.ft.com/cms/s/ ba65e892-68f6-11db-b4c2-0000779e2340.html. Accessed November 7, 2006.

Fisher, William F. 1997. "Doing Good? The Politics and Antipolitics of NGO Practices." *Annual Review of Anthropology* 26: 439–64.

Fishkin, James S. 1993. *Democracy and Deliberation: New Directions for Democratic Reform*. New Haven, CT: Yale University Press.

Florini, Ann M., ed. 2000. *The Third Force: The Rise of Transnational Civil Society*. Tokyo: Japan Center for International Exchange; Washington, DC: Carnegie Endowment for International Peace: Brookings Institution Press.

Flyvbjerg, Bent. 1991. *Rationality and Power: Democracy in Practice*. Chicago, IL: University of Chicago Press.

Foucault, Michel. 1977. *Discipline and Punish: The Birth of the Prison*. New York: Vintage Books.

———. 1988. "Technologies of the Self." In *Technologies of the Self: A Seminar with Michel Foucault*, ed. Luther H. Martin, Huck Gutman, and Patrick H. Hutton, 16–49. Amherst: University of Massachusetts Press.

———. 1991. 'Governmentality." In *The Foucault Effect: Studies in Governmentality*, ed. Graham Burchell, Colin Gordon, and Peter Miller, 87–104. Chicago, IL: University of Chicago Press.

———. 2003. "The Subject and Power." In *The Essential Foucault: Selections from the Essential Works of Foucault 1954–1984*, ed. Paul Rabinow and Nikolas Rose, 126–44. New York: New Press.

Friedman, Milton, with the assistance of Rose D. Friedman. 1962. *Capitalism and Freedom*. Chicago, IL: University of Chicago Press.

Frost, Yuko Iida. 1993. "A Key to Open Japan? Japan's Nonprofit Sector on the Move." *The Brookings Review* 11(4): 28–29.

Fujii, Atsushi. 2002. "Shakaigakusha wa borantia wo donoyōni katattekitanoka" (In What Way Do Sociologists Talk about Volunteerism?). *Borantia Kenkyū* 11: 13–28.

Fukuda, Kan'ichi. 1971. *Kindai seiji genri seiritsushi josetsu (Introduction to the History of Modern Political Principles)*. Tokyo: Iwanami shoten.

Fukuyama, Francis. 1995. "The Primacy of Culture." *Journal of Democracy* 6(1): 7–14.

Garon, Sheldon M. 2002. *The Evolution of Civil Society: From Meiji to Heisei*. Cambridge, MA: Harvard University Program on U.S.-Japan Relations Occasional Paper Series.

Gastil, John, and Peter Levine, eds. 2005. *The Deliberative Democracy Handbook: Strategies for Effective Civic Engagement in the Twenty-first Century*. San Francisco: Jossey-Bass.

Gayle, Curtis Anderson. 2001. "Progressive Representations of the Nation: Early Postwar Japan and Beyond." *Social Science Japan Journal* 4(1): 1–19.

Gellner, Ernest. 1994. *Conditions of Liberty: Civil Society and Its Revival*. New York: Allen Lane.

Gendai yōgo no kiso chishiki (Basic Knowledge for Contemporary Vocabulary). Various years. Tokyo: Jiyū kokumin sha.

George, Timothy S. 2001. *Minamata: Pollution and the Struggle for Democracy in Postwar Japan*. Cambridge, MA: Harvard University Asia Center, distributed by Harvard University Press.

Giddens, Anthony. 1984. *The Constitution of Society: Outline of the Theory of Structuation*. Cambridge, UK: Polity Press.

———. 1998. *The Third Way: The Renewal of Social Democracy*. Cambridge, UK: Polity Press.

Gidron, Benjamin, Ralph M. Kramer, and Lester M. Salamon. 1992. "Government and the Third Sector in Comparative Perspective: Allies or Adversaries?" In *Government and the Third Sector: Emerging Relationships in Welfare States*, ed. Benjamin Gidron, Ralph M. Kramer, and Lester M. Salamon, 1–30. San Francisco: Jossey-Bass.

Gill, Tom. 2001. *Men of Uncertainty: The Social Organization of Day Laborers in Contemporary Japan*. Albany: State University of New York Press.

Goodman, Roger. 1993. *Japan's "International Youth": The Emergence of a New Class of Schoolchildren*. Oxford: Oxford University Press.

———. 2000. *Children of the Japanese State: The Changing Role of Child Protection Institutions in Contemporary Japan*. Oxford: Oxford University Press.

———, ed. 2002. *Family and Social Policy in Japan: Anthropological Approaches*. Cambridge: Cambridge University Press.

Gordon, Bill. 1998. *Lifelong Learning in Japan*. http://gordon.web.wesleyan.edu/papers/lifelrn.htm. Accessed January 11, 2006.

Graham, Fiona. 2005. *A Japanese Company in Crisis: Ideology, Strategy, and Narrative.* London; New York: RoutledgeCurzon.

Greenhouse, Carol J., and Davydd J. Greenwood. 1998. "Introduction: The Ethnography of Democracy and Difference." In *Democracy and Ethnography: Constructing Identities in Multicultural Liberal Arts,* ed. Carol J. Greenhouse, 1–24. Albany: State University of New York Press.

Greenwood, Davydd J. 1999. "Theory-Practice Relations in Anthropology: A Commentary and Further Provocation." *NAPA Bulletin* 18: 164–75.

———. 2002. *Naturalizing Social Capital: Social Darwinism—Again and Again and Again.* Paper presented at Cornell University/University of Turin Workshop on Social Capital. September 13.

Greenwood, Davydd J., and Morten Levin. 1998. *Introduction to Action Research: Social Research for Social Change.* Thousand Oaks, CA: Sage Publications.

Habermas, Jürgen. 1987. "The Theory of Communicative Action." Vol. 2, *Lifeworld and System: A Critique of Functionalist Reason.* Boston, MA: Beacon Press.

———. 1989. *The Structural Transformation of the Public Sphere: An Inquiry into a Category of Bourgeois Society.* Cambridge, MA: MIT Press.

———. 1996. *Between Facts and Norms: Contributions to a Discourse Theory of Law and Democracy.* Cambridge, MA: MIT Press.

Haddad, Mary Alice. 2007. *Politics and Volunteering in Japan: A Global Perspective.* Cambridge: Cambridge University Press.

Hall, John A., ed. 1995. *Civil Society: Theory, History, Comparison.* Cambridge, UK: Polity Press.

Hamabata, Matthews Masayuki. 1990. *Crested Kimono: Power and Love in the Japanese Business Family.* Ithaca, NY: Cornell University Press.

Hamada, Tomoko. 1991. *American Enterprise in Japan.* Albany: State University of New York Press.

Han, Seung-Mi. 2004. "From the Communitarian Ideal to the Public Sphere: The Making of Foreigners' Assemblies in Kawasaki City and Kanagawa Prefecture." *Social Science Journal Japan* 7(1): 41–60.

Hann, Chris M. 1996. "Introduction: Political Society and Civil Anthropology." In *Civil Society: Challenging Western Models,* ed. Chris M. Hann and Elizabeth S. Dunn, 1–26. London: Routledge.

Hann, Chris M., and Elizabeth S. Dunn, eds. 1996. *Civil Society: Challenging Western Models.* London: Routledge.

Harvey, David. 2003. *The New Imperialism.* Oxford: Oxford University Press.

———. 2005. *A Brief History of Neoliberalism.* Oxford: Oxford University Press.

Hasegawa, Koichi. 2004. *Constructing Civil Society in Japan: Voices of Environmental Movements.* Melbourne: Trans Pacific Press.

Hastings, Sally Ann. 1995. *Neighborhood and Nation in Tokyo, 1905–37.* Pittsburgh, PA: University of Pittsburgh Press.

Hegel, Georg Wilhelm Friedrich. [1821] 1967. *Hegel's Philosophy of Right.* Translated by T. M. Knox. Oxford: Clarendon Press.

Hein, Laura. 2004. "Thinking Globally, Acting Locally: The Tokyo Governorship." In *Reasonable Men, Powerful Words: Political Culture and Expertise in Twentieth-Century Japan,* 182–211. Berkeley: University of California Press.

Hemment, Julie Dawn. 2000. *Gender, NGOs and the Third Sector in Russia: An Ethnography of Post-Socialist Civil Society*. Ph.D. dissertation, Department of Anthropology, Cornell University.

———. 2004. "The Riddle of the Third Sector: Civil Society, International Aid, and NGOs in Russia." *Anthropological Quarterly* 77(2): 215–41.

Hendry, Joy. 1981. *Marriage in Changing Japan: Community and Society*. New York: St. Martin's Press.

Himmelstein, Jerome L. 1993. "The Place and Meaning of the Nonprofit Sector." *Qualitative Sociology* 6(3): 319–29.

Hiraishi, Nao'aki. 2003. "The Formation of Maruyama Masao's Image of Japanese Intellectual History during the War Period." Translated by Moriya Fumiaki. *Social Science Japan Journal* 6(2): 241–54.

———. 2004. "Maruyama Masao, National Democrat." *Social Science Japan Newsletter* 30: 11–13.

Hirata, Keiko. 2002. *Civil Society in Japan: The Growing Role of NGOs in Tokyo's Aid and Development Policy*. New York: Palgrave/Macmillan.

Hirata, Kiyoaki. 1969. *Shimin shakai to shakai shugi (Civil Society and Socialism)*. Tokyo: Iwanami shoten.

Hirowatari, Seigo. 2002. "On 'Civil Society.' " *Social Science Japan Newsletter* 23: 3–4.

Hirst, Paul Q. 1989. The Pluralist Theory of the State: Selected Writings of G. D. H. Cole, J. N. Figgis, and H. J. Laski. London; New York: Routledge.

———. 1994. *Associative Democracy: New Forms of Economics and Social Governance*. Cambridge, UK: Polity Press.

———. 1997. *From Statism to Pluralism: Democracy, Civil Society, and Global Politics*. London: UCL Press.

Hobbes, Thomas. [1660] 1996. *Leviathan*. Cambridge: Cambridge University Press.

Hodgson, Lesley. 2004. "Manufactured Civil Society: Counting the Cost." *Critical Social Policy* 24(2): 139–64.

Hoffman, Lisa, Monica Dehart, and Stephen J. Collier. 2006. "Notes on the Anthropology of Neoliberalism." *Anthropology News* 47(6): 9–10.

Honma, Masaaki, and Masayuki Deguchi. 1996. *Borantia kakumei: Daishinsai deno keiken wo shimin katsudō ye (Volunteer Revolution: Toward Promoting Citizens' Activities Based on the Experience of the Great Earthquake)*. Tokyo: Tōyō keizai shimpōsha.

Hood, Christopher P. 2001. *Japanese Education Reform: Nakasone's Legacy*. London; New York: Routledge.

Hoshino, Masako. 2000. "Who Wants to Be a Volunteer?" *Look Japan* (August): 14–16.

Hourigan, Naiamh. 2003. *Escaping the Global Village: Media, Language, and Protest*. Lanham, MD: Lexington Books.

Husserl, Edmund. 1970. *The Crisis of European Sciences and Transcendental Phenomenology: An Introduction to Phenomenological Philosophy*. Evanston, IL: Northwestern University Press.

Hyatt, Susan Brin. 2001. " 'Service Learning,' Applied Anthropology, and the Production of Neoliberal Citizens." *Anthropology in Action* 8(1): 6–13.

Illich, Ivan. 1972. *Deschooling Society*. New York: Harrow Books.

Imada, Makoto. 2001. "From the Iron Triangle to Civil Society: Changing Japan's Society." *The Japan Foundation Newsletter* XXVIII(2): 1–9.

Imai, Hiromichi. 1998. *"Shimin" no jidai: hō to seiji karano sekkin (The Era of Citizens: Approaches from Law and Politics)*. Sapporo: Hokkaidō daigaku tosho kankōkai.

———, ed. 2001. *Shin shimin shakai ron (New Arguments on Civil Society)*. Tokyo: Fūkōsha.

Imamura, Anne E. 1987. *Urban Japanese Housewives: At Home and in the Community*. Honolulu: University of Hawaii Press.

Inda, Jonathan Xavier, ed. 2005. *Anthropologies of Modernity: Foucault, Governmentality, and Life Politics*. Malden, MA: Blackwell.

Inoguchi, Takashi. 2000. "Social Capital in Japan." *Japanese Journal of Political Science* 1(1): 73–112.

———. 2002. "Broadening the Basis of Social Capital in Japan." In *Democracies in Flux: The Evolution of Social Capital in Contemporary Society*, ed. Robert D. Putnam, 359–92. Oxford: Oxford University Press.

International Encyclopedia of the Social and Behavioral Sciences. 2001. Amsterdam; New York: Elsevier, s.v. "Concept and History of Civil Society."

International Monetary Fund. 1999. "Real Gross Domestic Product (annual percent change), Advanced Economics—Japan." In *The World Economic Outlook (WEO) Database April 1999*. Washington, DC: International Monetary Fund. http://www.imf.org/external/pubs/ft/weo/1999/01/data/growth_b.csv. Accessed May 18, 2005.

Iokibe, Makoto. 1999. "Japan's Civil Society: An Historical Overview." In *Deciding the Public Good: Governance and Civil Society in Japan*, ed. Tadashi Yamamoto, 51–96. Tokyo: Japan Center for International Exchange.

Iriyama, Akira. 2004. *Shimin shakairon: NGO-NPO wo koete (Civil Society Arguments, beyond NGO-NPO)*. Tokyo: Akashi shoten.

Irokawa, Daikichi. 1988. "Popular Movements in Modern Japanese History." In *The Japanese Trajectory: Modernization and Beyond*, ed. Gavan McCormack and Yoshio Sugimoto, 69–86. Cambridge: Cambridge University Press.

Irwin, Greg. 1998. *Japan's Best Loved Songs of the Season; Eigo de utau nihon no uta*. Tokyo: Japan Times.

Ishida, Takeshi. 1984. " 'Shimin' no funshutsu to gendai shakai kagaku no kadai" (The Emergence of Shimin and Agendas for Contemporary Social Sciences). In *Nihon no shakaikagaku (Social Sciences in Japan)*, 195–223. Tokyo: Tokyo daigaku shuppankai.

———. 1997. "Maruyama Masao to shimin shakai" (Maruyama Masao and Civil Society). In *Maruyama Masao to Shimin Shakai*, ed. Kokumin bunka kaigi (National Congress of Culture Japan), 5–62. Tokyo: Seori Shobō.

Ishitsuka, Shoji. 1998. "The Postmodern Situation in Present-Day Japanese Civil Society—Towards a Theoretical Synthesis in the Civil Society Discussion." In *Japan in Transition: Sociological and Psychological Aspects*, ed. Gisela Trommsdorff, 83–86. Lengerich, Germany: Pabst Science Publishers.

Iwasaki, Nobuhiko, Tadaichi Ueda, Manabu Ajisaka, Masao Takagi, and Naoki Yoshihara, eds. 1989. *Chonaikai no kenkyū (Studies on Neighborhood Associations)*. Tokyo: Ochanomizu shobō.

Japan Association of Charitable Organizations (Koeki hōjin kyōkai). 2001. *Kōeki hōjin no setsuritsu, un'ei, kantoku no tebiki (Guidebook for Establishing, Operating, and Supervising Public-Interest Legal Persons)*. Tokyo: Kōeki hōjin kyōkai.

———. 2006. The Reform of Public Benefit Corporation Law. http://www.kohokyo.or.jp/english/eng_02/reform2006-06.pdf. Accessed January 31, 2007.

Japan Center for International Exchange. 2003. "Unofficial Translation, Law to Promote Specified Nonprofit Activities." *Civil Society Monitor* 8 (December). http://www.jcie.or.jp/civilnet/monitor/npo_law.pdf. Accessed March 5, 2004.

Japan Consumers' Co-operative Union (Nihon seikatsu kyōdō kumiai rengōkai). 2002. *Gendai nihon seikyō undō shi, jō kan, ge kan (History of Contemporary Japanese Co-operative Union Movements)*. Tokyo: Nihon seikatsu kyōdō kumiai rengō kai.

———. 2006a. *Our History*. http://www.jccu.coop/English_here/aboutus/o_history_01.htm. Accessed October 5, 2006.

———. 2006b. *Our Members*. http://www.jccu.coop/English_here/aboutus/o_members_01.htm. Accessed October 5, 2006.

———. 2006c. *Our Mission*. http://www.jccu.coop/English_here/aboutus/o_mission.htm. Accessed October 5, 2006.

Japan NPO Research Association (Nihon npo gakkai). 2001. *Nihon no NPO rōdō shijō (The Japanese Nonprofit Labor Market)*, ed. Naoto Yamauchi. Osaka: Japan NPO Research Association.

Japanese Red Cross Society (Nippon sekijūji sha). 2006. *Review of Activities 2006*. Tokyo: Japanese Red Cross Society.

Jarvis, Peter. 1993. *Adult Education and the State*. London; New York: Routledge.

Junkerman, John, Gavan McCormack, and David McNeill. 2004. *Japan's Political and Constitutional Crossroads*. June 10. http://www.japanfocus.org/products/details/2175. Accessed January 24, 2007.

Kaldor, Mary, Helmut Anheier, and Marlies Glasius, eds. 2003. *Global Civil Society*. Oxford: Oxford University Press.

Kanagawa Information Center for Citizen's Activities (Alice Center). 2003. *Tātoru Tsūshin No. 11* (July 31). Yokohama, Kanagawa: Kanagawa Information Center for Citizen's Activities.

Kaneko, Ikuyou. 1992. *Borantia: Mō hitotsu no johō shakai (Volunteer: Another Information Society)*. Tokyo: Iwanami shoten.

Kant, Immanuel. [1784] 1963. "What Is Enlightenment?" In *On History*, ed. Lewis White Beck, 3–10. Translated by Lewis White Beck, Robert E. Anchor, and Emil L. Fackenheim. New York: Macmillan.

Kawahara, Akira. 2006. *Gendai shimin shakairon no shin chihei: "arento teki momento" no saihakken (New Dimension of Civil Society Arguments: Searching for the Arendtian Moment)*. Tokyo: Yushindokobunsha.

Kawano, Satsuki. 2005. *Ritual Practice in Modern Japan: Ordering Place, People, and Action.* Honolulu: University of Hawaii Press.

Kawanobe, Satoshi. 1994. "Lifelong Learning in Japan." *International Review of Education* 40(6): 485–93.

Kawashima, Takeyoshi. 1949. *Shoyūkenhō no riron (Theories of Property Rights Law).* Tokyo: Iwanami shoten.

Keane, John, ed. 1988. *Civil Society and the State: New European Perspectives.* London: Verso.

———. 1998. *Civil Society: Old Images, New Visions.* Stanford, CA: Stanford University Press.

Kelly, William W. 1985. *Deference and Defiance in Nineteenth-Century Japan.* Princeton, NJ: Princeton University Press.

———. 1993. "Finding a Place in Metropolitan Japan: Ideologies, Institutions, and Everyday Life." In *Postwar Japan as History,* ed. Andrew Gordon, 189–238. Berkeley: University of California Press.

Kersten, Rikki. 1999. "Neo-nationalism and the 'Liberal School of History.'" *Japan Forum* 11(2): 191–203.

Kersten, Rikki, and David Williams, eds. 2006. *The Left in the Shaping of Japanese Democracy: Essays in Honour of J. A. A. Stockwin.* London; New York: Routledge.

Kingston, Jeff. 2001. *Japan in Transformation 1952–2000.* New York: Longman.

———. 2004. *Japan's Quiet Transformation: Social Change and Civil Society in the 21st Century.* London; New York: Routledge.

Koe Naki Koe no Kai, ed. 1962. *Mata demo de aō: Koe naki koe no ninenkan (See You at the Demonstration: Two Years of the Voiceless Voices' Movements).* Tokyo: Tokyo shoten.

Kokumin bunka kaigi (National Congress of Culture Japan), ed. 1997. *Maruyama Masao to Shimin Shakai (Maruyama Masao and Civil Society).* Tokyo: Seori Shobō.

Kondo, Dorrine K. 1990. *Crafting Selves: Power, Gender, and Discourses of Identity in a Japanese Workplace.* Chicago, IL: University of Chicago Press.

Koschmann, J. Victor, ed. 1978. *Authority and the Individual in Japan.* Tokyo: University of Tokyo Press.

———. 1981. "The Debate on Subjectivity in Postwar Japan: Foundations of Modernism as a Political Critique." *Pacific Affairs* 54(4): 609–31.

———. 1993. "Intellectuals and Politics." In *Postwar Japan as History,* ed. Andrew Gordon, 395–423. Berkeley: University of California Press.

———. 1996. *Revolution and Subjectivity in Postwar Japan.* Chicago, IL: University of Chicago Press.

———. 1998. "The Spirit of Capitalism as Disciplinary Regime in the Postwar Thought of Ōtsuka Hisao." In *Total War and "Modernization,"* ed. Yasushi Yamanouchi, J. Victor Koschmann, and Ryūichi Narita 97–115. Ithaca, NY: Cornell University East Asia Program.

Krauss, Ellis S. 1974. *Japanese Radicals Revisited: Student Protest in Postwar Japan.* Berkeley: University of California Press.

Krauss, Ellis S., Thomas P. Rohlen, and Patricia G. Steinhoff, eds. 1984. *Conflict in Japan*. Honolulu: University of Hawaii Press.

Kumar, Krishan. 1993. "Civil Society: An Inquiry into the Usefulness of an Historical Term." *British Journal of Sociology* 44(3): 375–95.

Kunda, Gideon. 1992. *Engineering Culture: Control and Commitment in a High-Tech Corporation*. Philadelphia, PA: Temple University Press.

Kuno, Osamu. 1960. "Shimin shugi no seiritsu—hitotsu no taiwa" (Development of Citizen-ism: A Dialogue). *Shisō no kagaku* 19: 9–16.

Kurasawa, Susumu, and Ritsuo Akimoto, eds. 1990. *Chōnaikai to chiiki shūdan (Neighborhood Associations and Local Groups)*. Kyoto: Mineruba shobō.

Kurihara, Akira. 1999. "New Social Movements in Present-Day Japan." Translated by J. Victor Koschmann. *Journal of Pacific Asia* 5: 7–22.

Kuwayama, Takami. 2004. *Native Anthropology: The Japanese Challenge to Western Academic Hegemony*. Melbourne: Trans Pacific Press.

Kyodo News.
    2004. (April 16). "Koizumi Criticizes Freed Hostages for Wish to Work in Iraq.
    2004. (April 17). "68% of Japanese Back Gov't. Handling of Iraq Hostage Crisis: Kyodo Poll."
    2005. (September 1). "Disputed History Textbook To Be Used by 0.4% of Junior High School Students."

Laclau, Ernesto, and Chantal Mouffe. 1985. *Hegemony and Socialist Strategy: Towards a Radical Democratic Politics*. London: Verso.

Layland, Penelope. 2001. "A Comic Book View of History." *Quarterly Bulletin* 2(2): 6–9.

LeBlanc, Robin M. 1999. *Bicycle Citizens: The Political World of the Japanese Housewife*. Berkeley: University of California Press.

Lehning, Percy B. 1998. "Toward a Multicultural Civil Society: The Role of Social Capital and Democratic Citizenship." *Government and Opposition* 33(2): 221–42.

Lemke, Thomas. 2001. " 'The Birth of Bio-Politics': Michel Foucault's Lecture at the College de France on Neo-Liberal Governmentality." *Economy and Society* 30(2): 190–207.

Lesbirel, S. Hayden. 1998. *NIMBY Politics in Japan: Energy Sitting and the Management of Environmental Conflict*. Ithaca, NY: Cornell University Press.

Levi, Margaret. 1996. "Social and Unsocial Capital: A Review Essay of Robert Putnam's Making Democracy Work." *Politics and Society* 24(1): 45–55.

Levy, Jonah D. 1999. *Tocqueville's Revenge: State, Society, and Economy in Contemporary France*. Cambridge, MA: Harvard University Press.

Locke, John. [1690] 1980. *The Second Treatise of Government*. Indianapolis, IN: Hackett.

London, Nancy R. 1992. *Japanese Corporate Philanthropy*. New York: Oxford University Press.

Maki, Shōhei. 1976. "The Postwar Consumer Movement: Its Emergence from a Movement of Women." *Japan Quarterly* XXIII(2): 135–39.

Marcus, George E. 1994. "After the Critique of Ethnography: Faith, Hope, and Charity, but the Greatest of These Is Charity." In *Assessing Cultural Anthropology*, ed. Robert Borofsky, 40–54. New York: McGraw-Hill.

Maruyama, Masao. 1944. "Kokumin shugi no riron keisei" (Theoretical Formation on Nationalism) (1). *Kokka gakkai zasshi* 58(3): 93–112.

———. 1954. "Nihon seiji shisōshi kenkyū" (Studies on Japanese Political Thoughts). Tokyo: Tokyo daigaku shuppankai.

———. [1951] 1964a. "Nihon ni okeru nashonarizumu: Sono shisō teki tenbō." In *Gendai seiji no shisō to kōdō*, 152–70. Tokyo: Miraisha. An English translation, "Nationalism in Japan: Its Theoretical Background and Prospects," is available in *Thought and Behavior in Modern Japanese Politics*, ed. Ivan Morris, 135–56. London; New York: Oxford University Press.

———. [1947] 1964b. "Nihon fashizumu no shisō to undō." In *Gendai seiji no shisō to kōdō*, 29–87. Tokyo: Miraisha. An English translation, "The Ideology and Dynamics of Japanese Fascism," is available in *Thought and Behavior in Modern Japanese Politics*, ed. Ivan Morris, 25–83. London; New York: Oxford University Press.

———. 1969. "Fuhen genri no tachiba" (On the Position of Universalism). In *Kataritsugu sengoshi*, ed. Tsurumi Shunsuke, vol. 1, 80–107. Tokyo: Shisō no kagakusha.

———. [1943] 1976a. "Fukuzawa ni okeru chitsujo to ningen" (Order and Human Beings by Fukuzawa). In *Senchū to sengo no aida 1936–1957*, 143–46. Tokyo: Misuzu shobō.

———. [1949] 1976b. "Jyon Rokku to kindai seiji genri" (John Locke and Modern Political Principle). In *Senchū to sengo no aida 1936–1957*, 391–420. Tokyo: Misuzu shobō.

Marx, Karl. [1845] 1978a. "The German Ideology." In *The Marx-Engels Reader*, ed. Robert C. Tucker, 146–200. New York: W. W. Norton & Company.

———. [1843] 1978b. "On the Jewish Question." In *The Marx-Engels Reader*, ed. Robert C. Tucker, 26–52. New York: W. W. Norton & Company.

Masujima, Toshiyuki. 2005. "Administrative Reform in Japan: Past Developments and Future Trends." *International Review of Administrative Sciences* 71(2): 295–308.

Mathews, Jessica T. 1997. "Power Shift." *Foreign Affairs* 76(1): 50–66.

Matsushita, Keiichi. 1966. "Shimin teki ningen gata no gendaiteki kanōsei" (Modern Possibilities for Citizen-like Human Types). *Shisō* 504: 16–30.

———. 1971a. *Shibiru minimamu no shisō (Theory of the Civil Minimum)*. Tokyo: Tokyo daigaku shuppankai.

———. 1971b. "Shimin sanka to sono rekishiteki kanōsei" (Civic Participation and Its Historical Possibilities). In *Shimin Sanka*, ed. Matsushita Keiichi, 175–243. Tokyo: Tōyō keizai shimpōsha. An English translation of this article, "Politics of Citizen Participation," is available in *Japan Interpreter* 9(4): 451–65.

———. 1991. *Seisakugata shikō to seiji (Policy-Oriented Ways of Thinking and Politics)*. Tokyo: Tokyo daigaku shuppankai.

————. 1994. *Sengo seiji no rekishi to shisō (History and Thoughts in Postwar Politics)*. Tokyo: Chikuma shobō.

McCormack, Gavan. 1971. "The Student Left in Japan." *New Left Review* I/65 (January–February): 37–53.

McKean, Margaret A. 1981. *Environmental Protest and Citizen Politics in Japan*. Berkeley: University of California Press.

McVeigh, Brian J. 2004. *Nationalisms of Japan: Managing and Mystifying Identity*. Lanham, MD: Rowman and Littlefield.

Melucci, Alberto. 1989. *Nomads of the Present: Social Movements and Individual Needs in Contemporary Society*, ed. John Keane and Paul Mier. Philadelphia, PA: Temple University Press.

MEXT (Ministry of Education, Culture, Sports, Science, and Technology, Monbu kagaku shō). 2002. *Monbu kagaku hakusho (White Paper on Education, Culture, Sports, Science, and Technology)*. Tokyo: Ministry of Finance Printing Bureau.

————. 2003. *Chiiki to gakkō ga renkei shita hōshi katsudō, taiken katsudō suishin jigyō (Program on Social Service Experiences through the Linkage of Communities and Schools)*. http://www.mext.go.jp/a_menu/hyouka/kekka/020908/006.pdf. Accessed January 15, 2007.

MHLW (Ministry of Health, Labor, and Welfare, Kōsei rōdō shō). 2005. *Heisei 17 nen jinko dōtai toukei no nenkan suikei (Vital Statistics in 2005)*. http://www.mhlw.go.jp/toukei/saikin/hw/jinkou/ suikei05/index.html. Accessed December 22, 2005.

MIAC (Ministry of Internal Affairs and Communications, Soumu shō). 2004. *Heisei 16 nendo Kakei chōsa (Household Economies Survey for Fiscal 2004)*. http://www.stat.go.jp/data/kakei/2004dn/index.htm. Accessed June 28, 2006.

————. 2006. *Kōeki hōjin hakusho (White Paper on Public-Interest Corporations)*. Tokyo: National Printing Bureau.

Mie Prefectural Government (Mie ken). 2001. *Jūmin, NPO to gyōsei no kyōdō jireishū (Collection of Collaborative Cases by Local Residents, NPOs, and the Prefectural Government)*. Tsu, Mie: Mie Prefectural Government Department of Social Affairs.

Miller, Char Roone. 2002. *Taylored Citizenship: State Institutions and Subjectivity*. Westport, CT: Praeger.

Minobe, Ryōkichi. 1979. *Tochiji 12 nen (Twelve Years as Tokyo Governor)*. Tokyo: Asahi shimbunsha.

Miyajima, Takashi. 2004. *Yōroppa shimin no tanjō: hirakareta shitizunshippu ye (The Birth of Citizens in Europe: Toward Opening Up Citizenship)*. Tokyo: Iwanami shinsho.

Miyazaki, Hirokazu. 2003. "The Temporalities of the Market." *American Anthropologist* 105(2): 255–65.

Mizuta, Hiroshi. 1954. *Kindaijin no keisei: kindai shakaikan seiritsu shi (Formation of Modern Man: History of Modern Social Views)*. Tokyo: Tokyo daigaku shuppankai.

Moon, Okpyo. 2002. "Voluntary Associations in Japan: A Functional Factor in the System or a Changing Force?" In *The Culture of Association and Associations in Contemporary Japanese Society*, ed. Hirochika Nakamaki, 25–39. Suita, Osaka: National Museum of Ethnology. Senri Ethnological Studies, no. 62.

Moore, Sally Falk. 1987. "Examining the Present: Theoretical Dilemmas in Processual Anthropology." *American Ethnologist* 14(4): 727–36.

Morgan, Gareth. 1986. *Images of Organization*. Beverly Hills, CA: Sage Publications.

Mori, Masatoshi. 1998. "Gendai nihon shimin shakai ron: Sono hihan to kōsō" (Arguments on Contemporary Civil Society: Its Critique and Design). In *Gendai nihon no paburikku firosofī*, ed. Yamawaki Naoshi, 23–59. Tokyo: Shinseisha.

Muramatsu, Michio, and Frieder Naschold, eds. 1997. *State and Administration in Japan and Germany: A Comparative Perspective on Continuity and Change*. Berlin; New York: Walter de Gruyter.

Murphy, Mark. 2001. "The Politics of Adult Education: State, Economy and Civil Society." *International Journal of Lifelong Education* 20(5): 345–60.

Nader, Laura. 1972. "Up the Anthropologist—Perspectives Gained from Studying Up." In *Reinventing Anthropology*, ed. Dell Hymes, 284–311. New York: Vintage Books.

Nagai, Kafū. [1937] 1969. *Bokutō kitan (A Strange Tale from the East Side of the River)*. Tokyo: Nihon Kindai Bungakkan.

Nakamaki, Hirochika, ed. 2002. *The Culture of Association and Associations in Contemporary Japanese Society*. Senri, Osaka: National Museum of Ethnology. Senri Ethnological Studies, no. 62.

Nakamura, Karen. 2002. "Resistance and Co-optation: The Japanese Federation of the Deaf and Its Relations with State Power." *Social Science Japan Journal* 5(1): 17–35.

———. 2006. *Deaf in Japan: Signing and the Politics of Identity*. Ithaca, NY: Cornell University Press.

Nakamura, Yoichi, and Japan NPO Center. 2001. *Nihon no NPO (Japanese NPOs)*. Tokyo: Nihon hyorōnsha.

Nakane, Chie. 1967. *Tate shakai no ningen kankei: Tan'itsu shakai no riron (Interpersonal Relationships in a Vertically Structured Society: A Theory of Homogenous Society)*. Tokyo: Kōdansha.

———. 1970. *Japanese Society*. London: Weidenfeld & Nicolson.

Nakano, Lynne Y. 2000. "Volunteering as a Lifestyle Choice: Negotiating Self-Identities in Japan." *Ethnology* 39(2): 93–107.

———. 2005. *Community Volunteers in Japan: Everyday Stories of Social Change*. London; New York: RoutledgeCurzon.

Nakano, Toshio. 1999. "Borantia dōin gata shimin shakai ron no kansei" (The Pitfalls of Volunteer-Mobilized Types of Civil Society). *Gendai shisō* 27(5): 72–93.

———. 2001. *Ōtsuka Hisao to Maruyama Masao: Dōin, shutai, sensou sekinin (Ōtsuka Hisao and Maruyama Masao: Mobilization, Subject, and War Responsibility)*. Tokyo: Seidosha.

Naruse, Osamu. 1984. *Kindai shimin shakai no seiritsu: Shakai sisōteki kōsatsu (The Formation of Modern Civil Society: Socio-ideological Inquiry).* Tokyo: Tokyo daigaku shuppankai.

Naschold, Frieder. 1996. *New Frontiers in Public Sector Management: Trends and Issues in State and Local Government in Europe.* Translated by Andrew Watt. Berlin; New York: Walter de Gruyter.

Nash, June. 2005. "Introduction: Social Movements and Global Processes." In *Social Movements: An Anthropological Reader,* ed. June Nash, 1–26. Malden, MA: Blackwell.

NCLL (National Council for Lifelong Learning, Shogai gakushū shingikai). 1992. *Kongo no shakai no dōkō ni taiōshita shōgai gakushū no shinkō hōsaku ni tsuite (On the promotion of lifelong learning for the future).* Tokyo: National Council for Lifelong Learning.

National Tax Agency (Kokuzei chō). 2003. *Heisei 15 nen heikin kyūyo (Average Salaries in 2002).* http://www.nta.go.jp/category/toukei/tokei/menu/minkan/h15/pdf/1.pdf, p6. Accessed June 1, 2006.

———. 2007. *Nintei NPO hōjin seido (Approved Specified Nonprofit Corporations).* http://www.nta.go.jp/category/npo/04/01.htm. Accessed May 25, 2007.

Newman, Janet. 2001. *Modernising Governance: New Labour, Policy and Society.* London; Thousand Oaks, CA: Sage Publications.

NHK (Nihon hōsō kyōkai). 2002. *Kurashi to keizai—NPO de hatarakitai, kyūyo taigū wa? (Want to Work at an NPO? How are Salaries and Benefits?).* November 9.

Nihon Keizai Shimbun.

1985. (September 16). "Shitamachi nimo atarashii miryoku wo" (Creating New Images of Downtown Tokyo).

2002. (June 14). "Gakusei borantia shōchū gakkō ni haken" (Student Volunteers To Be Dispatched to Elementary and Junior High Schools).

2003. (January 26). "Hanko bijinesu naze hanjō" (Why Is the Hanko Business Prosperous?).

2003. (January 31). "Shushō shisei hōshin enzetsu no zenbun" (Full Script of the Prime Minister's Policy Speech).

2003. (June 16). "NPO dōnyū maemuki rokuwari" (60% of Local Governments Consider Introducing NPOs to Public Administration).

2004. (February 28). "Shimin to renkei sonzoku wo mosaku" (Exploring Collaboration with Citizens for Continuing Social Services).

2006. (March 25). "Daini Tokyo tawā, sumida taitō eria ni kettei" (Second Tokyo Tower To Be Built in the Sumida-Taitō Area).

9-jō no Kai (Kyujō no kai). 2006. *"Kai" no kazu 5 sen toppa shi, zenkoku kōryū shūkai (The Number of Groups Now Exceeds 5,000, Organizing a Nationwide Gathering).* A newsletter titled "9-jō no Kai," issued June 13. Available at http://www.9-jo.jp/news/9jouNews/9jouNews70-060613.pdf. Accessed January 24, 2007.

Oda, Makoto. [1965] 1974. "Futsū no shimin ni dekirukoto, 'kō' to 'shi' no mondai" (What Ordinary Citizens Can Do, a Problem of Public and Private). In *Shiryō "Beheiren" Undō.* Betonamu ni heiwa o! shimin rengō, ed. Jō-kan,

10–12. Tokyo: Kawade Shobō Shinsha. Originally appeared in the *Mainichi Shimbun*, May 7, 1965, evening edition.

Ogasawara, Yuko. 1998. *Office Ladies and Salaried Men: Power, Gender, and Work in Japanese Companies*. Berkeley: University of California Press.

Ogawa, Akihiro. 1997. "Scandals Provide Chance to Clean Up Finance System." *Japan Times Weekly International Edition*, October 20–26.

———. 2004. "Invited by the State: Institutionalizing Volunteer Subjectivity in Contemporary Japan." *Asian Anthropology* 3: 71–96.

———. 2005. "Shimin shakai ron ye no atarashii apurōchi" (New Approach to Civil Society Studies). *Gekkan Minpaku* (April): 6.

———. 2006a. "Initiating Change: Doing Action Research in Japan." In *Dispatches from the Field: Neophyte Ethnographers in a Changing World*, ed. Andrew M. Gardner and David M. Hoffman, 207–21. Long Grove, IL: Waveland Press.

———. 2006b. "Shōgai gakushū to shitizunshippu" (Lifelong Learning and Citizenship) with Okubo Kuniko. *Shakai kyōiku* 725 (November): 4–11.

———. 2007a. "Otona no manabi no puroguramu" (Learning Program for Adults) with Kuniko Okubo. *Shakai kyōiku* 730 (April): 42–49.

———. 2007b. "Taiseiyō wo kakeru posudoku shūshoku katsudōki" (Job Hunting Notes by a Postdoc Fellow over the Atlantic) with Kuniko Okubo. *Shakai kyōiku* 727 (January): 42–48.

———. 2008. " 'Induced' Voluntarism: A New Role for Schools?" In *The Demographic Challenge: A Handbook about Japan*, ed. Florian Coulmas, Harald Conrad, Annette Schad-Seifert and Gabriele Vogt, 721–32. Leiden, the Netherlands: Brill Academic Publishers.

Ogawa, Seiko. 2005. "Lifelong Learning and Demographics: A Japanese Perspective." *International Journal of Lifelong Education* 24(4): 351–68.

Ogawa, Tadashi. 1991. *Gendai shogai kyoiku tokuhon (Modern Lifelong Learning Reader)*. Tokyo: Eidell Institute.

Oguma, Eiji. 2002. *Minshu to aikoku: Sengo nihon no nashonarizumu to kōkyōsei (Democracy and Patriotism: Nationalism and Publicness in Postwar Japan)*. Tokyo: Shinyōsha.

Okada, Akito. 2002. "Education of Whom, for Whom, by Whom? Revising the Fundamental Law of Education in Japan." *Japan Forum* 14(3): 425–41.

Okimoto, Daniel I., and Thomas P. Rohlen. 1988. *Inside the Japanese System: Readings on Contemporary Society and Political Economy*. Stanford, CA: Stanford University Press.

Ōkouchi, Kazuo. 1954. *Sumisu to risuto (Smith and List)*. Tokyo: Kōbundo.

Okui, Fukutaro. 1940. *Gendai daitoshi ron (Contemporary Theories on Big Cities)*. Tokyo: Yūhikaku.

Orr, Julian E. 1990. *Talking about Machines: An Ethnography of a Modern Job*. Ithaca, NY: Cornell University Press.

Osborne, David, and Ted Gaebler. 1992. *Reinventing Government: How the Entrepreneurial Spirit Is Transforming the Public Sector*. Reading, MA: Addison-Wesley.

Osborne, Stephen P., ed. 2003. *The Voluntary and Non-Profit Sector in Japan: The Challenge of Change*. London; New York: RoutledgeCurzon.

Oshiba, Ryo. 2002. "National Symbols, History Textbooks, and Neo-Nationalism in Japan." In *We the People in the Global Age: Re-examination of Nationalism and Citizenship*, ed. Ryo Oshiba, Edward Rhodes and Chieko Kitagawa Otsuru, 125–35. Suita, Osaka: Japan Center for Area Studies, National Museum of Ethnology. JCAS Symposium Series, no. 18.

Ōtsuka, Hisao. 1946. *Kindai ōshū keizaishi josetsu (Introduction to Modern European Economic History)*. Tokyo: Nihon hyōronsha.

———. [1946] 1969a. "Kindaiteki ningen ruikei no sōshutsu, seiji teki shutai no minshū teki kiban no mondai." In *Ōtsuka Hisao chosakushū* 8, 169–75. Tokyo: Iwanami shoten. An English translation of this article, The Formation of Modern Man: The Popular Base for Democratization," is available in *Japan Interpreter* 6(1): 1–5.

———. [1947] 1969b. "Robinson Kurūsō no ningen ruikei" (Human Type of Robinson Crusoe). In *Ōtsuka Hisao chosakushū* 8, 214–21. Tokyo: Iwanami shoten.

———. [1944] 1969c. "Saikōdo 'jihatsusei' no hatsuyō, keizai rinri to shite no seisan sekinin ni tsuite" (Generating a Supreme "Inner Originality," on production responsibility as economic ethics). In *Ōtsuka Hisao chosakushū* 8, 339–44. Tokyo: Iwanami shoten.

Packard, George R. 1966. *Protest in Tokyo: The Security Treaty Crisis of 1960*. Princeton, NJ: Princeton University Press.

Park, Peter. 1997. "Participatory Research, Democracy, and Community." *Practicing Anthropology* 19 (3): 8–13.

Peacock, James L. 2001. *The Anthropological Lens: Harsh Light, Soft Focus*. Cambridge: Cambridge University Press.

Pekkanen, Robert. 2000. "Japan's New Politics: The Case of the NPO Law." *Journal of Japanese Studies* 26(1): 111–48.

———. 2003. "Molding Japanese Civil Society: State-Structured Incentives and the Patterning of Civil Society." In *The State of Civil Society in Japan*, ed. Frank J. Schwartz and Susan J. Pharr, 116–34. Cambridge: Cambridge University Press.

———. 2004a. "After the Developmental State: Civil Society in Japan." *Journal of East Asian Studies* 4: 363–88.

———. 2004b. "Japan: Social Capital without Advocacy." In *Civil Society and Political Change in Asia: Expanding and Contracting Democratic Space*, ed. Muthia Alagappa, 223–55. Stanford, CA: Stanford University Press.

———. 2006. *Japan's Dual Civil Society: Members without Advocates*. Stanford, CA: Stanford University Press.

Pekkanen, Robert, and Karla Simon. 2003. "The Legal Framework for Voluntary and Non-Profit Activity." In *The Voluntary and Non-Profit Sector in Japan: The Challenge of Change*, ed. Stephen P. Osborne, 76–101. London; New York: RoutledgeCurzon.

Pérez-Diaz, Victor M. 1993. *The Return of Civil Society: The Emergence of Democratic Spain*. Cambridge, MA: Harvard University Press.

Pharr, Susan J. 2003. "Conclusion: Targeting by an Activist State: Japan as a Civil Society Model." In *The State of Civil Society in Japan*, ed. Frank J. Schwartz and Susan J. Pharr, 316–36. Cambridge: Cambridge University Press.

Plath, David W. 1964. *The After Hours: Modern Japan and the Search for Enjoyment.* Berkeley: University of California Press.

Pollitt, Christopher. 1990. *Managerialism and the Public Services: The Anglo-American Experience.* Oxford: Blackwell.

Putnam, Robert D., with Robert Leonardi and Raffaella Y. Nanetti. 1993. *Making Democracy Work: Civic Traditions in Modern Italy.* Princeton, NJ: Princeton University Press.

———. 1995. "Tuning In, Tuning Out: The Strange Disappearance of Social Capital in America." *PS: Political Science & Politics* 28:4 (December): 664–83.

———. 2000. *Bowling Alone: The Collapse and Revival of American Community.* New York: Simon & Schuster.

Pynes, Joan E. 2000. "Are Women Underrepresented as Leaders of Nonprofit Organizations?" *The Review of Public Personnel Administration* 20(2): 35–50.

Rausch, Anthony S. 2003. "A Case Study of Lifelong Learning in Japan: Objectives, Curriculum, Accountability, and Visibility." *International Journal of Lifelong Education* 22(5): 518–32.

———. 2004. "Lifelong Learning in Rural Japan: Relevance, Focus, and Sustainability for the Hobbyist, the Resident, the Careerist, and the Activist as Lifelong Learner." *Japan Forum* 16(3): 473–93.

Redclift, Michael R. 2006. *Frontiers: Histories of Civil Society and Nature.* Cambridge, MA: MIT Press.

Reinhold, Susan. 1994. *Local Conflict and Ideological Struggle: "Positive Images" and Section 28.* D.Phil. thesis, University of Sussex.

Ren, Hai. 2005. "Modes of Governance in Neo-Liberal Capitalism: An Introduction." *Rhizomes* 10. http://www.rhizomes.net/issue10/introren.htm. Accessed March 10, 2006.

Rhodes, R. A. W. 2005. "Everyday Life in a Ministry: Public Administration as Anthropology." *American Review of Public Administration* 35(1): 3–25.

RIETI (Research Institute of Economy, Trade, and Industry, Keizai sangyō kenkyūjo). 2003. *NPO hōjin ankēto chōsa hōkoku (A Survey Report of the NPO).* September 2003. Tokyo: Research Institute of Economy, Trade, and Industry.

Rix, Alan G. 1975. "Tokyo's Governor Minobe and Progressive Local Politics in Japan." *Asian Survey* 15(6): 530–42.

Roberts, Glenda S. 1994. *Staying on the Line: Blue-Collar Women in Contemporary Japan.* Honolulu: University of Hawaii Press.

Robertson, Jennifer Ellen. 1991. *Native and Newcomer: Making and Remaking a Japanese City.* Berkeley: University of California Press.

———. 1998. *Takarazuka: Sexual Politics and Popular Culture in Modern Japan.* Berkeley: University of California Press.

Rohlen, Thomas P. 1974. *For Harmony and Strength: Japanese White-Collar Organization in Anthropological Perspective.* Berkeley: University of California Press.

———. 1983. *Japan's High Schools.* Berkeley: University of California Press.

Rom International. 2004. *Tokyo wo edo no kochizu de aruku hon (A Guidebook to Walking Tokyo by Old Maps).* Tokyo: Kawade shobō.

Rose, Nikolas S. 1999. *Governing the Soul: The Shaping of the Private Self*. 2d ed.. London; New York: Free Association Books.

Rosenblum, Nancy L., and Robert C. Post, eds. 2002. *Civil Society and Government*. Princeton, NJ: Princeton University Press.

Roth, Joshua Hotaka. 2002. *Brokered Homeland: Japanese Brazilian Migrants in Japan*. Ithaca, NY: Cornell University Press.

Rucht, Dieter. 1984. *Comparative New Social Movements, Organizations, and Strategies in a Cross-sectional and a Cross-national View*. Paper presented at the Conference of the European Group of Organizational Sociologists on New Social Movements. Aarhaus, Denmark, August.

Rueschemeyer, Dietrich, Marilyn Rueschemeyer, and Bjèorn Wittrock, eds. 1998. *Participation and Democracy, East and West: Comparisons and Interpretations*. Armonk, NY: M. E. Sharpe.

Ryfe, David M. 2005. "Does Deliberative Democracy Work?" *Annual Review of Political Science* 8: 49–71.

Saaler, Sven. 2005. *Politics, Memory, and Public Opinion: The History Textbook Controversy and Japanese Society*. Munich: Iudicium.

Saeki, Keishi. 1997. *"Shimin" to wa dare ka, sengo minshushugi wo toinaosu (Who Are "Shimin"?, Revisiting Postwar Democracy)*. Tokyo: PHP shinsho.

Saito, Hideharu. 1998. *Kokka wo koeru shiminshakai: Dōin no seiki kara nomado no seiki ye (Civil Society beyond the State: From the Era of Mobilization to the Era of Nomad)*. Tokyo: Gendai kikakushitsu.

Sakamoto, Yoshikazu. 1997. "Civil Society and Democratic World Order." In *Innovation and Transformation in International Studies*, ed. Stephen Gill and James H. Mittelman, 207–19. Cambridge: Cambridge University Press.

Sakuta, Keiichi. 1966. "Shiminshakai to taishūshakai" (Civil Society and Mass Society). *Shisō* 509: 31–46.

Salamon, Lester M. 1994. "The Rise of the Nonprofit Sector." *Foreign Affairs* 73(4): 109–22.

———. 2001. "An 'Associational' Revolution." *The UNESCO Courier*.

Salamon, Lester M., Helmut K. Anheier, Regina List, Stefan Toepler, S. Wojciech Sokolowski, and Associates. 1999. *Global Civil Society: Dimensions of the Nonprofit Sector*, vol. 1. Baltimore, MD: Johns Hopkins Center for Civil Society Studies.

Salamon, Lester M., S. Wojciech Sokolowski, and Associates. 2004. *Global Civil Society: Dimensions of the Nonprofit Sector*, vol. 2. Bloomfield, CT: Kumarian Press.

Sanday, Peggy Reeves, ed. 1976. *Anthropology and the Public Interest: Fieldwork and Theory*. New York: Academic Press.

———. 1998. *Defining Public Interest Anthropology*. Opening statement presented at the Annual Meeting of the American Anthropological Association, December 3, Philadelphia. http://www.sas.upenn.edu/~psanday/pia.99.html. Accessed April 26, 2006.

Sasai, Hiromi. 1998. "An Analysis of Lifelong Learning Policy in Japan." In *International Perspectives on Lifelong Learning*, ed. John Holford, Peter Jervis, and Colin Griffin, 180–85. London: Kogan Page.

Sasaki, Takeshi. 1997. "Maruyama Masao and the Spirit of Politics." *Japan Quarterly* 44(1): 59–63.

Sasaki-Uemura, Wesley. 2001. *Organizing the Spontaneous: Citizen Protest in Postwar Japan*. Honolulu: University of Hawaii Press.

Sato, Barbara Hamill. 2003. *The New Japanese Women: Modernity, Media, and Women in Interwar Japan*. Durham, NC: Duke University Press.

Sato, Ikuya. 1991. *Kamikaze Biker: Parody and Anomie in Affluent Japan*. Chicago, IL: University of Chicago Press.

Sato, Katsuko. 1998. *Shogai gakushū to shakai sanka: Otona ga manabu koto no imi (Lifelong Learning and Social Participation: The Meaning of Adult Learning)*. Tokyo: Tokyo daigaku shuppankai.

Sato, Yoshiyuki. 2002. *NPO to shimin shakai (NPOs and Civil Society)*. Tokyo: Yūhikaku.

SBSZ (Sumida bunka shinkō zaidan). 2003. *Heisei 15 nendo jigyō hōkoku oyobi shūshi kessansho (Annual Business Report and Closing Accounts of Revenue and Expenditures)*. Tokyo: Sumida bunka shinkō zaidan.

Schwartz, Frank J., and Susan J. Pharr, eds. 2003. *The State of Civil Society in Japan*. Cambridge: Cambridge University Press.

Schwartzman, Helen B. 1989. *The Meeting: Gatherings in Organizations and Communities*. New York: Plenum Press.

———. 1993. *Ethnography in Organizations*. Newbury Park, CA: Sage Publications.

Scott, James C. 1998. *Seeing Like a State: How Certain Schemes to Improve the Human Condition Have Failed*. New Haven, CT: Yale University Press.

SCT (Sakura Cable Television). 2006. *Jupitā terekomu, sumidaku no sakura kēburu terebi no keieiken shutoku kanryō (Jupiter Telecom Competed to Acquire Sakura Cable Television in Sumida Ward)*. Press release distributed at the JASDAQ Securities Exchange, April 6.

Seibel, Wolfgang, and Helmut K. Anheier. 1990. "Sociological and Political Science Approaches to the Third Sector." In *The Third Sector: Comparative Studies of Nonprofit Organizations*, ed. Helmut K. Anheier and Wolfgang Seibel, 7–20. Berlin; New York: Walter de Gruyter.

Seikatsusha Network. 2006. *Tokyo seikatsusha nettowāku, katsudō shōkai (Introduction of Our Activities, Tokyo Seikatsusha Network)*. http://www.seikatsusha.net/index.html. Accessed October 5, 2006.

Seligman, Adam B. 1992. *The Idea of Civil Society*. New York: Free Press.

Shigetomi, Shin'ichi, ed. 2002. *The State and NGOs: Perspective from Asia*. Singapore: Institute of Southeast Asian Studies.

Shils, Edward. 1991. "The Virtue of Civil Society." *Government and Opposition* 26(1): 3–20.

Shimizu, Ikutarō. 1951. *Shimin shakai (Civil Society)*. Tokyo: Sōgen bunko.

Shinohara, Hajime. 2004. *Shimin no seijigaku: Tōgi demokurashī to wa nanika (Political Science of Citizen: What Is Discursive Democracy?)*. Tokyo: Iwanami shoten.

Shore, Cris, and Susan Wright, eds. 1997. *Anthropology of Policy: Critical Perspectives on Governance and Power*. London; New York: Routledge.

———. 2000. "Coercive Accountability: The Rise of Audit Culture in Higher Education." In *Audit Cultures: Anthropological Studies in Accountability, Ethics, and the Academy*, ed. Marilyn Strathern, 57–89. London; New York: Routledge.

Shūkan Tōyō Keizai. 2003. (March 29). "Gen'eki salaryman mo sunaru NPO to iu ikikata" (Participating in NPOs as Salaried Men as a Way of Life).

Simon, Herbert A. 1997. *Administrative Behavior: A Study of Decision-Making Processes in Administrative Organizations*. New York: Free Press.

SKBS (Sumida kyōdo bunka shiryōkan). 2000. *Sumidagawa no densetsu to rekishi (Legends and History of Sumidagawa River)*. Tokyo: Tokyōdō shuppan.

Skocpol, Theda, and Morris P. Fiorina, eds. 1999. *Civic Engagement in American Democracy*. Washington, DC: Brookings Institution Press.

Smith, Adam. [1776] 1974. *The Wealth of Nations*. Harmondsworth: Penguin.

Smith, Philip D. 2002. *The Virtue of Civility in the Practice of Politics*. Lanham, MD: University Press of America.

Smith, Robert J. 1974. *Ancestor Worship in Contemporary Japan*. Stanford, CA: Stanford University Press.

———. 1978. *Kurusu: The Price of Progress in a Japanese Village, 1951–1975*. Stanford, CA: Stanford University Press.

Smith, Robert J., and Ella Lury Wiswell. 1982. *The Women of Suye Mura*. Chicago, IL: University of Chicago Press.

Snow, Crocker. 1973. "Tokyo's Governor Minobe." *Japan Interpreter* 8(2): 185–94.

Social Epistemology. 2003. *Roundtable on Social Capital*. 17(4): 325–400.

Social Science Japan Newsletter. 2004. *Nationalism, Number 30*. Tokyo: Institute of Social Science, University of Tokyo.

Steiner, Kurt, Ellis S. Krauss, and Scott C. Flanagan, eds. 1980. *Political Opposition and Local Politics in Japan*. Princeton, NJ: Princeton University Press.

Steinhoff, Patricia G. 1989. "Protest and Democracy." In *Democracy in Japan*, ed. Takeshi Ishida and Ellis S. Krauss, 171–98. Pittsburgh, PA: University of Pittsburgh Press.

Stevens, Carolyn S. 1997. *On the Margins of Japanese Society: Volunteers and the Welfare of the Urban Underclass*. London; New York: Routledge.

SWBE (Sumida Ward Board of Education, Sumida ku kyōiku iinkai). 1986. *Sumidaku kyōikushi (History of Education in Sumida Ward)*. Tokyo: Sumida Ward Government.

SWG (Sumida Ward Government, Sumida ku). 1978a. *Sumidakushi ge (History of Sumida Ward, the Third Volume)*. Tokyo: Sumida Ward Government.

———. 1978b. *Sumidakushi jō (History of Sumida Ward, the Second Volume)*. Tokyo: Sumida Ward Government.

———. 1978c. *Sumidakushi zenshi (History of Sumida Ward, the First Volume)*. Tokyo: Sumida Ward Government.

———. 1985. *Sumida kusei gaiyō 1985 (Outline of Sumida Ward Administration 1985)*. Tokyo: Sumida Ward Government.

———. 1990. *Kōryū, sōzō, mirai (Interactions, Creation, and Future)*. April. Tokyo: Sumida Ward Government.

———. 1997. *Discovering Sumida: Sumida City Guide Book*. Tokyo: Sumida Ward Government, Cultural Affairs Department.

———. 1999a. *Kumin ni yoru shōgai gakushū soshiki no arikata ni tsuite (On Creating an Organization Promoting Lifelong Learning by Local Residents)* October. Tokyo: Sumida Ward Government.

———. 1999b. *Kumin ni yoru shōgai gakushū soshiki no hōjinka ni mukete (Toward Incorporating Resident-Based Lifelong Learning Organization by Local Residents)*. August 1999. Tokyo: Sumida Ward Government.

———. 2006. *Sumida, jinkō, setai (Population and Households in Sumida)*. http://www.city.sumida.lg.jp/sumida_info/population/index.html. Accessed June 1, 2006.

SWTL (Sumida Ward Terashima Library, Sumida kuritsu terashima toshokan). 1990. *Sumida bungaku chizu (A Map of Where Writers Lived in Sumida)*. Tokyo: Sumida Ward Terashima Library.

Takabatake, Michitoshi. 1971. *Seiji no ronri to shimin (Political Logic and Citizens)*. Tokyo: Chikuma shobō.

———. 1978. "Citizens' Movements: Organizing the Spontaneous." In *Authority and the Individual in Japan: Citizen Protest in Historical Perspective*, ed. J. Victor Koschmann, 189–99. Tokyo: University of Tokyo Press.

———. 2001. "Shimin shakai mondai: Nihon ni okeru bunmyaku" (Civil Society Problem: Japanese Context). *Shisō* 924: 4–23.

———. 2004. *Shimin seiji saikō (Citizens' Politics Revisited)*. Tokyo: Iwanami shoten.

Takao, Yasuo. 2001. "The Rise of the 'Third Sector' in Japan." *Asian Survey* 41(2): 290–309.

Takashima, Zenya. 1953. *Keizaishakaigakusha to shiteno sumisu to risuto (Smith and List as Socio-economists)*. Tokyo: Nyosui shobō.

———. 1991. *Shimin shakairon no kōsō (The Design of Civil Society Arguments)*, ed. Hideo Yamada. Tokyo: Shinhyōron.

Tanaka, Hisashi. 2005. *Seikyō tono hanseiki (A Half Century with Co-op)*. Tokyo: Co-op shuppan.

Tester, Keith. 1992. *Civil Society*. London; New York: Routledge.

Thang, Leng Leng. 2001. *Generations in Touch: Linking the Old and Young in a Tokyo Neighborhood*. Ithaca, NY: Cornell University Press.

Theiss, Elizabeth, and John R. Hibbing. 2005. "Citizenship and Civic Engagement." *Annual Review of Political Science* 8: 227–49.

Thomas, J. E (James Edward). 1985. *Learning Democracy in Japan: The Social Education of Japanese Adults*. London; Beverly Hills, CA: Sage Publications.

Thomas, J. E., Takamichi Uesugi, and Shuichi Shimada. 1997. "New Lifelong Learning Law in Japan: Promise or Threat?" *International Journal of Lifelong Education* 16(2): 132–40.

Thurow, Lester C. 1996. *The Future of Capitalism: How Today's Economic Forces Shape Tomorrow's World*. New York: W. Morrow and Co.

Tocqueville, Alexis de. [1840] 1980. *Democracy in America*. Vol. 2. New York: Alfred A. Knopf. The first volume was published in 1835 and the second in 1840.

Todd, Malcolm J., and Gary Taylor. 2004. "Introduction." In *Democracy and Participation: Popular Protest and New Social Movements*, ed. Malcolm J. Todd and Gary Taylor, 1–28. London: Merlin Press.

Tokyo Council of Social Welfare (Tokyoto shakai fukushi kyōgikai). 2006. *Tōshakyō no koto (On the Tokyo Council of Social Welfare).* http://www.tcsw.tvac. or.jp/about/index.html. Accessed September 14, 2006.

Tokyo Junior Chamber (Tokyo seinen kaigisho). 1999. *Aratanaru 50 nen ni mukete (For the Next 50 Years).* Tokyo: Tokyo seinen kaigisho.

———. 2006. *Shadan hōjin Tokyo seinen kaigisho towa (What Is Tokyo JC?).* http:// www.tokyo-jc.or.jp/2006/jc/gaiyou.html. Accessed October 5, 2006.

Tokyo Metropolitan Government, Tokyo to. 2000a. *Kyōdō no suishin shishin sakutei ye no teigen (Proposal for Promoting Policy Collaboration).* Tokyo: Tokyo Metropolitan Government Bureau of Citizens and Cultural Affairs.

———. 2000b. *Tokutei hieiri katsudō hōjin gaido bukku (Guidebook for NPOs).* Tokyo: Tokyo Metropolitan Government Bureau of Citizens and Cultural Affairs.

Tokyo Shrine Agency (Tokyoto jinja chō). 2006. *Shūkyō hōjin Tokyoto jinja chō (Religious Corporation, Tokyo Shrine Agency).* http://www.tokyo-jinjacho. or.jp. Accessed October 6, 2006.

Tokyoto Irei Kyōkai. 2005a. *Kanto daishinsai (Great Kanto Earthquake).* Tokyo: Tokyoto irei kyōkai.

———. 2005b. *Tokyo daikūshū no kiroku (Records of Tokyo Air Bombardment).* Tokyo: Tokyoto irei kyōkai.

Touraine, Alain. 1971. *The Post-Industrial Society; Tomorrow's Social History: Classes, Conflicts and Culture in the Programmed Society.* Translated by Leonard F. X. Mayhew. New York: Random House.

Traphagan, John W. 2000. *Taming Oblivion: Aging Bodies and the Fear of Senility in Japan.* Albany: State University of New York Press.

———. 2004. *The Practice of Concern: Ritual, Well-being, and Aging in Rural Japan.* Durham, NC: Carolina Academic Press.

Tsujinaka, Yutaka, ed. 2002. *Gendai nihon no shimin shakai, rieki dantai (Civil Society and Interest Groups in Contemporary Japan).* Tokyo: Bokutakusha.

Turner, Christena L. 1995. *Japanese Workers in Protest: An Ethnography of Consciousness and Experience.* Berkeley: University of California Press.

TVAC (Tokyo Voluntary Action Center). 2001. *Volunteer Booklet.* Tokyo: Tokyo Voluntary Action Center.

Uchida, Yoshihiko. 1953. *Keizaigaku no seitan (The Birth of Economics).* Tokyo: Miraisha.

Ueno, Chizuko. 1988. "The Japanese Women's Movement: The Counter-values to Industrialism." In *The Japanese Trajectory: Modernization and Beyond,* ed. Gavan McCormack and Yoshio Sugimoto, 167–85. Cambridge: Cambridge University Press.

———. 1994. *Kindai kazoku no seiritsu to shūen (Development and End of Modern Family).* Tokyo: Iwatani shoten.

Ueno, Yōko. 2003. "Futsū no shimin-tachi ni yoru 'tsukuru-kai' no esunogurafī" (An Ethnography on History Textbook Making by Ordinary People). In *"Iyashi" no nashonarizumu: Kusanone no hoshu undō no jisshō kenkyū (Nationalism as Healing: Empirical Studies on Grassroots Conservative Movements).* Tokyo: Keio gijuku daigaku shuppankai.

Urbinati, Nadia. 2006. *Representative Democracy: Principles and Genealogy.* Chicago, IL: University of Chicago Press.

Van Maanen, John. 1991. "The Smile Factory: Work at Disneyland." In *Reframing Organizational Culture*, ed. Peter J. Frost, Larry F. Moore, Meryl Reis Louis, Craig C. Lundberg, and Joanne Martin, 58–76. Newbury Park, CA: Sage Publications.

Verba, Sidney, Kay Lehman Schlozman, and Henry E. Brady. 1995. *Voice and Equality: Civic Voluntarism in American Politics*. Cambridge, MA: Harvard University Press.

Vogel, Ezra F. 1963. *Japan's New Middle Class: The Salary Man and His Family in a Tokyo Suburb*. Berkeley: University of California Press.

———, ed. 1975. *Modern Japanese Organization and Decision Making*. Berkeley: University of California Press.

———. 1987. "Japan: Adaptive Communitarianism." In *Ideology and National Competitiveness: An Analysis of Nine Countries*, ed. George C. Lodge and Ezra F. Vogel, 141–71. Boston, MA: Harvard Business School Press.

Vos, Frits. 1957. *A Study of the Ise-Monogatari, with the Text According to the Den-Teika-Hippon and an Annotated Translation by Frits Vos*. Vol. 1. The Hague: Mouton and Co.

Vosse, Wilhelm. 1999. "The Emergence of a Civil Society in Japan." *Japanstudien* (11): 31–53

Waley, Paul. 2005. Ruining and Restoring Rivers: The State and Civil Society in Japan. *Pacific Affairs* 78(2): 195–215.

Walzer, Michael. 1992. "The Civil Society Argument." In *Dimensions of Radical Democracy: Pluralism, Citizenship, Community*, ed. Chantal Mouffe, 89–107. London: Verso.

Wanner, Barbara. 1998. "Japan's Growing Nonprofit Sector Responds to Government Shortfalls." *Japan Economic Institute (JEI) Report No. 21A* (June 5): 1–12.

Warren, Mark E. 2001. *Democracy and Association*. Princeton, NJ: Princeton University Press.

Watanabe, Hideo. 2005. "Changing Adult Learning in Japan: The Shift from Traditional Singing to Karaoke." *International Journal of Lifelong Education* 24(3): 257–67.

Weber, Max. 1978. *Economy and Society: An Outline of Interpretive Sociology*. Vols. 1 and 2. Berkeley: University of California Press.

———. 1992. *The Protestant Ethic and the Spirit of Capitalism*. London; New York: Routledge.

Wedel, Janine R., Cris Shore, Gregory Feldman, and Stacy Lathrop. 2005. "Toward an Anthropology of Public Policy." *The Annals of the American Academy* 600: 30–51.

Wedel, Janine R., and Gregory Feldman. 2005. "Why an Anthropology of Public Policy?" *Anthropology Today* 21(1): 1–2.

Weick, Karl E. 1995. *Sensemaking in Organizations*. Thousand Oaks, CA: Sage Publications.

White, Merry I. 1987. *The Japanese Educational Challenge: A Commitment to Children*. New York: Free Press.

———. 1991. *Challenging Tradition: Women in Japan*. New York: Japan Society.

———. 2002. *Perfectly Japanese: Making Families in an Era of Upheaval.* Berkeley: University of California Press.

Wilson, John Dewar. 2001. "Lifelong Learning in Japan—A Lifeline for a 'Maturing' Society?" *International Journal of Lifelong Education* 20(4): 297–343.

Witteveen, Guven Peter. 2004. *The Renaissance of Takefu: How People and the Local Past Changed the Civic Life of a Regional Japanese Town.* New York: Routledge.

Wright, Susan. 2006. "Anthropology of Policy." *Anthropology News* 47(8): 22.

Wuthnow, Robert. 1998. *Loose Connections: Joining Together in America's Fragmented Communities.* Cambridge, MA: Harvard University Press.

Yagi, Kiichiro, Toshio Yamada, Shigeyoshi Senga, and Toshiharu Nozawa, eds. 1998. *Fukken suru shimin shakairon: Atarashii soshietaru paradaimu (Civil Society Arguments Reinstated: A New Societal Paradigm).* Tokyo: Nihon hyōronsha.

Yamaguchi, Yasushi. 2004. *Shimin shakairon: Rekishiteki isan to shintenkai (Civil Society Arguments: Historical Inheritance and New Developments).* Tokyo: Yūhikaku.

Yamamoto, Tadashi, ed. 1996. *Emerging Civil Society in the Asia Pacific Community: Nongovernmental Underpinnings of the Emerging Asia Pacific Regional Community.* Singapore: Institute of Southeast Asian Studies; Tokyo: Japan Center for International Exchange, in cooperation with the Asia Pacific Philanthropy Consortium.

———. 1998. "The State and the Nonprofit Sector in Japan." In *The Nonprofit Sector in Japan,* ed. Tadashi Yamamoto, 119–44. Manchester; New York: Manchester University Press.

———. 1999. "Emergence of Japan's Civil Society and Its Future Challenge." In *Deciding the Public Good: Governance and Civil Society in Japan,* ed. Tadashi Yamamoto, 97–124. Tokyo; New York: Japan Center for International Exchange.

Yamanouchi, Yasushi. 1993. "Senjiki no isan to sono ryōgisei" (Wartime Legacy and Its Ambivalence). In *Nihon shakai kagaku no shisō (Thoughts on Japanese Social Sciences),* vol. 3, ed. Yasushi Yamanouchi, 131–70. Tokyo: Iwanami shoten.

———. 1996. "Sengo hanseiki no shakai kagaku to rekishi ninshiki" (Social Sciences and Historical Consciousness in Postwar Japan). *Rekishigaku Kenkyū* 689: 32–43.

———. 1998. "Total-War and System Integration: A Methodological Introduction." In *Total War and "Modernization,"* ed. Yasushi Yamanouchi, J. Victor Koschmann, and Ryūichi Narita, 1–39. Ithaca, NY: Cornell University East Asia Program.

Yamaoka, Yoshinori. 1999. *Jidai ga ugokutoki, shakai no henkaku to NPO no kanōsei (When the Times Move, Social Reform and Possibilities of NPO).* Tokyo: Gyōsei.

———. 2000. *Present and Future Trends of NPOs in Japan.* Paper presented at the International Conference on the Role of Non-Profit Organizations in Civil Society in the 21st Century, Institute for International Policy Studies, Tokyo, December 12–14.

Yamashita, Shinji. 2004. *Establishing "Anthropology in Action" in Japan.* Opening address at the International Symposium—The Social Use of Anthropology in the Contemporary World, October 29–30. National Museum of Ethnology, Osaka, Japan.

Yamashita, Yusuke, and Mashiho Suga. 2002. *Shinsai borantia no shakaigaku (Sociology of Disaster Volunteers).* Kyoto: Mineruba shobō.

Yamauchi, Naoto. 1999a. *NPO nyūmon (Introduction to NPOs).* Tokyo: Nikkei bunko.

———. 1999b. *NPO saizensen. A Japanese translation of Holding the Center: America's Nonprofit Sector at a Crossroads by Lester M. Salamon with Analysis of the Development of NPOs in Japan.* Tokyo: Iwanami shoten.

———. 2000. *NPO kenkyū no kadai to tenbō (Agenda and Prospects in NPO studies).* Tokyo: Nihon hyōronsha.

———. 2001. "Japanese Nonprofit Sector in Comparative Perspective." *Global Economic Review* 29(4): 106–28.

Yamauchi, Naoto, and Hiroko Shimizu. 1999. "Kokusai hikaku kara mita nihon no NPO" (Japanese NPOs in International Comparative Perspectives). *Kōeki hōjin* (March): 2–15.

Yamauchi, Naoto, Hiroko Shimizu, S. Wojciech Sokolowski, and Lester M. Salamon. 1999. "Japan." *In Global Civil Society: Dimensions of the Nonprofit Sector,* vol. 1, ed. Lester M. Salamon et al., 243–59. Baltimore, MD: Johns Hopkins Center for Civil Society Studies.

Yamauchi, Naoto, and Masayuki Deguchi, eds. 2000. *Kēsu sutadi nihon no NPO (Case Studies on Japanese NPOs).* Osaka: Osaka University School of International Public Policy.

Yomiuri Shimbun. 2006. *Fukushimaken ni amakudari yō NPO, hashi tenken nado kenjigyō 3 okuen juchū (Fukushima Prefecture Establishes an NPO for Amakudari, Receives 300 Million Yen Orders for Inspecting Bridges etc.).* http://www.yomiuri.co.jp/national/news/20061006ic01.htm. Accessed October 6, 2006.

Yoshida, Masatoshi. 2005. *Shimin shakairon: Sono riron to rekishi (Civil Society: Theory and History).* Tokyo: Otsuki shoten.

Japanese Glossary

amakudari (天下り) literally means "descent from heaven" or the practice of retired bureaucrats landing cushy jobs in the private sector

Anpo (安保, 日米安全保障条約) U.S.-Japan Security Treaty

atarashii kōkyō (新しい公共) new public

Atarashii Rekishi Kyōkasho wo Tsukuru Kai (新しい歴史教科書をつくる会) Japanese Society for History Textbook Reform

Beheiren/Betonamu ni heiwa wo! shimin rengō (ベ平連、ベトナムに平和を！市民連合) Peace for Vietnam! Citizens' Committee

bōhan (防犯) crime prevention

borantia (ボランティア) volunteer/volunteering

borantia sentā or *borasen* (ボランティアセンター、ボラセン) volunteer center

bunka dantai rengō (文化団体連合会) cultural groups federation

bunkasai (文化祭) cultural festival

bunka shinkō zaidan (文化振興財団) culture-promoting foundation

buraku (部落) outcast communities

bushidō (武士道) way of the warrior

byōbu (屏風) paper-folded screens

chi-en (地縁) territorial bonds

chōkai, chōnaikai, or *jichikai* (町会, 町内会, 自治会) neighborhood association

chūshingura (忠臣蔵) the tale of Forty-Seven *Rōnin*

daisan sekutā (第三セクター) third sector

dodoitsu (都々逸) Japanese storytelling

dōtoku (道徳) moral education

fuku-kaichō (副会長) vice president

fuku-rijichō (副理事長) vice president

futsū (普通) ordinary

futsū no hito (普通の人) ordinary people

gakkō hōjin (学校法人) private-school corporation

gakusei undō (学生運動) students' movements

gyōsei yōgo (行政用語) administrative language

hagoita (羽子板) battledore, decorated wooden paddle

haiku (俳句) Japanese-style poetry

hanko (はんこ) seal

hansen undō (反戦運動) antiwar movements

heiwa undō (平和運動) peace movements

hieiri hōjin (非営利法人) nonprofit organization (NPO)

hinomaru (日の丸) rising-sun flag

hiseifu soshiki (非政府組織) nongovernmental organization (NGO)

hodokoshi wo ukeru (施しを受ける) given to

hojo kin (補助金) aid money

hōmukyoku (法務局) Legal Affairs Bureau

hōshi (奉仕) service

igyōshu kōryūkai (異業種交流会) business exchange

ippan shadan hōjin (一般社団法人) general incorporated association

ippan zaidan hōjin (一般財団法人) general incorporated foundation

iryō hōjin (医療法人) medical services corporation or hospital

ishi-kai (医師会) medical association

itaku kin (委託金) entrustment money

izakaya (居酒屋) Japanese-style bar

jidōkan (児童館) juvenile welfare institution

jiko-sekinin (自己責任) self-responsibility

jimu kyoku (事務局) secretariat

jimu kyokuchō (事務局長) secretary general

Jinja honchō (神社本庁) Association of Shrines

Jōruri (浄瑠璃) a traditional Japanese puppet theater

josei-bu or *fujin-bu* (女性部, 婦人部) women's association

jūmin (住民) residents

jūmin undō (住民運動) local residents' movements

kabuki (歌舞伎) a traditional Japanese form of theater

kaichō (会長) president

kaigo (介護) elderly care, nursing

kaikei (会計) accounting

kairanban (回覧板) circular notice

kakushin (革新) progressive

kankan settai (官々接待) lower-level bureaucrats entertaining higher-level bureaucrats at the taxpayers' expense

kankyō undō (環境運動) environmental movements

karuchā sentā (カルチャーセンター) culture center

kawanote (川の手) riverside, waterfront

keizai senryaku kaigi (経済戦略会議) Economic Strategy Council

keizokuteki (継続的) continuous

kendama (けんだま) cups and balls

kentei (検定、教科書検定) textbook examination

ketsu-en (血縁) kinship

kigyō shimin (企業市民) corporate citizens

kimigayo (君が代) His Majesty's reign

kindai shugi sha (近代主義者) modernists or advocates of modernity

kinrōsha fukushi sentā (勤労者福祉センター) workers' welfare service center

kiri (桐) paulownia

kisei kanwa (規制緩和) deregulation

kodomo-kai (子ども会) children's association

kōeki (公益) public interest

kōeki hōjin (公益法人) public-interest legal person/public-interest corporation

Koe Naki Koe no Kai (声なき声の会) The Voiceless Voice

kōen-kaiin (後援会員) supporting membership

kokusai kōryū (国際交流) international exchange

kokutai (国体, 国民体育大会) National Sports Festival

koma (こま) tops

kōmin (公民) public person

kōminkan (公民館) citizens' public halls

kōreisha jinzai sentā (高齢者人材センター) senior citizens' manpower center

kōsei hogo hōjin (更正保護法人) offender rehabilitation corporation

kōza-ha (講座派) Marxism of Lecturers Faction

kōzō kaikaku (構造改革) structural reform

kusabue (草笛) grass reed

kyōdō (協働) collaboration

kyōiku kihon hō (教育基本法) Fundamental Law of Education

kyoka (許可) permission

machizukuri (まちづくり) community development

manabi (学び) learning

manga (漫画) cartoon

matsuri (祭り) seasonal festival

messhi hōkō (滅私奉公) sacrificing personal interests for the good of the state

minyō (民謡) Japanese traditional folk song

nemawashi (根回し) discussion in advance

9-jō no Kai (９条の会) Article 9 Association

ningen ruikei (人間類型) human type

nin'i dantai (任意団体) informal private group

ninka (認可) approval

ninshō (認証) recognition

nintei NPO hōjin (認定NPO法人) approved specified nonprofit corporation

Nippon Keidanren (日本経団連, 日本経済団体連合会) Japan Business Federation

ohigan (お彼岸) equinoctial week

OL (オーエル) female office workers doing clerical work

omoiyari (思いやり) kindness

origami (折り紙) traditional paper folding

otagaisama (お互いさま) for each other

rakugoka (落語家) comic storyteller

rengōkai (連合会) federation

riji (理事) director

riji chō (理事長) president

riji-kai (理事会) board of directors

rōdō undō (労働運動) labor movements

rōjin-kai (老人会) elderly association

rōnin (浪人) masterless samurai

rōnō-ha (労農派) Marxism of Worker-Farmer Faction

ryōsai-kenbo (良妻賢母) good wife and wise mother

ryōtei (料亭) traditional first-class Japanese restaurant

sairento majoritī (サイレントマジョリティー) silent majority

salaryman (サラリーマン) white-collar workers, generally used for men

samurai (侍) Japanese warrior

sanka (参加) participation

sanyaku (三役) three key officials

sei-kaiin (正会員) regular membership

seikyō (生協) co-op

seinen-bu (青年部) young men's association

seinen kaigisho (青年会議所) Junior Chamber

seinenkan (青年館) youth hall

seishōnen ikusei iinkai (青少年育成委員会) youth development committee

sekijūji (赤十字) Red Cross

senja-fuda (千社札) fortune seals

sentaku-en (選択縁) the relation that people can choose

sentō (銭湯) Japanese public bath

seppuku (切腹) ritual suicide

shadan hōjin (社団法人) incorporated association

sha-en (社縁) corporate network

shakai fukushi hōjin (社会福祉法人) social welfare services corporation

shakai fukushi kyōgikai or *shakyō* (社会福祉協議会) social welfare council

shakai kōken (社会貢献) contribution to making society better

shakai kyōiku (社会教育) social education

shakaiteki shinyō (社会的信用) social trust

shaonkai (謝恩会) thank-you parties for the teachers

shikaishi-kai (歯科医師会) dental association

shimin (市民) citizen(s)

shimin dantai (市民団体) citizens' group

shimin gurūpu (市民グループ) citizens' group

shimin shakai (市民社会) civil society

shiminshakai-ha (市民社会派) civil-society school

shiminshakai-seinen (市民社会青年) civil-society youth

shimin undō (市民運動) citizens' movements

shinsetsu (親切) kindness

shitamachi (下町) downtown

shōgai gakushū (生涯学習) lifelong learning

shōgai kyōiku (生涯教育) lifelong education

shōhisha undō (消費者運動) consumer movements

shūkyō hōjin (宗教法人) religious corporation

sobaya (蕎麦屋) Japanese noodle shop

sōkai (総会) general meeting

taiikukan (体育館) public gym

taiiku kyōkai (体育協会) amateur sports association

taiken (体験) experience

taiwa (対話) dialogue

taiwa shūkai (対話集会) dialogue assembly

takeuma (竹馬) stilts

tasaina hitotachi (多彩な人たち) various kinds of people

teikan (定款) articles of association

tejime (手締め) closing hand-clapping ceremony

Tetsuwan Atomu (鉄腕アトム) Astro Boy

tokushu hōjin (特殊法人) special corporation

tokutei hieri katsudō hōjin (特定非営利活動法人, NPO) specified nonprofit corporation

tokutei hieiri katsudō sokushin hō (特定非営利活動促進法/NPO 法) Law to Promote Specified Nonprofit Activities

tōki (登記) registration

tsunagari (つながり) networking

undōkai (運動会) school athletic meet

waka (和歌) a Japanese poetic form

yakuzaishi-kai (薬剤師会) Association for Pharmacists

yamanote (山の手) a popular residential area in Tokyo

yukata (浴衣) light Japanese robe

zaibatsu (財閥) a conglomerate

zaidan hōjin (財団法人) incorporated foundation

Index

Printed in Japan
落丁、乱丁本のお問い合わせは
Amazon.co.jp カスタマーサービスへ